THE
EVERYTHING®
SPROUTED GRAINS
BOOK

Dear Reader,

The Everything® Sprouted Grains Book is a practical guide and cookbook that I wish I'd had when I first began my adventures with whole grains.

After seeing family members dealing with health issues a few years ago, I decided to really take charge of my health. The starting point for this change, for me, was food. The kitchen is such an important place in my own life and in my family's, and I knew that making any kind of change would need to start there.

I slowly began to seek out whole grains and started adding them into the regular rotation of recipes. Adding whole grains, in raw, cooked, and sprouted form, gave me much more energy, helped me get more restful sleep, and has kept my body in balance over the last few years.

Sprouting your own food doesn't have to be scary or intimidating, and I hope this book shows you just how easy and accessible it is.

Happy sprouting!

Brandi Evans

Welcome to the EVERYTHING® Series!

These handy, accessible books give you all you need to tackle a difficult project, gain a new hobby, comprehend a fascinating topic, prepare for an exam, or even brush up on something you learned back in school but have since forgotten.

You can choose to read an Everything® book from cover to cover or just pick out the information you want from our four useful boxes: e-questions, e-facts, e-alerts, and e-ssentials.

We give you everything you need to know on the subject, but throw in a lot of fun stuff along the way, too.

We now have more than 400 Everything® books in print, spanning such wide-ranging categories as weddings, pregnancy, cooking, music instruction, foreign language, crafts, pets, New Age, and so much more. When you're done reading them all, you can finally say you know Everything®!

QUESTION

Answers to
common questions

FACT

Important snippets
of information

ALERT

Urgent
warnings

ESSENTIAL

Quick
handy tips

PUBLISHER Karen Cooper

MANAGING EDITOR, EVERYTHING® SERIES Lisa Laing

COPY CHIEF Casey Ebert

ASSISTANT PRODUCTION EDITOR Melanie Cordova

ACQUISITIONS EDITOR Lisa Laing

ASSOCIATE DEVELOPMENT EDITOR Hillary Thompson

EDITORIAL ASSISTANT Matthew Kane

EVERYTHING® SERIES COVER DESIGNER Erin Alexander

LAYOUT DESIGNERS Erin Dawson, Michelle Roy Kelly, Elisabeth Lariviere

Visit the entire Everything® series at *www.everything.com*

THE
EVERYTHING®
SPROUTED GRAINS
BOOK

A complete guide to the miracle of sprouted grains

Brandi Evans

Avon, Massachusetts

*For Nick, my shelter in the storm. Thank you for believing in
me, for supporting me, for encouraging me in everything.*

An Everything® Series Book.
Everything® and everything.com® are registered trademarks of F+W Media, Inc.

Published by Adams Media, a division of F+W Media, Inc.
57 Littlefield Street, Avon, MA 02322 U.S.A.
www.adamsmedia.com

ISBN 10: 1-4405-3343-1
ISBN 13: 978-1-4405-3343-3
eISBN 10: 1-4405-3409-8
eISBN 13: 978-1-4405-3409-6

Printed in the United States of America.

10 9 8 7 6 5 4 3 2 1

Library of Congress Cataloging-in-Publication Data
Evans, Brandi.
The everything sprouted grains book / Brandi Evans.
p. cm.
Includes bibliographical references and index.
ISBN 978-1-4405-3343-3 (pbk. : alk. paper) –
ISBN 1-4405-3343-1 (pbk. : alk. paper) –
ISBN 978-1-4405-3409-6 (ebook) – ISBN 1-4405-3409-8 (ebook)
1. Grain. 2. Cooking (Sprouts) I. Title.
TX808.E93 2012
641.3'31–dc23
                                    2012004404

This publication is designed to provide accurate and authoritative information with regard to the subject matter covered. It is sold with the understanding that the publisher is not engaged in rendering legal, accounting, or other professional advice. If legal advice or other expert assistance is required, the services of a competent professional person should be sought.

—From a *Declaration of Principles* jointly adopted by a Committee of the American Bar Association and a Committee of Publishers and Associations

The information in this book should not be used for diagnosing or treating any health problem. Not all diet and exercise plans suit everyone. You should always consult a trained medical professional before starting a diet, taking any form of medication, or embarking on any fitness or weight-training program. The author and publisher disclaim any liability arising directly or indirectly from the use of this book.

Many of the designations used by manufacturers and sellers to distinguish their products are claimed as trademarks. Where those designations appear in this book and Adams Media was aware of a trademark claim, the designations have been printed with initial capital letters.

Nutritional statistics by Leah Traverse, RD.

This book is available at quantity discounts for bulk purchases. For information, please call 1-800-289-0963.

Contents

Acknowledgments

Thank you to my family, above all, for always believing in me and supporting all the crazy endeavors I throw myself into. Despite the heartache over the past few years, thank you most of all for persevering and making healthier choices along the way with me.

Thank you to Lisa Laing, my editor throughout this process, who answered my endless questions and encouraged me from the very beginning.

Thank you to Susan, a friend and someone who had walked through this process already, for your tips, for always lending an ear to my nervous chatter, and for pushing me to do my best.

Thank you, God, for giving me the strength, motivation, and dedication to write my first book. I can only pray that there are many more to be written and that You will give me the words to do it.

And the biggest thanks is for my husband, Nick. Through the months of writing this book, you never questioned the time I was spending writing. Thank you for giving me the time and space to do my work while supporting me and encouraging me all the while.

Introduction

EACH TIME THE NEW nutritional guidelines and updated food pyramids are released, it seems that whole grains are given a more prominent place in the diet goals set forth for the country. As more research is done on whole grains, sprouted grains, and the incredible health benefits held within those tiny seeds, it's no surprise that whole grains—no matter what form they're in—need a permanent spot on our kitchen tables. Filling and hearty, grains can be served with any meal.

They are proven to reduce the risks for heart diseases such as coronary heart disease, stroke, and heart attacks, and have also shown measurable effects helping manage diabetes, liver disease, depression, stress, anxiety, digestion issues, and weight loss. The need for grains and their effects on our health in our daily life is confirmed more and more every day as more research is done.

Whole grains have been used since ancient times as nourishment, as medicine, and as energy. Hundreds of years ago, people were eating whole grains in their daily lives, taking advantage of the protein, fiber, and other nutrients in the grains. Even in those times, there were people who were sprouting grains for consumption, but at that time they weren't aware of the increase in nutrition that the sprouting process presents.

As the years passed, sprouting for consumption began to take hold. The most popular period for the "rebirth" of whole grains and the idea of sprouting in the Western world was in the 1970s. At this point in time, the United States was leaning into more healthful habits and began to research ways to add healthier foods to the American diet. While sprouting grew in popularity, experts emerged with books, kits, and prepared sprouted-grain foods that allowed more consumers to add sprouted grains to their diets without having to do the sprouting themselves.

Whether or not you want to use a store-bought kit or prepared foods, sprouting at home is something that anyone can do and the basic process does not require any type of special equipment. Sprouting does take time. The grains are put into an environment that encourages the plant embryo to begin building the new plant life held within the seed, and this first sprout (the tip of the plant root) triggers the grain to release more nutrients that are now available to you through those sprouts. But the time spent on waiting for those little sprouts to emerge is worth all the health benefits and fantastic flavors you end up with.

Almost every whole grain, seed, and legume can be sprouted, giving you a variety of options when it comes to adding sprouted grains to your diet. Adding sprouts will not only give you more energy, but the nutrients make your heart healthier, can lower your cholesterol, and can help you manage your weight.

The role of whole grains in the American diet is becoming more important each year. As the rate of obesity rises, and diabetes and heart disease become two of the most widespread health issues in this country, the need for healthy and balanced diets steps to the forefront of every health and medical recommendation on how to turn the situation around in this country. Eating a diet rich in nutrients, antioxidants, and fiber is a proven way to create a balance in your body and keep all of your organs working in the way they were designed to work.

CHAPTER 1

Introduction to Sprouted Grains

Many people know what whole grains are, but they don't understand what a sprouted grain is. Whole grains are grains that still include each part of the original grain and have all the nutrients that the grain naturally has to offer. Sprouted grains are whole grains that have gone through the process that triggers them to begin growing a new plant. These sprouts can be grown from almost every whole grain, seed, and legume.

Whole Grains

All grains begin and grow as whole grains. The grain contains everything within it to begin a new plant. Whole-grain foods (those products made with whole grains) can be considered whole-grain if the food contains all the essential vitamins, minerals, and nutrients that are typically found in the whole grain itself.

What Makes Up a Whole Grain?

Whole grains are made up of three parts: the bran, the germ, and the endosperm. The bran is the outer shell of the grain, which provides a protective layer that keeps the germ and endosperm safe from sunlight until the sprout is ready, and safe from pests, water, and disease. The bran also contains many antioxidants and nutrients, B vitamins, and fiber.

FACT

Eating grains in their whole form is one of the easiest ways to up your nutritional intake. Whole grains, sprouted or not, have a much higher fiber count than refined grains. Eating whole grains is one way to quickly add heart-healthy nutrients, keep your digestive tract working properly, and keep you feeling full and satisfied.

The germ is located inside the grain and is the seed, or embryo, part that can be planted to grow a new plant. This part of the grain also contains many different vitamins, minerals, proteins, and healthy fats, which are essential for the plant's growth.

The endosperm is inside the bran, or outer shell, but is also what surrounds the germ or seed of the grain. The endosperm is the largest part of the seed and is also called the kernel. It contains mostly starchy carbohydrates and proteins, and serves as the seed's food and energy supply. Without the endosperm, the germ would not have enough stored food and energy for a new plant to send out sprouts and roots for sunlight and water absorption.

The Whole-Grain Distinction

While all grains begin as whole grains, they are only considered "whole grains" if they still contain the three parts—the bran, germ, and endosperm—once they are harvested. Most refined grains have had the germ and bran removed, and when those two are removed in the refining process, it means the grain is losing more than 25 percent of its naturally occurring proteins along with dozens of nutrients.

ESSENTIAL

The majority of grain-based products use refined grains, which have been processed so much that they've lost almost all of their nutritional qualities. As whole grains are processed further and further—in order to lessen the cooking time or to remove their natural nutty flavor—all of the health benefits are stripped away.

Whole grains are always a healthier choice than refined grains because whole grains still contain all the naturally occurring proteins, healthy fats, vitamins, and minerals that they have to offer. When you remove parts of the grain, you're also removing many of the health benefits.

Sprouted Grains

Sprouted grains are whole grains that have been left to soak and germinate, which causes the grain to release enzymes and, depending on the grain, grow the "tail" that most people associate with a sprout. The long tails you normally see on sprouts have their own nutritional values, but waiting for the long "tail" on a sprouted grain isn't necessary to reap the benefits of the enzymes working inside the grain. Many people believe that sprouting is the only way to release all of the important nutrients that are stored in grains because the process activates enzymes that turn grains into a living food that is active and nutrient-rich.

Sprouted grains have other benefits as well. They are known to be nutritious and packed with antioxidants. Sprouting grains yourself offers some of the freshest foods you'll eat in your own home. The grains you need for sprouting at home are typically inexpensive per pound and can be found in bulk in many grocery stores. Besides being economical, sprouts are easy to grow. They need things you already have at home: water, light, and oxygen. While the process is a bit more involved than those three things, if you have those, you can have sprouts growing in no time. Sprouting at home also gives you the chance to try new foods, new grains, new flavors, and new textures. There are so many grains, legumes, and seeds to sprout that you can keep your meals varied and diverse.

A Marvel of Nature

Like all other seeds, whole grains, in their small and unassuming form, contain everything needed to produce an entirely new plant. The nutrients, vitamins, and energy that are necessary to grow a new plant are just sitting underneath the outer shell of the grain, waiting for the right amount of light and water to begin the new life of the plant.

ESSENTIAL

Watching the sprouting process is a great way to show your family, especially kids, how plants begin new plant life. You can explain the process, but putting your grains in a place where your kids can see the grain sprouting more each day will let your family experience the awesome power of nature for themselves.

Once the germination and sprouting process begins, you can literally watch the sprouts grow out of the grains. Catching this act in progress is definitely something to watch for—it's not often you get to see nature working in such a small vessel and to truly be able to see the changes from minute to minute.

Just the Right Amount of Sprouting

Sprouting different grains or other seeds and legumes takes different amounts of time to get to the point where each type of grain is at its best. For optimal health from each grain, the right timing leaves you with the perfect balance for the highest vitamins and mineral count and active enzymes for easier digestion.

If your sprouts are not watched closely or if you're not keeping track of when you started a batch and how long they've been germinating, you could end up with rotten or inedible sprouts. Longer sprouts do not necessarily mean more health benefits, either. Letting sprouts get too long can increase chances of fermentation, and, if sprouts get long enough and turn into small grass stalks, they lose their digestibility as well. It is very important to keep track of how long you have a batch of sprouts working so that you are getting the healthiest sprout.

Types of Sprouted Grains

Almost every type of whole grain can be sprouted, as well as some seeds and legumes. Because whole grains contain everything needed for new plant growth, all types of grains go through the germination and sprouting process in their own way.

While every grain has the possibility to sprout, there are some varieties of seeds, grains, and legumes that are not safe to eat as sprouts. There are, however, many more options that are safe to sprout than those that aren't.

Whole Grains to Sprout

The majority of whole grains are safe to eat once sprouted, whether you choose to eat them raw or to cook them a bit more once they have been sprouted. The most popular grains used for sprouting are amaranth, barley, rice (brown, colored, and wild), buckwheat, bulgur, corn, farro, Kamut, millet, oats, quinoa, sorghum, spelt, triticale, rye, and wheat.

FACT

Gluten-free diets are becoming more popular as more people are being diagnosed with celiac disease or gluten intolerance. (*Gluten* is a protein composite found in wheat and some cereal grains.) But being gluten-free doesn't mean you have to avoid all grains. Add some oomph to your diet with naturally gluten-free grains like amaranth, rice, buckwheat, corn, millet, oats, quinoa, and brown and wild rice.

Amaranth

Amaranth was originally a basic staple in the diet of the Aztec people until it was banned by Cortez in order to destroy their civilization. After being carried to other countries, the seeds took off and amaranth is now gaining popularity again thanks to its high protein content and the fact that it is a naturally gluten-free grain. Amaranth grains are extremely tiny and look like small brown caviar when they are cooked. Not a true whole grain, amaranth is actually part of a botanical family of plants, genus *Amaranthus*, but is considered a grain because of the way it is most often used.

Barley

Barley use can be traced back to the Egyptians, and it is one of the oldest known cultivated grains. Because it has such a tough outer hull, most purchased barley is not technically a "whole grain," as removing the hull often takes some or all of the bran with it. Even without the distinction of being a whole grain, barley is extremely high in fiber and is still healthier than any other type of refined grain.

ESSENTIAL

To sprout barley, make sure you don't get the quick-cooking variety. Barley that has been processed for quicker cooking won't sprout like regular, raw barley. The quick-cooking type is a great option for soups and stews when you don't have time to cook the dish for very long, but it won't give you good sprouts.

Brown, Colored, and Wild Rice

While whole-grain rice is usually brown, it can also be a variety of other colors including purple, red, and black. Rice is one of the most popular grains not only in the United States but also around the world because it thrives in warmer climates. It is also one of the most easily digestible grains.

Wild rice is typically categorized with other varieties of rice, but it is actually a type of grass. The grain of the plant has a similar shape and texture as rice and is used in the same way.

Buckwheat

Buckwheat is treated like and served like a whole grain, but it is actually not a grain at all. It is related to rhubarb, but the texture, flavor, and appearance of buckwheat are so similar to whole grains that many people have accepted that it serves the same role as a whole grain. Buckwheat can be eaten raw or cooked (with or without sprouting). It is also the main ingredient in Japanese soba noodles and in kasha, a cereal commonly eaten in Eastern Europe.

QUESTION

Does it matter if buckwheat is eaten raw, cooked, or sprouted?
No matter how you like your buckwheat prepared, you'll be reaping great health benefits from it. While sprouting does increase some nutrients in the grain, eating it raw in yogurt or salads, or cooked in a grain dish or granola, will also offer more health benefits than if you were eating some type of refined grain instead.

Bulgur

Bulgur is wheat kernels that have been cooked, dried, and then cracked. Because bulgur has been precooked for a short amount of time, it only needs to cook for another 5–10 minutes, which makes it a quick whole-grain option to make at home. The slightly nutty flavor and fluffy texture make it a great grain base for all kinds of dishes, but it is most widely known as the base of tabbouleh salad. Since bulgur has been precooked, it will not actually sprout, but the soaking and germination process can still be used with bulgur to increase the nutritional value and enzymes within the grain before eating it.

Corn (and Whole Cornmeal)

Corn as a whole grain can be used in many different forms: whole corn kernels, cornmeal, masa (corn dough), polenta (cornmeal mush), popcorn, and tortillas. As long as the end result began with the entire grain, you'll still get all the benefits of the corn in things like cornmeal and polenta. Naturally sweet and tender, using corn as a whole grain in your diet offers a different texture and flavor from almost every other whole grain.

Farro

Farro, originally called emmer, is an ancient variety of wheat that was once a mainstay in the diets of people in the Fertile Crescent and in Italy. It lost popularity once those cultures learned that other varieties of wheat were easier to hull, but it is slowly regaining its popularity as an alternative whole grain to regular wheat. Farro can be labeled either as "whole" or as "pearled"; pearled means that the grains have been processed in some way. To make sure you're getting the entire grain, look for whole farro.

Kamut

Kamut is an heirloom grain and one that is making a comeback on the food scene after being abandoned years ago. It is often said to have a buttery flavor, which is very different from any other whole grains, which are typically nutty or slightly sweet. Kamut is one of the most popular grains used to make whole-grain products that are available in grocery stores.

Millet

Millet is one whole grain that is more often fed to birds than humans. It is a common ingredient in most birdseed mixes, but it's also one of the most popular grain choices in China, South America, Russia, and India. Toasting the grain before cooking it helps to bring out the slightly sweet flavor.

FACT

Millet is one grain that is gaining more attention lately and it's a delicious one to add to your diet. It has a slightly sweet flavor that is similar to corn and, when it's cooked, it has a fluffy, tender texture that makes it fun to use in your favorite side dish or grain salad. Millet isn't just for the birds!

Whole Oats and Oatmeal

Oats are one of the best whole grains to add to your diet. Even in processing, oats rarely have the bran and germ removed, which means that eating oats (in any form) is one of the best ways to make sure you are, in fact, having a whole grain. Whole oats are processed into many different textures, from steel-cut to rolled, with each texture requiring a different cooking time. Oats have a sweet flavor that makes them a delicious choice for breakfast or a healthy addition to baked goods.

Quinoa

Quinoa is another item that is used as a "whole grain" but isn't actually a grain. Originally eaten by the Incas, quinoa is a very tiny round seed that cooks in 10 minutes and turns fluffy once it's ready to eat. It is related to Swiss chard, but its light texture makes it a perfect addition to any meal as a grain option. Quinoa is also one of the few foods that is a complete protein on its own. There are three main types of quinoa that are cultivated: white (most common), red, and black. (White quinoa is used for the recipes in this book, unless specifically noted.)

Sorghum

Sorghum hasn't taken hold in the United States as a choice for food consumption as well as it has in other countries. Yet it is one of the most versatile grains and can be eaten as hot cereal and a popcorn-like snack or ground into flour for baking. Sorghum is a naturally gluten-free grain and has a completely edible hull, giving even more health benefits than some other grains.

Spelt

Spelt is a variety of wheat that can be used in place of regular wheat or other varieties of wheat in most recipes. It is higher in protein than common wheat and comes in both whole spelt or refined forms for cooking and eating. Spelt flour also is becoming more popular in baked goods and is available in many grocery stores for purchase.

Triticale

Triticale is not like other grains—it is actually a hybrid of durum wheat and rye. Triticale is almost always grown commercially and has only been available for about thirty years. Because it grows easily without fertilizers and pesticides, triticale is a great option for sustainable and organic whole-grain farming.

Whole Rye

Rye is most common in Northern European countries and in Russia because of its ability to thrive in cold, wet environments. Whole rye has a much higher level of fiber in its endosperm compared to other whole grains, which gives rye and rye products a lower glycemic index than those made from other whole grains. While most people know rye for its use in breads and crackers, it is also used as the base for salads and soups.

Whole and Cracked Wheat

Wheat, no matter the variety, is the most popular grain because of the amount of gluten contained in the grain. Wheat is not only used in whole forms, but wheat flour is the main ingredient in breads, pasta, and a large variety of baked goods and products. Wheat is usually split into categories based on when it is sown (winter or spring), the color of the wheat kernels (red or white), and the amount of protein it contains (hard or soft endosperms; hard wheat contains higher amounts of protein).

ESSENTIAL

There are more categories of wheat than there are any other whole grain, but the majority of people only eat one kind: refined, white flour. Each type of wheat—soft, hard, winter, spring—has its own flavor and texture, but those are lost when the grains are refined down into normal, all-purpose flour.

Bulgur, wheatberries, cracked wheat, and wheat flakes all consist of whole-wheat grains that are in presented in different forms and with different cooking methods.

Seeds You Can Sprout

Similar to grains, seeds already have everything inside that they need to begin new plant life. To make sure you have the right seeds, buy those that are meant to be used for eating rather than planting. Seeds meant for sowing are often treated with chemicals or processed in different ways that could make them unsafe to eat. Seeds most commonly used for sprouting are alfalfa, broccoli, celery, radish, and sunflower.

Alfalfa

Alfalfa is part of the pea family. It is a flowering plant that looks like clover and has groups of small purple flowers. Its most common use is as feed for cattle because of its high protein content and digestible fiber, but it is also eaten in sprout form on sandwiches and salads.

Broccoli

Broccoli is most commonly enjoyed in its fully mature form, but broccoli seeds can also be sprouted for three to four days before eating. As sprouts, broccoli has a flavor similar to radishes rather than the fully grown form of broccoli.

Celery

Celery seeds are often used as seasoning in dishes and the vegetable has a permanent place on the veggie tray, but celery sprouts aren't eaten as much as other sprouts. Celery sprouts have a bitter flavor that pairs well with sweet and acidic foods such as dried fruits, fresh fruits (especially citrus), and simple homemade vinaigrettes made with vinegar, oil, and spices.

Radish

When planting radishes from seed, one of the most important steps is to thin the seedlings to keep the growing plants healthy and give them room to develop their peppery bulbs. The seedlings and leaves that are removed or culled from the plot are tender and have a slightly spicy flavor that's similar to the radish as a whole. Once they are rinsed and cleaned, the sprouts are delicious in salads or used as a topping or garnish. You can also sprout radish seeds indoors in the same way as you do other seeds.

Sunflower

Sprouting sunflower seeds requires a bit more work than most other sprouts do because sunflower seeds need to be germinated and sprouted on soil. However, sunflower seeds have a great flavor once sprouted and are filled with protein, potassium, and a variety of vitamins.

Legumes You Can Sprout

Legumes are some of the easiest things to sprout at home. Because many legumes don't have a hard, thick outer shell, they sometimes need less soaking time before the sprouting begins. The most common legumes sprouted for food are lentils, mung beans, and chickpeas, or garbanzo beans.

Lentils

Lentils are, in their most basic form, already nutritional powerhouses that are full of protein, vitamins, and minerals. Once sprouted, lentils become even more nutritious. Brown, green, and red lentils can all be sprouted to use in salads, soups, or casseroles.

Mung Beans

Mung beans are small, green, oval-shaped beans that are used for cooking whole and for sprouting. Sprouting mung beans at home is one of the easiest to start with, as they don't require too much time or special equipment. The sprouts are used in stir-frys, spring rolls, salads, and garnishes.

Chickpeas

Chickpeas are one of the most easily digestible beans, making them one of the most popular beans to sprout. While sprouted chickpeas can be cooked, the raw sprouted beans can be blended into hummus or other chickpea-based dips and spreads as well.

A Wide Variety of Choices

Most people associate sprouts with alfalfa, but as you can see, there are many grains, seeds, and legumes you can sprout. This mix will open up a variety of recipe options for sprouting at home and trying some new foods.

It's worth trying different grains, both cooked from their raw state and sprouted, to figure out which flavors you enjoy the most and to find new ways to add them to your diet. Once you've sprouted the first time at home, the process becomes easier to follow each time.

CHAPTER 2

Sprouting: An Ancient Tradition

The sprouting of grains is a natural occurrence that happens every day in plant life, and in terms of sprouting grains for consumption, it began as an accident simply because of the way grains were stored in years past. Once people realized they could sprout grains and reap the benefits of those whole grains, they began to use them regularly as a low-cost, high-energy food. They also used them as medicine to heal the body from the inside out. As the health benefits became clear, sprouting grew in popularity.

An Accidental Beginning

Like many things in our current food system, sprouted grains and seeds first happened simply because of nature and their specific characteristics. Thousands of years ago, people didn't have as much storage space or things like refrigerators. Because of the way grains were stored after harvest, sprouting occurred in response to the environment and was not done on purpose. Sprouting grains and seeds on purpose has become rather popular and is beginning to show up in more mainstream areas, but the first sprouting of grains was more of a happy accident.

The First Sproutings

Traced back for thousands of years, sprouts have been referenced in history for medical and other nutritional reasons. In 1282 B.C., Shen-Nung, the Emperor of China, reported how good he was at growing mung beans himself. Whether or not he used the term "sprouted" or even knew what this report would do for the future of sprouting in the world, this record shows that sprouting was happening domestically thousands of years ago.

Sprouts of seeds and grains have been a large part of the history in Eastern cultures and are still a main staple in certain areas of the world. Sprouts and sprouting are also mentioned a few times in the Bible. However, sprouting took much longer to take off in Western cultures and is just now hitting its stride in certain areas of the world.

FACT

The main references to sprouted grains in the Bible come from Genesis 1:29 and Ezekiel 4:9. Food for Life Baking Company, a firm that makes sprouted-grain products, offers a variety of sprouted-grain foods that use the mixes of grains mentioned in the Bible, as well as other blends, to create tasty prepared sprouted-grain foods.

Accident or Luck?

In ancient times, and even just until a few hundred years ago, most grains were tied together and stored either in the field until the families were ready to use them or stored in some sort of barn or shelter. In those conditions, it was only a matter of time before the grains began to sprout on their own, leaving the families with already-sprouted grains to use in their diet. And these "accidental" sproutings were not as beneficial as when you deliberately sprout grains for yourself at home. Because the conditions for these early sproutings were not controlled or done on purpose, not every grain would sprout, but even a mix of sprouted and nonsprouted grains had more nutritional value than all nonsprouted grains.

Traditional Cultures and Sprouted Grains

Throughout history, some cultures and groups have documented using seed, legume, and grain sprouts for medicinal cures and nutritional reasons, as well as recording simple things like how they grew new plants or sprouts on their own. Historically, in Chinese culture, many families were known to grow sprouts themselves because sprouts, whether from seeds, legumes, or grains, were a low-cost food to produce and provided impressive nutritional benefits.

FACT

Scurvy is a human disease caused by a severe vitamin C deficiency. This lack of vitamin C can cause extreme weakness, swollen and painful joints, anemia, gum disease, and skin problems. Eating a diet high in vitamin C—which includes citrus fruits, berries, melons, peppers, tomatoes, dark greens, and some whole grains—can cure the disease.

One other historic recorded use of sprouts is from the 1770s. Captain James Cook was looking for cures and solutions for his ship's crew because the sailors were getting sick while out at sea. When a large number of his crew were found to have scurvy caused by the extreme lack of vitamin C, Captain Cook began to use sprouts as one way to easily give his men more vitamin C to help keep them healthy while they were onboard the ship. Along with citrus fruits and other vegetables, the regular use of sprouts in the men's diets cleared up the scurvy and solved one of the biggest health problems they were facing.

Historical Uses of Sprouted Grains

Throughout history, food has been used not only as nourishment but also to heal. In early civilizations, food and plants were the only things available to people when it came to curing diseases or treating infections, headaches, and stomachaches. Many of those early people found that certain foods did have healing powers and began to use them for medicinal purposes, as well as to feed their families and keep them healthy throughout the year.

Common Uses of Sprouted Grains

Sprouted grains are used today in many of the same ways as they were centuries ago. Whole grains, whether sprouted or not, are a relatively low-cost food that provides many different nutritional values. Grains can serve as the main part of a meal, the base of a salad, and the star of your breakfast, all depending on how you cook them and what you combine with them.

Because grains have all the basics to start a new plant life within the grain itself, sprouted grains are known to have a variety of vitamins and minerals that can cure illnesses and keep people healthy. Along with curing diseases or using them to help with certain nutritional deficiencies, sprouted grains are also eaten because they offer high levels of energy within the grains themselves. Because sprouted grains are complex carbohydrates, they are also one of the best sources of energy for our bodies.

ESSENTIAL

The most common way sprouts are used, both throughout history and today, is to add them to sandwiches, wraps, or salads. As sprouted beans, seeds, and grains grow in popularity, they are also making their way into new recipes and becoming the main ingredient of many dishes rather than a garnish or an afterthought.

One reason people began eating sprouted grains hundreds of years ago may simply have been because they couldn't afford to waste their grains. When the grains began sprouting on their own while they were being stored, families were still intent on eating all the food they had available to them, including these grains that they may have thought were ruined.

Historically, sprouted grains were often used for medical reasons, but they were also used as a healthy, filling food option that didn't cost much and that didn't require special processing or storage. Sprouting at home became a staple in Eastern cultures because the families could do everything themselves and have a healthy food on their tables.

A Rebirth in the Seventies

For years, the majority of the Western world didn't pay much attention to sprouting, or whole grains for that matter, but the movement steadily spread over the last century. As things began changing and shifting in the 1970s, people began to think more about their health, bringing sprouting and whole grains to a new level of awareness and into the homes and lives of people all over the country.

A Focus on Health

Until the 1970s, the Western world wasn't as concerned or as interested in health or in the health of the planet as we are today. But public awareness changed during the decade of the 1970s, and as health consciousness reached new levels, activities like sprouting and juicing began to spread like wildfire.

This decade was somewhat of a turning point in terms of health and nutrition, and the general interest in these topics. As families began turning more and more to convenience foods on the market and to fast-food restaurants, it was noticeable that the shape of America was changing. To help combat the growing costs of convenience foods and the ever-growing waistbands, many people began to accept more responsibility and take action for their food costs and especially for their personal health.

Running started to become popular as an exercise regimen in the 1970s, and eating healthier at home began to take hold. Getting back to basics in terms of food was more important in certain areas of the country, including making things at home again like bread and desserts.

For some families, sprouting became one of those hobbies to do at home. Sprouting grains, seeds, and legumes is easy enough to do at home with items you already have in your kitchen, and once people tasted sprouts and heard about the health benefits, sprouting at home became a normal occurrence in many kitchens around the country.

Sprouts, Grass, Seeds

In the 1970s, bean sprouts were the most popular sprout that people were eating on a regular basis. The health movement happening during that decade also gave birth to companies that created sprouts to sell in local markets and, eventually, to national stores.

ALERT

While store-bought sprouts make adding them to your diet more convenient, it's also important to be careful with them. Because store-bought sprouts have traveled across the country to get onto your grocery store shelf, they have a higher risk of carrying food-borne illnesses. When possible, it's always a healthier and safer choice to sprout your own at home.

As interest in health became more widespread, bean sprouts became available in the produce section of some grocery stores in certain areas of the country. Many people were still sprouting for themselves at home, but the availability of sprouts as a convenience food helped make them even more popular. Things like wheatgrass juice, sprouted grains, and an abundance of vitamins began to make their way into the homes of families and onto store shelves as companies started to cash in on the health trend.

New Techniques for Sprouting

As more and more companies got into the sprouting business, whether through mass production of sprouts to sell in stores or by selling sprouting kits or books on the subject for do-it-yourselfers, the techniques used for sprouting began to grow and change. Sprouting at home with a kit gave people new options that were exciting and different from their normal options. Trays and containers were trendier and looked good on a countertop compared to a big bowl or jar. Sprouting on a larger level to sell in stores offered even more challenges, as mass production of large quantities requires some changes in the process to make sure the sprouts are still healthy and ready for consumers.

Mass Production for Store-Bought Sprouts

With the expansion of the health movement in the 1970s, companies felt the demand for healthier options, including sprouts. While some people were sprouting at home, others were looking for quick options that could be bought at the store with their flour and sugar. To fill the demand, mass production of sprouting became part of the story. But sprouting at home on a small scale is simple to do. Since you can see every sprout in the batch on your countertop, you don't have to worry much about rot or fermentation. Sprouting on a larger scale, however, brought new complications and issues.

Factory sprouting on a large scale requires much more forethought and needs controls in place that aren't needed at home. Companies that are sprouting seeds, legumes, and grains on a large scale use very carefully and purposefully climate-controlled conditions, along with a scrutinizing quality control program to make sure that the sprouts they're making are harvested at the right time and will offer the most health benefits possible to the consumer picking them up off the shelf.

Not only do the companies need to make sure large batches of sprouts are harvested at the right time, they also need to have the correct containers and storage options. Since sprouts typically do not last more than one to two weeks, they do not have a long shelf life. This makes it very important for companies to harvest, store, and ship sprouts as quickly and safely as possible.

Kits and Books Emerge for Home Use

As sprouting gained momentum, sprouting kits and books hit the market, giving people even more reasons to sprout at home and take charge of their health. Before kits became available, most people were using jars, bowls, screens, or colanders to sprout their own grains and seeds. These options are still in use today, but the emergence of sprouting during the 1970s opened the door for kitchen tools designed specifically for sprouting.

ESSENTIAL

Store-bought sprouters and kits work in much the same way that a jar would at home—they allow air to get to the sprouts, let excess water drain away from the grains, and provide space for the sprouts to grow. Some kits make the process a little easier and less messy, but you'll end up with sprouted grains no matter what method you use.

One tool called the Easy Sprout, invented by Gene Monson, is rumored to have come to him in a dream one night in the 1970s. His hard work made that dream a reality, and the Easy Sprout is still being sold today as one of the most useful sprouting tools to have in your own kitchen.

Sprout enthusiast and author Steve Meyerowitz, a.k.a. Sproutman, among others, began writing books and manuals on the health benefits of sprouting and how to sprout your own seeds, legumes, and grains at home. Meyerowitz's book on sprouting, *Sprouts: The Miracle Food*, was first published in 1983 and is now in its sixth-edition printing. There are many other books about sprouting at home, including manuals and cookbooks as well.

CHAPTER 3

Nutritional Powerhouses

From a nutritional standpoint, whole and sprouted grains are one of the healthiest foods available. The whole grain is already high in nutrients and antioxidants, including fiber, vitamin B, vitamin C, folate, manganese, and amino acids. Sprouting whole grains activates enzymes within the grain that actually increase many of these nutrients, making the grains even more nutritious in their sprouted state. The nutrients found in whole grains are proven to aid heart disease, diabetes, and depression, and can help with weight loss and weight maintenance.

Nutrients in Whole Grains

When it comes to healthy foods, most people know that fruits and vegetables are full of vitamins, minerals, and nutrients that are essential for a healthy life. But many people don't realize how much whole grains have to offer. Whole grains are a fantastic source of disease-fighting antioxidants and other nutrients that aren't found in the same combinations in other foods.

Most Common Nutrients

Most whole grains have some level of vitamin B, vitamin E, magnesium, iron, and fiber, along with other phytochemicals and nutrients. (Phytochemicals are chemicals in plants that help prevent diseases and cell damage.) Because of the scientific makeup of the grain, there are certain combinations of nutrients and antioxidants that are found in whole grains and in whole grains only. This also occurs in fruits and vegetables, and these combinations of nutrients aid each other in making sure your body absorbs as much of them as it possibly can.

ESSENTIAL

Like all other natural and whole foods, grains contain their own unique blend of vitamins, minerals, and antioxidants that make up the base of the grain. Your body is able to absorb more nutrients when you ingest them in foods rather than in pill form because many of those nutrients work together with others to help the body absorb everything it needs from the food.

Vitamin B

B vitamins are essential vitamins that are normally found in fish, eggs, shellfish, dairy, meat, and whole grains. The family of B vitamins, more commonly called the vitamin B complex, is especially important for your mind and nervous system. B vitamins are linked to mood and memory, and in the right amounts, can help with stress, fatigue, anxiety, and depression, and offer an increase in energy.

Vitamin E

Vitamin E is the name used for a collection of fat-soluble compounds with many different health benefits. The E vitamins are typically found in nuts, seeds, vegetables oils, and leafy greens, but like many other vitamins, they are also offered in pill form for people with specific deficiencies. Vitamin E is extremely important to the body's overall function as it has antioxidants that keep the immune system running smoothly, offers anti-inflammatory benefits, aids circulation, and helps protect cells from free radicals.

FACT

Vitamin E is found in many foods, including whole grains, but the highest levels are found in wheat germ oil, sunflower seeds, almonds, sunflower oil, safflower oil, and hazelnuts. Along with nuts and seeds, dark greens also contain large amounts of vitamin E, which is essential for immune function and is also important for the health of your skin and circulation.

Magnesium

Among minerals found naturally in the body, magnesium constitutes the fourth highest concentration, and is very important for overall good health. Roughly 50 percent of naturally occurring magnesium is found in the bones, while the remaining magnesium is typically in the cells of your organs and tissues. Magnesium can also be found coursing through the body in the bloodstream, but it's a very small amount. Your body is made to keep magnesium at low levels in the bloodstream for optimum health. Magnesium is necessary for helping to maintain muscle strength, nerve function, steady heart rhythms, strong immune systems, and strong bones.

Spinach and other green vegetables are good sources of magnesium, as well as beans, peas, nuts, seeds, and whole grains. Because the majority of magnesium is in the germ and bran sections of the whole grain, refined grains do not provide nearly as much of this nutrient as whole grains that still include the germ and bran.

Iron

Iron itself is one of the most prevalent metals and is essential to almost every life form and human function. It's an important part of enzymes and proteins that keep you healthy, including things like keeping oxygen flowing through your body, helping regular cell growth, and providing energy. The majority of iron in the body is found in the hemoglobin in your red blood cells that carry important oxygen to your tissues and organs, but your body also stores iron for future needs.

QUESTION

What is hemoglobin?
Hemoglobin is a protein molecule in your red blood cells that helps carry oxygen from your lungs to your tissues and also carries carbon dioxide from the tissues back to the lungs for more oxygen to continue the cycle. Healthy hemoglobin also helps your red blood cells keep their shape, which keeps your blood flowing the way it should.

To get iron from food, you need to focus on two things. In its simplest forms, iron concentrations are naturally the highest in meats and beans. Foods like chicken, beef, turkey, fish, and pork all provide one type of iron, while beans, lentils, and tofu offer a different type. There are also smaller amounts of naturally occurring iron in spinach and fortified cereals.

Fiber

Dietary fiber is found in fresh fruits, vegetables, whole grains, and legumes, and includes every part of the food that your body can't use or digest. Fiber isn't digested by the body, but it serves a big purpose in the digestive health of your body. When the undigested fiber passes through the stomach, small intestine, and colon, it takes other things along with it, cleansing your digestive system of other things that it doesn't need or won't absorb. A diet high in fiber not only keeps your digestive system working and balanced, but it can also help regulate your blood pressure and cholesterol, control your blood sugar, and help in weight loss, as the fiber helps rid the body of excess waste.

QUESTION

Is added fiber the same as naturally occurring fiber?
Fiber has become more popular over the past few decades as it's been touted as important for heart health and for weight loss and maintenance. But many prepared foods include added fiber rather than naturally occurring fibers. While any fiber is good for your diet, it is always better and healthier to add foods to your diet that have their own fiber rather than foods with artificially added fibers. The natural fiber-filled foods also include additional nutrients and vitamins for your body that the added-fiber foods don't offer.

Dietary fiber occurs naturally in two forms: soluble and insoluble. Soluble fiber can dissolve in water, creating a gel-like substance in the body that attaches to other excess substances in the body, helping to clear them out as both fiber and excess pass through your system. Soluble fiber is highest in foods like peas, beans, oats, barley, carrots, apples, and some citrus fruits, and can help lower cholesterol and blood-sugar levels if they are high. Insoluble fiber helps to keep food progressing through the digestive system and increases the stool, which can be helpful to people who deal with constipation or other digestive issues. Insoluble fiber is found in wheat bran, whole grains, whole-wheat flour, nuts, and most vegetables.

The amount of fiber in foods varies, and many natural foods like whole grains and beans contain both types of fiber. To have the best balance of fiber working through your system, you should eat a variety of foods with naturally occurring fiber for optimum health.

Whole Grains and Specific Nutrients

Whole grains as a category tend to offer similar essential nutrients, but among individual types there are some differences as well. Every grain has its own mix of vitamins and minerals because each grain requires different levels of certain nutrients for new plants to grow. The grains listed here are some of the types most commonly used in both raw and sprouted forms.

Oats

Whole oats, in almost every form, still have the germ and bran intact, leaving the most nutritional value within the grain itself. Oats offer manganese, selenium, tryptophan, phosphorous, vitamin B_1, dietary fiber, magnesium, protein, and fiber, making it a healthy and powerful option for breakfast or a side dish.

Quinoa

Quinoa, pronounced "KEEN-wa," is not a whole grain at all, but it is actually a seed that is rich in amino acids and protein. Quinoa contains almost half of your daily required value of manganese, plus magnesium, iron, tryptophan, copper, and phosphorous. There are over 100 known varieties of quinoa, but the most commonly cultivated are white (which is an ivory color), red, and black. While the health benefits of each variety of quinoa are similar, they do provide different textures and flavors in your recipes. Compared to white quinoa, the red variety tends to hold its shape better, making it a great choice for salad recipes or if you need the grains to keep their shape and stay separate from your other ingredients. Black quinoa has a sweeter flavor and keeps its deep color even after cooking.

Wheat

Whole wheat offers a large amount of essential nutrients, but the majority of these are only available when wheat is eaten in its unrefined and whole form. High in manganese, magnesium, tryptophan, and dietary fiber, whole wheat offers many more than just these nutrients: There are more than eighty nutrients documented in whole wheat.

FACT

Tryptophan is an amino acid that helps to break down proteins in the body. It helps to regulate mood, appetite, and sleep patterns. Many people realize that tryptophan is found in turkey, but don't realize that tryptophan is also found in nuts, seeds, whole grains, red meat, dairy products, bananas, and some soy products.

Buckwheat

Buckwheat is not a type of wheat at all. Buckwheat groats are fruit seeds, but they are often used in ways similar to the way wheat is used. Buckwheat is also a grain-type option for people who cannot tolerate gluten and wheat. Buckwheat, like whole wheat, is also highest in manganese, tryptophan, magnesium, and dietary fiber, but also offers smaller amounts of other essential nutrients.

Barley

In terms of nutrients, barley offers one of the highest levels of naturally occurring dietary fiber in all of the whole grains. Similar to wheat, barley is also high in manganese, tryptophan, phosphorous, selenium, and copper. These are the highest-occurring nutrients found in barley, but in total, it offers more than eighty different essential nutrients and vitamins in its whole-grain form.

Chickpeas

Chickpeas, or garbanzo beans, are one of the healthiest beans available. Just two cups of chickpeas provides the full daily requirement of dietary fiber for your body and includes more than eighty different nutrients. Chickpeas are high in molybdenum, manganese, folate, protein, copper, phosphorous, and iron, making it a superfood when it comes to nutrition.

Lentils

Lentils are legumes, like beans, but they contain different levels of nutrients that are specific to lentils themselves. As a legume, lentils are high in protein, which is what legumes are typically known for, but lentils are also high in molybdenum, folate, dietary fiber, tryptophan, manganese, iron, copper, vitamin B1, and potassium, all of which are necessary for your body to function well. The most common types in the United States are either green or brown, but lentils are also available in black, yellow, red, and orange.

Increases in Nutrients from Sprouting

Contained within every seed and whole grain is every essential part that is necessary to begin new plant growth. While the grains are dormant and resting in their whole-grain state, these nutrients are waiting under the surface for the growth stage to begin. The act of sprouting allows this process to start, letting you reap the benefits of higher levels of nutrients in your favorite whole grains.

Nutrient Activation

Most nutrients found in whole grains that are needed for their growth remain dormant in the grain until the germination process is under way. As the grain is preparing to start new life, these necessary vitamins and minerals begin to work within the seed itself, providing energy and nutrition that a new plant needs to survive.

FACT

Phytic acid helps store phosphorus in plants until they are ready to use it for new plant life. Phytic acid prohibits nutrients from being absorbed and that is its job—this acid works while the grain is in its dormant stages, keeping the plant in waiting until the environment is just right for sprouting.

Soaking and sprouting grains kicks off the germination process, waking up the nutrients that are waiting inside to begin their work. As the grains soak and begin to sprout, these essential vitamins and minerals are working in high gear to start new plant life. Before the germination process begins, growth inhibitors keep the grains from sprouting before the time and conditions are right. When grains are soaked for the right amount of time in prime conditions, germination starts. These growth inhibitors are then deactivated by the grain, letting the nutrients and enzymes take over and start the growth process. This activation in sprouting is what makes sprouted grains an even healthier option than whole grains that are simply cooked and eaten from their raw state.

Nutrients Increased with Sprouting

While almost all nutrients contained inside whole grains are at higher levels once sprouting has begun, the nutrient levels that are increased the most are those that are extremely essential to the life process of the plant itself.

Vitamins B and C are both important for plant growth and are two nutrients that are activated in the sprouting process. Nutrients like folate, fiber, and other essential amino acids are necessary for plant growth and are at higher levels in sprouted grains than in their raw state. All other vitamins and minerals contained in the grain are certainly still there—they do not leave at any point—but the ones needed for growth and nutrient absorption in the plant itself are ones that increase the most once the grain is sprouted. There are also some amino acids and other nutrients that are completely dormant in the raw whole grain and are only activated once sprouting has started.

Enzymes for Better Digestion

Each seed and grain has natural enzymes within the seed itself that are necessary to help new plants grow healthy and strong. These enzymes are typically in a resting state in the whole grain and are only active once the germination and sprouting stages have begun, as the grain itself does not need these enzymes until a new plant is beginning to grow.

Role of Enzymes

When grains and seeds are still in their sleeping, or dormant, state, there are growth inhibitors actively working to keep the grains intact. Until the germination process begins, these growth inhibitors make sure that the grain or seed stays dormant so that its protective shell or seed coat remains there and keeps the surroundings from damaging the essential minerals and nutrients within the grain.

Once the germination and sprouting process begins and conditions are right for growth, enzymes within the grain essentially "turn off" these growth inhibitors. When this happens, all the energy and starches that the grain has been holding in storage to keep the grain healthy are transformed by the enzymes into simpler forms that the young plant can easily use and digest.

More Enzymes, Better Digestion?

Enzymes in sprouted grains work to make the essential nutrients more easily digestible to the plant itself as it begins to grow. Because of this, sprouted grains are often viewed as being more easily digested by people than their raw and cooked counterparts.

ESSENTIAL

If you are sensitive to grain in your diet, you may want to try sprouted grains as opposed to regular cooked grains. While there still may be some varieties that bother you, the extra enzymes in sprouted grains may solve the digestive issues you have with certain grains.

As the enzymes work in the newly sprouted grain, everything within the grain is actively working on beginning new plant life. The molecules are broken down into only the necessary nutrients to enhance the growth process for the grain or seed, and those simpler versions are often more easily digested and absorbed into your body as well. The enzymes in the grain are basically one step ahead of you. These enzymes in sprouts are similar to what your body produces in the digestive process to help break down foods and release the nutrients that your body can use and absorb. Since the enzymes in the grain are already making these nutrients easy to digest and readily available, your body has one less step to do in the digestion of these foods, which is why sprouted grains are often easier to digest.

Because sprouting activates these enzymes and increases the nutrient values in the grain itself, sprouts offer more than just whole-grain goodness. Consuming sprouts gives you all of the nutritional benefit of that whole grain while also giving your body the best chance to digest and absorb the essential nutrients in the grain.

Recent Studies on the Benefits of Sprouted Grains

As whole-grain consumption and sprouting grow in popularity, research on the health benefits of eating whole grains and sprouts continues to develop. The variety of whole grains available and those that are easy to sprout has opened up many different avenues in research to see just how healthy whole grains are. The combination of nutrients found in whole grains make them miracle workers when it comes to keeping you healthy. Though the health benefits of whole and sprouted grains are explained and supported in the following text, always consult a physician or health care professional if you experience any unusual or persistent symptoms or suspect you may have ailments that require medical attention or treatment of any kind.

Heart Health

Risk factors for heart disease are high blood pressure, obesity, diabetes, high cholesterol, or a combination of these. When a body is battling with any of these issues, the heart is made to work harder than usual, which causes stress on the heart muscles and tissues, and can cause more inflammation in the arteries. These factors all affect the heart directly in some way, either through the blood that is pumping through the body or via the indirect strain placed on the heart in order to deal with these other conditions.

One of the most important nutrients for heart health is dietary fiber. Both soluble and insoluble fiber are necessary for keeping your body in balance for digestion and heart health. Fiber also helps to lower your cholesterol because part of its job is to carry the bad cholesterol out of your body, which keeps your heart healthy. Including soluble and insoluble dietary fiber in your daily diet also helps to lower blood pressure; lowering blood pressure takes some of the stress off your heart.

ESSENTIAL

When it comes to diet, two of the best ways to create a healthier heart are to increase the amount of fiber you eat and to limit the amount of saturated fats you consume. Eating a heart-healthy breakfast is as easy as trading your sugary cereal for a filling bowl of oats with fruit and chopped nuts.

Barley is one of the best grain options when it comes to fiber and eating for heart health. Compared to other whole grains, barley has the highest level of fiber because the fiber isn't isolated to certain parts of the grain—the fiber in barley can be found throughout the entire grain. But even though barley has the highest levels of fiber, any whole-grain choice is better than refined grains for keeping your heart healthy.

Oats have also been tied to lowering the risk of heart disease in many studies. Oats have high levels of fiber as well and offer anti-inflammatory effects that help keep the blood vessels and heart working optimally.

Diabetes

Diabetes, at its basic form, is a metabolic disorder in which the body is not able to break down, or metabolize, glucose (sugar) that is needed for energy. There are two different categories of diabetes, commonly referred to as type 1 and type 2. Type 1 diabetes is a condition in which the body is not producing its own insulin. Insulin is a naturally occurring hormone secreted by the pancreas that helps your body manage blood-sugar levels. This type of diabetes is not preventable and is irreversible, as there is no way to re-create the cells in the body that produce insulin. Type 1 diabetes is not affected by diet or lifestyle and is controlled by taking insulin regularly through external means.

FACT

Type 2 diabetes, formerly referred to as adult-onset diabetes, is no longer reserved for the adult population. With the rise of obesity in children, type 2 diabetes is quickly becoming one of the most diagnosed health problems in children due to a lack of healthy diet and physical activity.

In type 2 diabetes, the body is producing its own insulin, but either there isn't enough for the body to function correctly or the insulin itself isn't working the way it should. This type of diabetes is developed over time (normally later in life), mostly due to poor diet and an inactive lifestyle. Managing type 2 diabetes is possible and can include medications, but one of the most effective ways to control the effects of type 2 diabetes is through diet and lifestyle. If you have diabetes or suspect that you might, check with your physician for diet and treatment recommendations.

In almost every research study that has been done on the health effects of a diet rich in whole grains, fiber is always one of the factors that makes a measurable difference, especially when dealing with type 2 diabetes. Soluble fiber is an important nutrient for people dealing with diabetes, because soluble fiber helps to slow down the rate at which your body absorbs glucose from the foods you eat. This process helps to keep blood-sugar levels lower, making fiber essential for those who have diabetes or who need to keep their blood-sugar levels in check.

Not every grain has high levels of soluble fiber, but any whole grain will have some soluble fiber in its makeup. The effect of this fiber is a healthy choice for anyone either with or without diabetes. Oats, barley, wheat, legumes, and quinoa are all good options to help control diabetes and to lower blood-sugar levels.

Other Health Issues and Diseases

While whole grains are most notably associated with lowering the risk for heart disease and helping to manage diabetes, the variety of nutrients in whole grains also lowers the risks for other diseases and health issues.

Depression

When most people think of depression, they don't often think of food as being a way to help control it. The majority of whole grains contain tryptophan, an amino acid that helps trigger the body to produce serotonin, which is involved in the transmission of nerve impulses and can help create a mood-stabilizing effect in the body and mind. Grains are also high in B vitamins, which are essential for the nervous system and for having energy and feeling good. Without enough vitamin B, you can feel irritated, exhausted, and, ultimately, depressed. Manganese, a common nutrient found in whole grains, is needed to keep your nervous system working correctly and is necessary for combating depression. By adding whole grains that include these nutrients to your diet, it can make a difference in how you feel *and* improve your heart health.

Liver Disease

The liver serves many purposes in the body: It aids in digestion, helps the body absorb nutrients, stores some nutrients for later use, and filters toxins and other things that the body can't use and must get rid of. Liver disease—when the liver isn't working correctly—can occur for many reasons. Some liver disease is inherited through family health problems, and it can also develop if you are exposed to certain viruses or substances that attack the liver. While liver disease cannot fully be cured by diet alone, the way you eat and live does make a difference in managing liver diseases.

What is the difference between complex carbohydrates and simple carbohydrates?
Complex carbohydrates are those than contain three or more sugars, while simple carbohydrates have just one or two sugars. The higher number of sugars in the complex carbohydrates helps them break down more slowly in the body, meaning that you are satisfied longer, have more sustained energy, and don't get the "sugar rush" that you would expect from other simple carbohydrates like processed foods or sweet desserts.

Eating a diet rich in complex carbohydrates is one way to help combat the effects of disease. Complex carbohydrates, like whole grains, give the body a wide variety of vitamins, minerals, fiber, and antioxidants that help to support a healthy immune system, so your body will be working at its best to help keep you safe from illnesses and diseases.

High Cholesterol and High Blood Pressure

Not everyone who has high cholesterol or high blood pressure has heart disease, but both factors are directly related to heart disease and more serious heart problems. Cholesterol is a substance found in the fat in your blood, and the body uses cholesterol to build new cells. There are two types of cholesterol, also known as "good cholesterol" (HDL), which actually helps the heart, and "bad cholesterol" (LDL) because of their different effects on the body. Most cholesterol is LDL cholesterol, and this is the kind that is most likely to clog the blood vessels, keeping blood from flowing through the body the way it should. Working opposite of LDL, HDL cholesterol removes cholesterol from the blood vessels and carries it back to the liver, where it can be processed and sent out of the body. When you have high LDL cholesterol, it can cause problems because the excess can build up in your arteries and develop blockages that keep blood from flowing freely.

High blood pressure results when the force of the blood pumping through your body is higher than is healthy. When there is too much pressure on the artery walls, serious problems can develop, including coronary heart disease, stroke, and heart failure.

Grains that are high in fiber, like barley, oats, wheat, and legumes, are proven to help lower both high cholesterol and high blood pressure. The fiber in whole grains helps to rid the body of excess cholesterol, which lowers the total cholesterol in the body and keeps blockages from forming. While the body is being cleared of extra cholesterol, this also cleans the blood pumping through the body and reduces the amount of pressure the blood needs to get through the arteries efficiently.

Stress and Anxiety

Similar to depression in symptoms, added stress and anxiety can cause additional health problems that include sleeping disturbances, digestive concerns, and a stressed immune system. Including foods with high levels of tryptophan in your daily diet will help ensure that your body is creating enough serotonin, a neurotransmitter that helps keep your sleep cycle regular and provides a mood-stabilizing effect. Tryptophan is found in almost every whole grain, as well as in other foods such as lean protein and dairy.

Whole grains as a category are also one of the most satiating foods to eat. The combination of fiber, protein, and other nutrients found in whole grains helps to fill you up and keep you satisfied longer than refined grains do. Unlike refined grains, whole-grain foods do not spike blood sugar, so you won't experience the crash of energy you normally feel after having a sugary meal or snack.

Digestive Issues

One subject that people don't always want to talk about is digestion. But digestion is a huge part of your body's health. Digestion issues can spread into all other areas of your body and your life if they are not taken care of.

The most common digestion concerns tend to be things like gas, bloating, constipation, or loose stools. While there can be larger problems that cause digestion issues, your diet is one of the major factors influencing how your body digests and uses food.

If you are having digestion problems, it's a good sign that your body may not be absorbing the nutrients from the foods you are eating. A healthy digestive system should not be painful or uncomfortable, and it should work well without any help from you in the form of pills or liquids (unless medications are prescribed by a physician or health care professional).

One thing to consider is how much fiber you are getting and what sources that fiber is coming from. The best choice is to always pick foods with naturally occurring fiber, both soluble and insoluble, rather than foods with added fiber. Whole grains, beans, legumes, vegetables, and fruits all have naturally occurring fiber. Naturally occurring fiber helps your body break down these wholesome foods to get the nutrients it needs, and keeps the food moving through your system so it can rid itself of the excess that won't be used.

ESSENTIAL

The USDA now recommends that men get 38 grams and that women get 25 grams of fiber each day. If your diet relies mostly on whole grains and fresh fruits and vegetables, this number will be easy to reach. If, however, much of your food is processed or based on re-fined white flour, it will be harder to get the recommended amount of fiber to keep your digestive track moving smoothly.

Expanding Your Diet

If you're already eating whole grains as part of your diet, that's great! Whole grains, in their raw and cooked forms, give you great health benefits. Adding sprouted grains to your diet can give you even better results, including higher energy and increased levels of nutrient absorption. Expanding your diet to include some sprouted grains is an easy way to add more nutrients to your day and to try new foods and new combinations.

Add New Flavors and Textures

Compared to their refined forms, whole grains do have a different texture since they still contain the three parts of the grain. Some whole grains are fluffy and tender when cooked, some are chewy and hearty, others keep their form, and still others break down into a creamy texture. Whole grains can be substituted for any refined grain in a recipe, and they often bring a new level of flavor and texture to a dish that refined grains don't have.

Like refined grains, whole grains are often light in flavor and do not overwhelm a dish. In fact, most whole grains serve as a fantastic base for salads, casseroles, and other dishes because they take on any flavors you pair with the grains.

Nutritional Punch: Whole Grains Versus Refined

Refined grains are just that: grains that have been processed in a way that strips them of one or more parts of the grain. Refined grains are still considered grains, but because parts of the grain have been removed, they do not offer nearly as much nutritional benefit as the whole version.

Think of whole grains as you would a whole fruit or vegetable. An apple, for instance, has the peel and the flesh of the fruit. While the flesh contains many vitamins and minerals, a good amount of the fiber and other nutrients are found in the peel. When you peel your apples, you're losing many of the naturally occurring nutrients from the apple that the flesh itself doesn't offer. Eating whole grains (and fruits and vegetables) whenever possible gives you all the nutrients those foods have to offer.

Many of the essential nutrients seeds and grains need for growth are contained within the germ and bran of the grain. When those are removed in processing, most of the health benefits of that grain go with them and there is no way to get them back. Another major loss in refined grains is how the nutrients work together in both the grain and your body. When some nutrients are removed from the grain, that can prevent others in the grain from being absorbed in the body as easily as they would if all the nutrients were still intact.

Choosing whole grains and sprouted grains over refined is an easy way to add more vitamins and minerals to your diet. Thanks to more options in stores and online, whole grains are easy to find.

CHAPTER 4

Tools and Equipment

Sprouting your own grains at home is easy to do and requires only a few items, including the grains themselves, some type of container, and water. As long as you have those three items, you can sprout anything at home. There are sprouting kits available for purchase that may make the process easier or take up less room on your counter, but most sprouting can be done with things you already have in your kitchen.

Seeds

In order to sprout your own grains, the one item you need to have is the seeds themselves. The seed of any grain, bean, or lentil you purchase is basically a small plant embryo resting inside the seed coating. This seed coating serves as a protective layer for the seed, keeping all the necessary nutrients and stored energy safe from the surrounding environment. The size of seeds varies from plant to plant, from very tiny (chia seeds) to somewhat larger (butter beans, peanuts), and the seed coatings can be extremely different between each variety of plant. For example, peanuts have a paper-thin layer seed coating that is hidden beneath the hard outer shell, providing even more protection, but coconuts have a much more substantial shell that is extremely thick and tough to crack.

The stored energy and nutrients contained within each seed are triggered by certain forces of nature (i.e., water, sunlight) and when that energy is set into motion, the seed starts working to produce a new plant. The actual sprouting of any grain or seed happens once that energy and all the nutrients found within the seed have been activated. Some sprouts aren't eaten until they have the telltale "tail," but for most sprouts, the increase in nutrients and health benefits are available before the tail is visible.

Where to Get Them

Seeds and whole grains themselves are easy to find. Most grocery stores or markets will sell the more popular seeds you can use to sprout at home, like oats, wheat, rice, sunflower seeds, and lentils.

If you're looking for grains, seeds, or legumes that aren't as common, such as Kamut or buckwheat, there are specialty shops and online markets that offer the harder-to-find grains to purchase so you can sprout them yourself. Using whole grains and sprouting at home are becoming more popular with people all over the country, which means more varieties of grains and seeds will continue to show up on store shelves and online for purchase.

The Right Storage

When buying seeds, grains, and legumes to keep at home for sprouting, you'll usually find that the best deals will mean buying a larger quantity than you might buy normally. How you store your products will make a big difference in how long they will last, making sure that you get your money's worth.

Before Sprouting

Grains will keep extremely well in cooler temperatures, either in airtight containers or sealed in the freezer. Softer grains such as barley, oats, and quinoa won't keep as long as some of the harder grains like wheat, spelt, and corn, but all grains can potentially last for years as long as they are kept away from high heat.

ESSENTIAL

Once you have your whole grains, seeds, or legumes at home and are ready to begin sprouting, make sure that you have kept your grains away from heat. Warmer temperatures can cause the grains to begin sprouting before you are ready, which can cause rot or fermentation in your grain storage.

Legumes will last when kept in airtight containers, but they can also be frozen if you'd rather save shelf space for other items. For storing them frozen or in your pantry, try to remove as much air from the containers as possible before sealing. Using a vacuum sealer and recommended bags or material will ensure that all of the air is removed from your legumes before freezing.

Seeds should be kept in the freezer or in a completely airtight container. Depending on what seeds you want to keep on hand, consider testing a small batch of the seeds in different storage methods to see what you like best and how well they keep for future use.

After Sprouting

Sprouted grains, legumes, and seeds can be kept in the refrigerator for up to a week or longer. To ensure that they will last you throughout the week, store them in a plastic bag or open container and rinse them every two to three days.

Kept cool, the sprouts will retain the increase in nutritional value for a week or so, but after the first week, the levels will slowly begin to decrease as each day passes. It's always best to sprout smaller batches at home. Sticking with smaller batches means that they won't go waste and that you can make sure all the sprouts are healthy since you won't have to shuffle through a large container.

Germination

Germination is the process in which seeds or spores release their plant and begin to grow. This act is what brings new plants into being and can help to explain anything that is growing into being from a small start.

In order to get seeds to germinate, you need to create the right environment. Germination relies on things like the correct amounts of water, oxygen, temperature, and the balance between those factors.

Water

Water is one requirement for germination. Since the seeds or grains you want to sprout are dry, water is needed to soak in and start the growth process again. Once the seeds, grains, or legumes have absorbed enough water, the seed coat breaks down, which allows the physical sprout to become visible.

ALERT

Because the sprout is the root of the new plant reaching out to find a stronghold to anchor the new growth, your sprouts may end up in a tangled jumble of sprouted grains. As long as you're rinsing and draining them correctly, it should be easy to separate them so you can gather as much as you want at one time.

Letting seeds or grains soak in water is also a great way to test them to make sure they are still good. Seeds that are getting ready to germinate will soak up quite a bit of water. They need the water to activate the enzymes inside that trigger the cells to start growing and duplicating. Once the plant embryo inside the seed grows large enough, it bursts through the coat, letting the tip of the root (or the sprout) emerge. This happens so it can find a place to hold on to to keep the plant in place and to let the plant absorb water and nutrients from the soil.

Oxygen

Like all other living things, oxygen is necessary for metabolism and, in plants, is required to provide energy. For most seeds, grains, and legumes, oxygen is needed to keep the growth process going; if your seeds or grains become too waterlogged or don't have access to oxygen, they will not sprout.

Sprouting your grains in a controlled environment at home helps to ensure that all of your grains are getting the same amount of oxygen throughout the sprouting process. Using tools at home or a sprouting kit will allow air to get to the grains and circulate, which also keeps them from going bad before they're ready to eat.

ESSENTIAL

If you think about the normal life process of a plant, sprouting is no different. For most plant life, a new plant begins once it has been planted, is watered, and has sunshine to help the baby plant grow tall and strong. Germination is that process in which water, oxygen, and light work together with the seed or grain to start a new life.

Temperature

The temperature and environment can affect the growth rate of your sprouts. Depending on the type of seed or grain you're using, the optimal temperature will vary between each variety because of their specific characteristics.

For most seeds, grains, and legumes, keeping them at 75–90°F will allow them to begin the germination process and begin sprouting. This range works well for sprouting at home, as some area in most homes usually falls within this temperature range. Sprouting indoors also allows you to keep the grains at a consistent temperature. Finding the best temperature in your own home for sprouting will help give you healthy sprouts each time.

Sprouting Kits

As home sprouting becomes more and more popular, kits to use in your own kitchen are becoming easier to find. Sprouting kits come in a variety of shapes and sizes to fit any seed or grain you want to sprout. If you want to go with a store-bought kit, your options will be a tray system, a sprouting container, or a sprouting bag. Depending on what you want to sprout at home, you may find that certain kits work better for some grains than others; it may be worth having more than one sprouting option at home.

Trays

One type of sprouting kit you can purchase uses trays for sprouting the seeds or grains. Typically stacked on top of each other, the tray kits don't take up too much space on your counter. Sprouting tray kits typically come with three to four trays, a drain board, and a cover. Because you get more than one tray, the kit lets you sprout a few different seeds or grains at the same time in each tray, saving you time and using that space as efficiently as possible.

ESSENTIAL

Before buying one or more sprouting kits to use at home, try sprouting your own using items you already have in your kitchen. You may find that you enjoy sprouting your grains in a jar or using a bowl and colander. Knowing how it works, how much time it takes, and what space you'll need will help you decide later if you want to buy a premade sprouting kit.

Sprouting Canisters or Containers

Sprouting canisters or cylinders do the same work of the tray kits, but these canisters only sprout one type of seed or grain at a time. The containers are designed to utilize the energy and heat from the sprouting seeds and grains to help circulate air in the container, which keeps the sprouts healthy and allows the germination process to thrive. The vented lid also allows oxygen to get to the sprouts and eliminates excess moisture. Because these containers are smaller than the tray systems, they do take up less space for both usage and storage. They also are small enough that they are easy to take with you if you're traveling and want to have fresh sprouts.

Sprouting Bag

Woven hemp sprouting bags are another option to use at home. Because of the porous weave of the material used for the bags, the sprouts get a good amount of air circulation and the bag is able to drain well, keeping the sprouts in a healthy growing environment.

Since the bag needs to be hung up somewhere to fully drain, you will have to find a place to keep the bag—over a sink, bathtub, or basin—while the sprouts are working. Using hemp sprouting bags does ensure that the sprouts drain well, but they do need more frequent rinsing to keep them from drying out.

FACT

Hemp is a plant that is extremely versatile and can be grown in a variety of climates. The fiber from the plants can be used to make hemp fabric and plastic, which has been used in many different ways over the course of history, including for paper and cloth.

Hemp sprouting bags are the most convenient store-bought option since they are easy to fold up and put away. They take up a very small amount of space when you're not using them, which makes them a great choice for traveling as well. The bags are extremely durable, thanks to the strength of the hemp, and they will last for a very long time.

Using Common Household Items for Sprouting

Some sprouting kits and packages make the sprouting process easy to do at home, but you can also sprout any grain on your own with items you already have in your house. People have been sprouting seeds, grains, and legumes at home for centuries, and were doing it long before tray kits or sprouting bags were available. Sprouting at home is easy to do, and you may already have the equipment you need to start.

Glass Jars

Glass jars can be used for sprouting by securing some type of screen, mesh, cheesecloth, nylon stockings, or any other permeable materials to the lid with the ring. You can also buy mesh inserts or plastic sprouting lids with holes of various sizes that fit standard Mason glass canning jars. You want something that allows you to drain the water out of the jar without losing the sprouts themselves, so any mesh or screen needs to have small perforations to keep the sprouts inside the jar while draining.

To sprout in a glass jar, you'll want to fill the jar with cool water and your seeds, grains, or legumes and let them soak for the specific time for that variety of seed. After soaking, you will need to rinse the sprouts so you can pour all the soaking water out of the jar (using your screen, mesh, or cloth to keep the sprouts inside the jar) and fill the jar again with cool water. Swirl the water around in the jar with the sprouts and pour the water off. To fully rinse the sprouts, repeat this a few times to make sure all the soaking water has been rinsed off. Rinse the grains two to three times each day to keep the sprouts growing and to ensure that they are getting oxygen and fresh water. Once the sprouts are the size you want them, drain off as much of the water as you can. With the jars, the easiest way to do this is to hold the jar upside down with your screen or cloth in place on the lid and let the water run out of the jar. Shake the jar until you can no longer see water coming out of the jar.

ALERT

If you're using a glass jar for your first at-home sprouting and you don't have a screen or mesh that will fit over the lid of the jar, try stretching and securing some cheesecloth, a knee-high nylon stocking, or a paper towel over the top of the jar; make sure to replace the paper towel after each rinsing so you don't lose your grains down the drain.

Bowl and Colander Combination

For most grains and legumes, you can also sprout them at home using a bowl, colander, plate, and kitchen towel. To start, add your grains or legumes to a large bowl and cover them with cool water. Let them soak for eight to twelve hours (overnight, if you can) before draining in the colander and rinsing until the water coming through the sprouts is running clean. Fully drain the grains in the colander after rinsing, then move the colander onto a plate (to catch any remaining water from the grains) and cover the colander with a kitchen towel. Rinse the grains fully and drain them every eight to twelve hours—the easiest is to do this each morning and evening—until you begin to see the sprouts showing on the grains. Once you have the sprouts at the length you want, rinse and drain them one more time. Let them sit out for a few more hours to let all of the water drain off, until the sprouts are dry to the touch.

Making Space and Getting Ready to Sprout

While sprouting does take a few days, the actual hands-on time isn't much over the course of the process from start to finish. For the first few times you sprout, it might be helpful to collect everything you'll need and have it in one place for easy access while your sprouts are growing.

Basic At-Home Kit

The first time you want to sprout at home, gather all the things you'll need and set them aside a day before you start your batch of sprouts.

Before beginning your sprouting venture, you'll need:

- Grains, seeds, or legumes you want to sprout
- Sprouting kit (tray, container), jars with appropriate lids, or bowl/colander setup
- Cool water
- Container to store in once they are sprouted

Seeing all of the tools and ingredients you need to sprout will help get you ready for the first sprouting adventure. Once you have your basic kit together, and if you have the space, find a spot to keep all your sprouting tools together. When you're ready for the next batch of sprouts, everything will be ready and waiting for you and it will be easy to start the process.

The Perfect Space

Since the sprouting process requires you to rinse and drain the sprouts a few times a day, keeping them in a place near a sink or basin will make the process easier. The kitchen is the most obvious place, but if you have other options in your home that will work, feel free to move your sprouting area around until you find the perfect space for you.

ESSENTIAL

If your home stays warmer during the day or gets a large amount of sunshine, you may want to seek out other places to keep your sprouts while they're growing. Too much sunlight or heat can make the sprouts go bad, so keeping them at a comfortable temperature is the best option. Try a counter or table away from direct sunlight or in a basement with a window that stays cooler but offers some natural light during the day.

For instance, if you're using the sprouting bag, putting them in the bathroom with the bag hanging over the tub would be a great way to keep them while they're draining each time. You would still have access to water from the sink and the shower and tub, and since they're still inside the home, you won't have to worry about consistent oxygen and temperature levels like you would if you were trying to sprout grains outside.

Any spot in your home that easily keeps a consistent temperature and gives the sprouts some access to sunlight will work perfectly to help your sprouts grow. Experiment to find what works best for you!

CHAPTER 5

Sprouting Your Own

The basic process for sprouting your own grains, seeds, or legumes at home is essentially the same for whatever type you're using. Some grains will need more soaking time or legumes may need an extra rinse before they're ready, but once you get the process down, sprouting your own grains will be easy. The grains do the majority of the work by themselves, and there isn't much hands-on time to get the grains sprouted and ready to enjoy.

Basic Sprouting Techniques

No matter what you want to sprout at home, the basic process will be the same. Timing will differ between different grains, but getting a good sprouting setup ready will make each sprouting venture quicker and easier for you.

While the specifics may be slightly different for certain grains, sprouting at home will typically follow these steps:

1. Sort through your grain and make sure all the grains look whole and healthy before moving forward.
2. Rinse the grains completely.
3. Pour your grains into a container (large bowl, canister, jar, or other vessel) and add enough cool water so that the water level is a few inches above the grains. Let the grains soak in the water overnight.
4. In the morning, drain the grains and, using a colander or screened jar lid, rinse the grains with water a few times until the water runs clean.
5. Two to three times during the day, rinse the grains again and toss them around in the bowl or jar to make sure they are getting oxygen and water and that they are being fully rinsed each time.
6. Rinse the grains two to three times a day for a few days until the grains have sprouted to the stage where you want them.
7. Rinse and drain the sprouts one more time, and refrigerate them for use or dehydrate them to make flour.

ESSENTIAL

Learning to sprout your own grains, seeds, and legumes will give you a skill that many people today don't possess: the ability to feed your family on your own, from raw ingredients. So much of today's food options are ready-to-eat and processed, and don't give you the chance to do some of the work yourself. Knowing how to provide healthy food for your family is an important part of life.

Depending on the grain you are sprouting, you may not need to soak them as long or rinse and drain them as often, but if you can follow this process, you'll be able to sprout any grain, seed, or legume at home.

Oats

Oatmeal is known as a breakfast cereal, but the grain itself can be used in many different ways. Because of the slightly sweet and nutty flavor of the grain, oats make a great base for both sweet and savory dishes.

Oat Groats

Whole oat groats with the hull removed do not need to soak as long as other grains. To sprout your oat groats, pour ²/₃ cup of the grain into a large container and completely cover them with cool water. If you are using hulled oat groats, those without hulls, only let them soak for 2–3 hours; if you are using oat groats that still have the hulls intact, soak the grains for 6–8 hours to let the water soften the hulls.

After soaking the grains, rinse and drain them until the water runs clear as it runs off the grains. Let the grains sit at room temperature, and repeat the rinsing and draining two to three times a day until the grains are where you want them. After a day or two, you should be able to see small sprouts emerging from the grains. You can continue to let them grow if you'd like the "tail" a bit longer, or you can stop once you first see the sprouts. Once they're where you want them, rinse and drain the sprouts one last time, making sure they are relatively dry before storing. To fully dry the grains, spread them out on a baking sheet in a single layer and leave on your counter or table for a few hours. Sprouted oat groats will keep for one to two weeks in the refrigerator when stored in an airtight container or plastic bag.

Steel-Cut Oats

Steel-cut oats will not actually sprout in the way that other grains do; the "tail" will not emerge from the grain, but all grains, including steel-cut oats, still benefit from a soaking period before using.

Grains, beans, and legumes all contain phytic acid, which is meant to keep important vitamins and minerals contained in the grain to sprout a plant, rather than allowing your body to absorb those things. Soaking the grains in water helps to break down the active phytic acid, neutralizing the phytates so that the grains are more digestible and the vitamins and minerals are more easily absorbed into your body.

Quinoa

Quinoa is most widely recognized in its white or ivory variety, but there are more than 100 known varieties across the globe. The most common varieties are white, red, and black, and the type used in the recipes in this book are white unless stated otherwise.

The seed cover on quinoa isn't as thick and tough as it is on other grains, so it doesn't require as long of a soaking period as others. To sprout your quinoa, pour ²/₃ cup of the grain into a large container and completely cover it with cool water. Stir the quinoa and water together, and let it sit for thirty minutes to an hour.

ESSENTIAL

Quinoa is one of the easiest grains to sprout. Because quinoa has a thinner seed coat than other whole grains like wheat and oats, it doesn't take as long for the germination process to begin. Since quinoa is a softer grain, you can also eat quinoa sprouts immediately once they're ready. Some grains are still rather tough and can handle a bit of cooking, but quinoa is tender and ready to eat.

After soaking the quinoa, rinse and drain them until the water runs clear. Let the quinoa sit at room temperature, and repeat the rinsing and draining two to three more times. After just one to two times of rinsing and draining, you should be able to see small sprouts emerging from the quinoa. You can continue to let them grow if you'd like the "tail" a bit longer, or you can stop once you first see the sprouts. Once they're where you want them, rinse and drain the sprouts one last time, making sure they are relatively dry before storing. The longer you let quinoa sprout, the softer the grain will become. You can let them sprout a bit longer, but once the grains have softened, you'll need to use them soon as they won't last as long in the refrigerator. Sprouted quinoa will keep for one to two weeks in the refrigerator when stored in an airtight container or plastic bag.

Wheat

Wheat, in some form, is the basis for so many foods and recipes today. Breads, pastas, and baked goods typically begin with some type of wheat.

Wheatberries are the whole grain of the wheat plant, but they aren't only useful when they're ground into flour. Different cuts of the grain can be thrown into bread recipes for texture and used as the base for grain salads and side dishes.

Wheatberries

Wheatberries are the full grain from a wheat plant, whether it's a hard winter or soft spring variety. The shape and size of the wheatberry is similar to that of oat groats—it is usually oval-shaped and has a shiny seed covering.

To sprout your wheatberries, pour $^2/_3$ cup of the grain into a large container and completely cover them with cool water. Soak the grains for 6–8 hours to let the water soften the hull.

FACT

> Wheatberries are the entire wheat kernel and are usually brown or reddish in color. Wheatberries have a chewy, hearty texture that makes them a great base for a casserole or grain salad. They don't break down while cooking, and they are delicious mixed into breads.

After soaking the wheatberries, rinse and drain them until the water runs clear as it runs off the grains. Let them sit at room temperature, and repeat the rinsing and draining two to three times a day until the grains are where you want them. After a day or two, you should be able to see small sprouts emerging from the wheatberries. You can continue to let them grow if you'd like the "tail" a bit longer, or you can stop once you first see the sprouts. Once they're where you want them, rinse and drain the sprouts one last time, making sure they are relatively dry before storing. Sprouted wheatberries will keep for one to two weeks in the refrigerator when stored in a container or plastic bag.

Bulgur

Bulgur is another cut of wheat that is broken down from the whole wheatberry. When you purchase bulgur, you're buying a partially hulled wheatberry that has been parboiled, dried, and cracked into smaller pieces than the whole wheatberry.

Because bulgur has been partially cooked, some brands may not fully sprout, but like steel-cut oats, soaking the grains before using is a great way to up the nutritional value in the grain before eating. Depending on where you get your bulgur, you may find that you are able to get them sprouted. To make about 1 cup of sprouted bulgur, pour ⅔ cup of the grain into a large container and completely cover them with cool water. Let the bulgur soak in the water for 6–8 hours or overnight.

The next morning, rinse and drain them until the water runs clear as it runs off the grains. Let the bulgur sit at room temperature, and repeat the rinsing and draining two to three times a day until the grains are where you want them. After a day or two, you should be able to see small sprouts emerging from the grains. You can continue to let them grow if you'd like the "tail" a bit longer, or you can stop once you first see the sprouts. Once they're where you want them, rinse and drain the sprouts one last time, making sure they are relatively dry before storing. Sprouted bulgur will keep for one to two weeks in the refrigerator when stored in a container or plastic bag.

Buckwheat Groats

Despite what many people think, thanks to its name, the buckwheat groat is not actually wheat. In fact, it's not a whole grain at all! Buckwheat groats are actually a fruit seed related to the rhubarb plant. Because of the shape, texture, and flavor, buckwheat groats are used in similar ways as other whole grains.

To sprout your buckwheat groats, pour ⅔ cup of the grain into a large container and completely cover them with cool water, using about 3 cups of water total. Buckwheat groats only need to soak for twenty to sixty minutes, compared to the normal 6–8 hours for other whole grains. They absorb water more quickly, so you want to make sure you don't let them soak too long; otherwise they will absorb too much water, and that can keep them from sprouting.

After soaking the groats, rinse and drain them until the water runs clear as it runs off the grains. Buckwheat groats give off quite of bit of starchiness, so it may take a few good rinses each time to get the water running clean. Let the grains sit at room temperature, and repeat the rinsing and draining two to three times a day until the grains are where you want them. After a day or two, you should be able to see small sprouts emerging from the grains. You can continue to let them grow if you'd like the "tail" a bit longer, or you can stop once you first see the sprouts. Once they're where you want them, rinse and drain the sprouts one last time, making sure they are relatively dry before storing. Sprouted buckwheat groats will keep for one to two weeks in the refrigerator when stored in a container or plastic bag.

Barley

Barley isn't just for soup recipes anymore. Similar in texture to oats, barley adds a slightly sweet flavor to any dish. To sprout your barley, pour ⅔ cup of the grain into a large container and completely cover them with cool water. Soak the grains for eight to twelve hours or overnight.

ESSENTIAL

Barley and oats are the closest in flavor and texture when it comes to whole grains. For almost any recipe that calls for oats or barley, you could easily trade out one for the other option if you are out of one grain. Both barley and oats have a slightly sweet and nutty flavor that is light enough to go well in both sweet and savory dishes.

After soaking the grains, rinse and drain them until the water runs clear as it runs off the grains. Let the grains sit at room temperature, and repeat the rinsing and draining two to three times a day until the grains are where you want them. After a day or two, you should be able to see small sprouts emerging from the grains. You can continue to let them grow if you'd like the "tail" a bit longer, or you can stop once you first see the sprouts. Once they're where you want them, rinse and drain the sprouts one last time, making sure they are relatively dry before storing. Sprouted barley will keep for one to two weeks in the refrigerator when stored in a container or plastic bag.

Kamut

Kamut is an ancient grain that looks very much like long-grain brown rice and wheatberries. For about 1 cup of Kamut sprouts, pour ⅔ cup of the grain into a large container and completely cover them with cool water. Let the grains soak in the water 8–12 hours, overnight if you can.

FACT

Kamut is known for its buttery, rich flavor and smooth texture. Like some other whole grains, it is a good option for those who have other wheat sensitivities. Kamut is a nutritious whole grain that you can use in place of rice, pasta, or wheatberries.

After soaking the grains, rinse and drain them until the water runs clear as it runs off. Let the Kamut sit at room temperature, and repeat the rinsing and draining two to three times a day until the grains are where you want them. After a day or two, you should be able to see small sprouts emerging from the grains. You can continue to let them grow if you'd like the "tail" a bit longer, or you can stop once you first see the sprouts. Once they're where you want them, rinse and drain the sprouts one last time, making sure they are relatively dry before storing. Sprouted Kamut, like most sprouted grains, will keep for one to two weeks in the refrigerator when stored in a container or plastic bag.

Chickpeas

Chickpeas are commonly known as the base for hummus, but they have a light flavor and creamy texture that goes well in many different dishes. To get about 1 cup of sprouted chickpeas, add ½ cup into a large container and completely cover them with 2–3 cups of cool water. Soak the chickpeas for eight to twelve hours or overnight.

In the morning, rinse and drain them until the water runs clear as it runs off the chickpeas. Let them sit at room temperature, and repeat the rinsing and draining two to three times a day until the chickpeas are where you want them. After a day or two, you should be able to see small sprouts. You can continue to let them grow if you'd like the "tail" a bit longer, or you can stop once you first see the sprouts. Once they're where you want them, rinse and drain the sprouts one last time, making sure they are relatively dry before storing. Sprouted chickpeas will keep for one to two weeks in the refrigerator when stored in a container or plastic bag.

ESSENTIAL

Once you sprout chickpeas or other legumes, you have the option to stir them into salads or casserole dishes like other sprouted grains, or you can blend them up into dips and spreads. Since legumes typically have a creamy center and break down easily compared to grains, sprouting legumes will give you additional recipe options.

Lentils

Lentils have the most variety when it comes to sprouts. You can find different colors and sizes of lentils to sprout at home, giving your dishes a nice pop of color. To sprout lentils, start with a ½ cup in a large container. Pour 2–3 cups of cool water over the lentils and let them soak eight to twelve hours.

After soaking the lentils, rinse and drain them until the water runs clear as it runs off. Let the lentils sit at room temperature, and repeat the rinsing and draining two to three times a day until they are where you want them. After a day or two, you should be able to see small sprouts starting to show. You can continue to let them grow if you'd like the "tail" a bit longer, or you can stop once you first see the sprouts. Once they're where you want them, rinse and drain the sprouts one last time, making sure they are relatively dry before storing. Sprouted lentils will keep for one to two weeks in the refrigerator when stored in a container or plastic bag.

Dehydrating and Grinding Sprouts

Sprouted grains can be used in almost any recipe you make at home. Adding or substituting them into grain salads, casseroles, breakfast bakes, or just tossing them onto salads and sandwiches will give you some great options for using your sprouts. You can also dehydrate them and grind them into sprouted-grain flour at home, too.

To make your own sprouted-grain flour, you will need to have a grain mill or a milling/grinding attachment for a large stand mixer that is designed for grinding grains. A dehydrator is typically recommended, but a regular oven can also be used to dry/dehydrate the grains before grinding.

ALERT

If you want to try making your own sprouted-grain flour at home, you need to make sure that your sprouted grains are completely dried before grinding. If the grains have the tiniest bit of moisture left in them, you'll end up with a clumpy and soggy mixture that won't do well in baked goods.

Making your own sprouted-grain flour begins with the sprouts you've made. For flours, you only want to let the grains sprout for one to two days; the bigger and longer the tail is on the sprout, the harder it will be for the grain to be broken down for baking. Once you have your sprouts ready, pour them into a single layer on your dehydrator screen and dehydrate at 105–110°F until the grains are completely dry. If you do not have a dehydrator, place your grains in a single layer on a baking sheet and bake on the lowest level of your oven until the grains are completely dry. This process, no matter which appliance you are using, will take a few hours.

Once the grains are fully dry, grind them in your grain mill or with your stand mixer and attachment. Sprouted-grain flours, in most recipes, can be used in a 1:1 ratio for all-purpose or whole-wheat flours.

Sprouted-grain flours should be used as soon as possible after you dehydrate and grind them so you get the highest amount of nutrients. If you make a larger amount of flour and aren't able to use it all within the first few days, place it in a sealed container and keep it in the refrigerator or freezer until you are ready to use it.

CHAPTER 6

Incorporating Sprouted Grains Into Your Diet

It's easy to add sprouted grains to your daily routine once you have sprouts ready to use. You can add them to your favorite breakfast, lunch, and dinner dishes, or incorporate them into quick snack options when you're on the go. When you're first starting out, making an effort to try all kinds of sprouted grains will make it easier to add them into your diet. Pick the flavors and textures you enjoy, and swap them in for regular or refined grains.

Easy Swaps in Daily Meals

Adding sprouted grains into your daily routine is simple and rewarding. Because they are typically used in dishes like soups, salads, or sandwiches, most sprouted grains make great additions to almost any meal you make at home. Any grain-based dish can be transformed instantly into a healthier option, simply by swapping in sprouted grains.

Breakfasts

Most people tend to add sprouted grains to more savory dishes with lunches or dinners, but adding them to your first meal of the day is a fantastic way to sample sprouted grains with sweeter flavors. A variety of sprouted grains can be used in the same way in which you serve oatmeal or any other hot cereal. Depending upon the grains you're using, you can warm them up with a little extra liquid before serving, or cook them on the stovetop to make the grains even softer and creamier. Adding toppings like nuts, fruit, and sweet spices turns sprouted grains into a hearty breakfast meal.

QUESTION

Is it possible to add sprouted grains to my diet?
Making a change to your daily diet can seem intimidating, but it doesn't have to be! Adding sprouted grains to your day is easy if you have them on hand. Start small—toss a handful in your salad or sandwich, replace half of your grains in your side dish with sprouts, or make your favorite hot cereal with sprouted grains instead of regular. You'll reap the benefits of the sprouts without missing any of your favorite flavors.

Some grains have a lighter and sweeter taste on their own, like oats and wheat, which are good options to stir into yogurt or layer into a parfait with fresh fruit, yogurt, and nuts. You can take your favorite granola recipe and trade out the regular oats and other grains for the sprouted versions for an easy twist on something you already love.

One fast breakfast option is to toss a handful of sprouted whole grains into your favorite yogurt, stir in some fruit and nuts, and take it with you. For busy mornings, this mix is a quick and easy meal that will keep you satisfied and energized.

Lunches and Dinners

The easiest way to add sprouted grains into your diet is to swap them out for the normal grains you would use for lunches and dinners. Since grains are used in the majority of savory dishes, it's simple to substitute a sprouted-grain option for the base of a recipe.

If you are putting together a salad for lunch or dinner, toss a palmful of sprouts into the salad before mixing it together with your dressing. You can also make salads with a grain base, adding in chopped vegetables and fruits and a healthy dressing to bring everything together. The dish will have the same flavors you're expecting, but you'll be reaping the benefits of the added nutrition of the sprouted grains.

Sprouts can add oomph to soups, too. Add a handful to soup recipes before serving for some added texture and flavor. For vegetable-based soups, and brothy soups in particular, sprouts can help make them even more filling. They bring other vitamins and minerals to the soup that vegetables alone can't offer.

ALERT

Using sprouted grains instead of regular cooked grains will definitely give you a slightly different texture. If you're worried about losing the texture you're used to in certain recipes, try swapping out just half for sprouted grains at the beginning and slowly adjust the ratios until you find the mix that you like.

Casseroles are often based on grains like rice and pasta, making them a fantastic choice to use sprouted grains instead of nonsprouted and refined grains that the recipe might call for. If one of your favorite casserole recipes calls for white rice, try using sprouted brown rice instead. The texture will resemble the recipe you love, but the sprouted brown rice will add a nutty flavor to the dish. You'll be getting a more nutritious meal, too.

For pasta recipes, there are more options now than there were just a few years ago. You can purchase sprouted-grain dry pastas in many grocery stores and from companies that sell their products online. Sprouted-grain pastas can be used in any recipe that calls for regular white-flour pasta. The cooking time is almost the same and you can get the pasta in a few shapes, giving you more options to easily add sprouted grains—in any form—to your daily meals.

Snacks

Sprouted grains aren't something that most people associate with snacks. However, since many snack options and recipes include grains in some way, you can try different sprouted grains in their place. Fun treats like granola, cookies, and snack bars are quick and easy ways to add sprouted grains into your diet. Using sprouted grains in baked goods like muffins and cakes allows them to take on new flavors and textures, and makes your baked goods healthier at the same time.

Granola is one of the easiest recipes to modify in order to use sprouted grains. Most recipes call for a variety of whole grains, so swapping them for the sprouted version is quick and lets you decide what grains you want to use. Try a different mix each time until you find the best balance of flavor and texture to have with milk or stirred into yogurt.

ESSENTIAL

Many people don't think of snack foods when they think of sprouted grains, but you can easily incorporate sprouted grains into your afternoon or mid-morning snack time. Take your favorite snack, whether it's cereal and milk or a granola bar, and you can find ways to add in sprouted grains to your snack break.

If you have plans to make cookies, muffins, or breads, you can add some sprouted grains into your batter before baking. Certain grains will give crunchy textures, and others will completely bake into the batter, leaving your muffins or bread fluffy and tender. Homemade snack bars and granola bars are easy to make on a busy weeknight or on the weekend. They can be wrapped and kept in the fridge or freezer so you can grab one on the way out the door or take one to have as an afternoon snack at work.

A Plan for a Gradual Switch

Making the choice to add sprouted grains into your diet doesn't have to be intimidating or hard. By starting small, the switch to using sprouted grains can be an exciting process that will open your eyes to new flavors, textures, and recipes to use in your own home.

Make Some Lists

Before starting to add sprouted grains to your diet, you may want to make a list of recipes you find that you're interested in. Write down the ways you want to try to use sprouts. List some of your favorite recipes, and if they call for some kind of grain, write down what sprouted grain you want to try in its place. For recipes that don't call for grains, like soups and salads, think about the flavors in the dish and what sprouted grain might work well with them. These lists can be organized any way you want—by recipe, by meal type (breakfast, lunch, dinner, snack), by grain type, by main ingredient. Depending on how you organize your lists, they can also serve as make-shift grocery lists to keep track of what recipes you want to make in the next week and what ingredients you need to buy.

QUESTION

Where do I begin?
The biggest obstacle in making any change in your normal routine—especially when it comes to your daily diet—is finding the place to start. Making a change in your life doesn't have to require that everything in your life changes at the same time. Look for small ways to add sprouted grains by trying one new recipe a week or sprouting once a month at first before trying to make a lifestyle change. Starting small will give you the chance to figure out what you like and give you confidence to move forward to make the changes you want to see.

Having a simple plan of a few ways to start using sprouted grains will give you an easy list to follow and help you figure out which sprouted grains you like. Also, once you begin sprouting, this list will give you ideas to start with, and you can cross them off as you go.

Keep Stock

A well-stocked kitchen is a productive kitchen. In terms of cooking with grains, it is easier to use them more often when you can see them and know exactly what you have to work with in your pantry and refrigerator. Many whole grains are sold in bulk, meaning you will probably bring them home in a plastic bag. To keep them organized, consider keeping your raw grains in glass jars on a shelf or in glass or plastic containers that completely seal.

Having a counter full of grain-filled jars, a shelf in your pantry, or a section in a cabinet where you can see what the grains are can give you inspiration to use them more often. Using containers that show how much of the various grains that you have left will also help you keep them stocked, because you'll know right away when you're running low on oats or barley.

For grains like quinoa and lentils, you may not need labels to be able to tell what is in the jar or container. With other grains, like varieties of wheat, oats, barley, and beans, it may be helpful to label your containers or jars so you know exactly what you have. Some grains look very similar (wheatberries, Kamut, and oat groats, for example), so using labels will help ensure that you grab the grain you want in a specific recipe and that you're sprouting a grain for the right amount of time.

Sample, Sample, Sample

Above everything else, trying sprouted grains is the only way you'll ever begin to add them into your daily diet. If you don't eat many whole grains right now, that's okay! One first step you might want to take is to try some whole grains cooked directly from their raw state before trying to sprout them at home so you can see what their cooked texture is and find out if you like the flavor of the grain.

ESSENTIAL

Anytime you want to add new foods, it's a good idea to try all the options available. You don't want to plan a dinner around a grain that you don't like—the meal will be wasted, meaning you'll be losing out on money and the time you spent cooking. Take the time to sample the grains so you know which flavors you like, what meals certain grains will work with, and which ones to leave off your grocery list.

To start out sprouting, try working with grains that you already know you like. If you love barley in soups and stews, you'll probably love it sprouted in salads and casseroles, too. The texture of sprouted grains will be slightly different than when they're cooked straight from the raw state, but the subtle flavors you love will still be there in the final dish.

Buying grains in bulk gives you the option to buy as much or as little as you want of each type. If you want to sample Kamut but don't want to buy 3–4 cups of the grain, start out with just ¼–½ cup. That amount will be plenty to make a small batch of sprouts so you can try them and see if you like the texture and flavor before buying more.

Eat What You Love

The most important part of all of this—and with anything dealing with food—is to ultimately eat what you love. If you try barley and don't enjoy it, leave it out of your diet. If you want to try it again and have it in a different recipe, maybe you'll change your mind, but maybe you won't. There is no reason to eat foods that you don't enjoy.

There are so many whole-grain options; you'll be able to find the ones that you like to eat, with the flavors and textures you enjoy, and have fun in the kitchen cooking them. Leave out the grains you don't enjoy. Adding whole grains to your diet may already be a big change in your day, and you don't need added stress thinking that you should be eating every kind of whole grain. You'll still get incredible health benefits from the grains you do eat, regardless of the ones you avoid.

Store-Bought Options

Thanks to the popularity of sprouted grains in the past few years, there are a variety of store-bought options you can find in local markets and directly from company websites online. From flours to breads to pastas, adding sprouted grains to your daily diet has never been easier.

Sprouted-grain flours that are already ground and packaged will save you time in the kitchen, especially if you want to bake something and haven't had the time to sprout, dehydrate, and grind your own flour. If you have a pasta maker, you could make your own sprouted-grain pasta with a mix of flours, but the dried options are nice to keep in the pantry for busy nights.

ALERT

As more companies work to bring new sprouted-grain options to grocery store shelves, it's important to pay attention to the price tags. Store-bought options will definitely save you some time and help keep you stocked with sprouted-grain options, but you'll need to weigh the convenience against the money you'll be spending. If you have the time, sprouting at home will always be cheaper.

Sprouted-grain breads were one of the first store-bought sprouted-grain options, and companies continue to work on new blends of grains, new flavors, and new bread products like English muffins, tortillas, and hamburger buns. Sprouting grains at home will always be a bit cheaper, but having convenient options in stores makes it easier to add even more sprouted grains to your routine.

Quick Additions at Home or When Eating Out

Incorporating sprouts into your daily routine can be easy and quick, whether you're in your own home or on the go.

Once you have sprouts ready to eat, they can be used in a variety of ways:

- Add a palmful of sprouts to your salad at lunch or dinner.
- Stir some sprouts into your soup.
- Make a lentil soup and use sprouted lentils as the base.
- Use sprouted barley in a traditional ham and barley or mushroom barley soup recipe.
- Swap out rice for a sprouted grain like wheatberries or Kamut in a cheesy casserole for a family-pleasing meal.
- Add a layer of sprouts to your sandwich or wrap.
- Stir a handful of sprouts into yogurt with fresh fruit and nuts for breakfast or an afternoon snack.
- Toss a palmful of sprouts into your pot of oatmeal.

- Make your own healthy cereal mix with low-sugar cereal, sprouted grains, nuts, and spices.
- Fold sprouted grains into your favorite pancake or waffle batter.

Adding more sprouts to your diet doesn't have to be limited to the foods you prepare at home, either. Restaurants are beginning to offer sprouts and sprouted options, including sprouts for sandwiches and wraps and sprouted-grain breads. If you can find places that already have sprouted options on the menu, it will give you healthier choices for your lunch or dinner out.

If, however, you can't find places near you that offer sprouted items on the menu, you can always take your own. Add a handful of sprouts to a plastic bag and you'll be able to toss them onto salads, sandwiches, soups, or other grain dishes. If you don't want to take your own raw sprouts, you can always bring a snack with you from home that you've made with sprouted grains.

Smaller towns across the country may not have as many restaurant options when it comes to sprouts and whole grains, so incorporating them into your diet may happen at home more than anywhere else. As sprouting continues to grow as a mainstream kitchen activity, more places will pick up on the trend and offer more sprouted options.

The Versatility of Sprouted Grains

Sprouting grains sometimes changes their texture, but they can still be used in all the same ways you would use any nonsprouted grain. Unlike non-sprouted grains, some sprouted options can also be used immediately after sprouting and require no additional cooking. This makes it even easier to add them into dishes like sandwiches and salads.

ESSENTIAL

Sprouted grains may have a different texture that regular cooked whole grains, but they offer the same options for recipes. Sprouted oats can be used in all the different ways that regular raw or cooked oats can— sweet for breakfast, savory for dinner, or crumbled into a crisp topping on fruit for dessert. Try using sprouted grains in all your recipes and you'll be surprised at how many ways they can fit into your daily diet.

Because most whole grains are hearty and require twenty to thirty minutes' cooking time from their raw state, they also hold up well when they are baked into casseroles or simmered in soups for long periods. Depending on your preference in texture, you can eat your sprouted grains immediately after sprouting or cook them further.

For dishes like soups, you may want to add the sprouts at the last minute, or you could toss them in and let them cook for thirty minutes before serving to soften them up even more. Baking changes the texture of the grains, but you'll want them to be softer in baked goods. For recipes like granola or brittle or crisps, the grains bake without much liquid, so they keep their chewy and crunchy qualities.

CHAPTER 7

Prepared Sprouted-Grain Choices

As sprouting becomes more popular, companies are beginning to create more prepared sprouted-grain foods. A variety of sprouted-grain flours are now available that will give lots of choices for baking and cooking with sprouted grains at home. Bread products, pastas, snack foods, and cereals are being sold in most grocery stores now, with new flavors coming out every few months. Being able to make your favorite dish at home and incorporate sprouted grains is easier than ever.

Flours

Sprouted-grain flours can be made at home, but with the availability of flour options, keeping a stock of different flours is easy to do. For flours that you might use often, like wheat and oat, making your own at home would be worth the time because you could make a large batch to use. Other sprouted-grain flours that you use less often, like spelt or amaranth, may be ones that you want to buy if you don't think you'll use them as often.

ESSENTIAL

If you don't own a dehydrator or aren't normally home long enough to dehydrate your own sprouted grains, buying sprouted-grain flours will open up a variety of cooking options for you at home. Keeping a stock of sprouted-grain flours will let you throw in a handful to any baked good, adding a punch of nutrition to your regular pancake or muffin recipe.

Depending on what types of markets, grocery stores, or health-food cooperatives that you have in your area, you may be able to find sprouted-grain flours in stock. If not, there are a few companies that sell all different types of flours online. Local health-food cooperatives and "buying clubs" are rapidly gaining popularity and are often great sources for sprouted grains and sprouted-grain flours.

Not every brand or online store carries each variety, but you can find the following sprouted-grain flours for purchase:

- Amaranth flour
- Barley flour
- Buckwheat flour
- Corn flour
- Oat flour
- Millet flour
- Quinoa flour
- Rice flour
- Rye flour
- Spelt flour

If you're sprouting your own grains at home, you can make flour from any kind of sprout. Having sprouted-grain flour options to buy just makes it easier to keep them in stock in your kitchen and cuts out some of the prep time when you're in a rush.

Using Sprouted-Grain Flour in Your Recipes

With most sprouted-grain flours, you can substitute in the same amount for the regular flour that is called for in any recipe. Sprouted-wheat flour results are similar to nonsprouted-wheat flour, but varieties like corn flour and chickpea flour might create different textures in the final product.

When you're using a sprouted-grain flour for the first time, choose a recipe that calls for a sprouted-grain flour so you can see how it reacts in the recipe. There may be some flours that you don't enjoy the flavor or texture of, so testing them out in proven recipes is a great way to try them and decide which ones you want to keep for future use.

Measuring Your Flour

As usual, always measure your dry ingredients, including sprouted-grain flours, with measuring cups meant for dry ingredients. The easiest way to tell the difference is that "wet" measuring cups often have a spout for pouring.

To accurately measure your sprouted-grain flour, gently spoon the flour into the measuring cup until the level is above the top of the cup. Use a knife to level the flour off with the measuring cup. For even more accurate baking measurements, you can weigh your flour instead of measuring it in cups. If you are using a recipe that gives you both the weight and amount, take the extra minute to weigh the flour instead.

More than Baking

Sprouted-grain flours don't have to be reserved for baking, either. Sprouted-wheat flour has a light flavor similar to regular all-purpose flour and can be used in the same ways in smaller doses. Toss a spoonful of flour into some sautéed vegetables before adding stock to create a thick, creamy sauce. Make a batter or coating to bake chicken or fish, using sprouted-grain flour in place of regular.

Socca is a flatbread, typically made in a skillet, with a chickpea-flour base. A quick-cooking bread option, socca is also gluten-free and makes a nice addition to a lunch or dinner as a side dish or to add texture to a soup or stew.

Oat flour has a sweeter flavor and is delicious when added to baked goods like muffins, cupcakes, and biscuits. The slight sweetness also makes for great pancakes and waffles, and can be mixed with whole oats, butter, and brown sugar for a fruit-crisp topping.

Corn flour, or corn masa, has sweet and savory qualities, thanks to the natural sweetness of the vegetable. Corn bread and muffins can have even more flavor when you use sprouted-corn flour in place of the all-purpose flour. For a fun twist on breakfast, substitute corn flour for half of the flour in your favorite pancake recipe and add a handful of blueberries.

Breads

Sprouted-grain breads are becoming more popular, with companies offering new flavors and mixes of grains every few weeks. Most brands use a mix of sprouted grains in their breads and also offer other baked-goods options like English muffins, hamburger and hot dog buns, tortillas, and bagels.

In most stores or health-food markets, sprouted-grain breads and baked goods will be in the refrigerated or freezer sections. Once you take these products home, you can keep them in the fridge if you plan to use them in the following week. If not, you can freeze them and toast the bread or English muffins straight from the freezer whenever you want them.

To add even more sprouts to your day, try these ways to use your sprouted-grain breads:

- Make a sandwich or wrap on sprouted-grain bread or tortillas with vegetables and extra sprouts.
- Use sprouted-grain breads for French toast or bread pudding, making your favorite comfort foods a bit healthier.

- For an extra punch of sprouts in your salad, toss in a handful of your favorite sprouts and use some sprouted-grain bread to make croutons.
- Make a grilled cheese sandwich on sprouted-grain bread and pair it with soup.
- Use a sprouted-grain English muffin or bagel for your normal breakfast sandwich.
- Take your favorite enchilada or burrito recipe and use sprouted-grain tortillas.

While the sprouted-grain breads may have a nuttier flavor than white bread and a heartier texture, they can be used in the same ways that you use any other bread product. Changing out your regular bread for sprouted-grain bread is a good way to add sprouted grains to your day without making a big change in your routine.

Pastas

Dried sprouted-grain pastas are increasingly showing up on store shelves and in a variety of shapes. You can now get spaghetti, fettuccine, linguini, and penne shapes from a few brands in stores or online that will easily fit in any pasta recipe you make at home.

ESSENTIAL

There are only a few sprouted-grain pasta shape options available today, but if you make or buy sprouted-grain flours, you can easily make your own sprouted-grain pasta in whatever form you prefer. Using a pasta maker or rolling out the dough and cutting your own will give you fantastic homemade pasta with your own mix of sprouted grains. For the first batch, try adding your favorite sprouted-grain flour for half of the all-purpose flour, adding a little more each time you make it until you find the balance you like.

The majority of dried sprouted-grain pastas are a mix of grains, like wheat, barley, lentils, spelt, quinoa, Kamut, and sometimes soybeans. Because some sprouted flours don't hold together the same way that all-purpose or semolina flour does, companies tend to use a variety of flours to ensure that the pasta will cook up to be tender and have a similar texture to regular pasta. This mix of grains also gives the pasta a balanced flavor of its own so it won't overpower your dish.

If you're making your own sprouted-grain flours at home, you can try making your own pasta as well, but store-bought dried pastas are just as healthy as what you could make yourself. The majority of brands that offer sprouted-grain pastas do not use any preservatives, artificial colors or flavors, or other additives.

Sprouted-grain pastas will have a slightly different texture than regular semolina pasta. Make sure to follow the directions for cooking time with the pasta; many sprouted-grain options need to cook a bit less than other pastas to keep them from becoming too soft and being overcooked.

Convenience Foods

There are a few brands that offer sprouted grain–based convenience foods such as bars and granolas, but they are not as popular and widespread as breads and pastas. Snack bars made with sprouted grains are good snacks to keep on hand at home, in the car, in your office, or in your bag for a quick pick-me-up on busy days. Many premade snack bars include three or four grains along with natural sweeteners, like agave or honey, and dried fruit, nuts, seeds, or chocolate.

Sprouted-grain granolas make a great quick breakfast or afternoon snack. You can serve the granola with your favorite yogurt or milk, and add in some additional spices, fruits, nuts, or seeds for a filling dish that's also delicious as dessert. Granola is always a good snack option because you can take a bag of it with you on the road, in the car, or to work.

Baked goods with sprouted grains are being sold in more stores, giving you options like muffins that you don't have to make yourself. Pairing a healthy muffin with some fresh fruit is a great afternoon pick-me-up, or could stand in as a quick breakfast. You could also heat up a muffin and serve it with a scoop of your favorite ice cream or whipped topping for a sweeter treat or dessert.

How can I get my kids and family to eat sprouted grains with me?
Getting your family on board with a change in their diet is one of the toughest parts about making a change yourself. How can you get your family and children to sample these new foods with you? Start out small by adding sprouted grains to your favorite family recipes like a fruity oatmeal breakfast or adding in sprouted-oat flour to your favorite muffin recipe. Making the switch gradually and in places where they won't notice at first will give them the benefits without making big changes all at once.

If you want snacks and easy grab-and-go foods that incorporate sprouted grains, it would be just as easy to make your own batch of sprouted-grain granola bars, muffins, or hearty breakfast cookies. Making a batch of baked goods on the weekends and freezing them will give you quick and healthy snack options all week long. When you don't have the time to make your own, these store-bought snacks make it easy to keep sprouted grains in your daily routine.

Cereal

Cold cereal options with sprouted grains as the base are popping up more often, and brands are offering a variety of flavors rather than just a plain cereal base. Flavors like cinnamon raisin and almond are on most grocery store shelves in the natural or organic sections. Some cold cereals come in flake form, some in nuggets, and some in clusters that are similar to granola in texture.

Whether you like hot or cold cereal for your morning meal or evening snack, sprouted grains can be incorporated into either option. Store-bought cold cereals are great to have on hand for busy mornings, and hot cereal mixes make your pot of oatmeal or multigrain cereal even easier to put together before work or on a lazy weekend.

Hot cereal is simple to make from any sprouted grain you have in the kitchen. With things like oats, wheat, quinoa, and Kamut, a hot breakfast bowl can be cooked in a short amount of time and topped with nuts or fruit for a hearty meal. The best part about hot cereal is that you can use a mix of your favorite grains to make your perfect breakfast bowl, full of different flavors and textures.

CHAPTER 8

Sprouted Oats Recipes

Strawberry Almond Overnight Oats

Five minutes of prep the night before gives you a healthy breakfast in no time!

INGREDIENTS | SERVES 2

1 cup sprouted rolled or steel-cut oats, or oat groats

1 cup milk

½ teaspoon salt

1 teaspoon cinnamon

¼ cup sliced almonds

1 cup fresh or frozen strawberries

½ cup low-fat plain Greek yogurt

2 teaspoons honey

In a medium bowl, stir the oats, milk, salt, and cinnamon together. Cover the bowl and let it sit in the refrigerator overnight.

In the morning, stir the almonds, berries, and yogurt into the oat mixture.

Divide into 2 bowls and top with a teaspoon of honey before serving.

PER SERVING | Calories: 289 | Fat: 7 g | Protein: 13 g | Sodium: 329 mg | Fiber: 7 g | Carbohydrates: 42 g | Sugar: 10 g

Blueberry Overnight Oatmeal Pancakes

These oatmeal pancakes are full of nutty whole-grain flavor that goes well with any berry or nut mix-in. Feel free to switch up the flavors with whatever you prefer or have on hand.

INGREDIENTS | SERVES 6

1½ cups sprouted rolled oats

1½ cups buttermilk

½ teaspoon salt

¼ cup sprouted oat flour

½ cup whole-wheat pastry flour

1 tablespoon baking powder

1 teaspoon cinnamon

2 tablespoons brown sugar

1 egg, beaten

½ cup milk

2 tablespoons oil

1 cup blueberries

Whole-Wheat Pastry Flour

While regular whole-wheat flour can make some recipes seem too heavy, whole-wheat pastry flour is made from soft wheat and is lower in gluten than regular whole-wheat flour. It gives a lighter texture in baked goods, pancakes, and waffles, and is a great whole-grain option to swap in your favorite recipes.

The night before, mix together sprouted oats, buttermilk, and salt in a large bowl. Cover the bowl and let it sit, overnight, in the fridge so the oats soak up the buttermilk and soften.

In the morning, stir in both flours, baking powder, cinnamon, and brown sugar.

In a separate bowl, whisk together the egg, milk, and oil.

Add egg mixture to the batter and stir until combined.

Fold in blueberries.

Heat a skillet or griddle over medium-high heat. Drop batter by ¼–⅓ cup scoops and cook for 3–4 minutes until the edges start to turn golden and the bubbles on the top of the pancakes stop popping. Flip the pancakes over and cook for 1–2 minutes more.

Repeat with remaining batter until all the pancakes are cooked. Serve warm with your favorite toppings.

PER SERVING | Calories: 327 | Fat: 9 g | Protein: 12 g | Sodium: 282 mg | Fiber: 6 g | Carbohydrates: 50 g | Sugar: 11 g

Sprouted Oat Risotto with Bacon and Peas

*Using sprouted oats instead of rice with the classic mix of bacon and peas
is a fun and healthy twist on a regular risotto.*

INGREDIENTS | SERVES 4

2 slices bacon

1 cup sprouted steel-cut oats

½ cup white wine

4 cups broth, simmering

½ cup Parmesan cheese, freshly grated

1 cup peas, steamed

2 tablespoons fresh parsley, chopped

Super Starches

Most people wouldn't think that oats could be used in a risotto recipe, but the cut of the oats and the cooking process lets the oats soften slowly and turn into a creamy dish.

Place a large skillet over medium heat and add the bacon.

Cook the bacon until it has rendered its fat and is crisp. Remove from the pan and set aside on paper towels to drain. Once cooled, crumble into small pieces.

Stir the steel-cut oats into the hot bacon fat, stirring to coat the oats. Cook for 2–3 minutes until the oats start to toast and are evenly coated in the fat.

Pour the wine into the pan, stirring, and let the mixture simmer until the wine is almost completely absorbed.

Add ½–1 cup of the warm broth to the pan, stirring occasionally, and let the broth absorb into the oats. Once one batch of broth has been mostly absorbed, add another cup of broth every 5 minutes or so, and mix until the oats are cooked and the mixture is creamy.

Once all the broth has been added and the oats are cooked and have released their starches, stir in the Parmesan, steamed peas, and crumbled bacon.

Top with a sprinkling of Parmesan and fresh parsley.

PER SERVING | Calories: 302 | Fat: 9 g | Protein: 18 g | Sodium: 318 mg | Fiber: 5 g | Carbohydrates: 34 g | Sugar: 2 g

Baked Apples with Sprouted Oats and Maple Topping

These baked apples can be made as an easy dessert or eaten leftover for a warm breakfast. Just reheat in the morning for a fun weekday treat.

INGREDIENTS | SERVES 4

4 medium apples, cored and peeled

½ cup maple syrup

1 tablespoon lemon juice

½ cup sprouted rolled oats or oat groats

½ teaspoon cinnamon

¼ teaspoon nutmeg

¼ cup walnuts, chopped

1 tablespoon butter or neutral oil (like safflower or canola)

Preheat the oven to 425°F.

Place cored apples in a baking dish. You can cut the bottoms of the apples to make them sit level in the dish, if needed.

In a bowl, mix together the maple syrup, lemon juice, oats, cinnamon, nutmeg, and walnuts.

Fill the center of each apple with the oat mixture.

Divide the butter (or oil) between the apples and place a piece of butter or drizzle of oil over the top of the filling.

Bake for 20–25 minutes.

PER SERVING | Calories: 343 | Fat: 9 g | Protein: 5 g | Sodium: 6 mg | Fiber: 6 g | Carbohydrates: 63 g | Sugar: 40 g

Peanut Butter Chocolate Chip Oatmeal Snack Bars

Snacks don't have to come from the vending machine!
Whip up these bars on the weekend, and you can have a healthy choice all week long.

INGREDIENTS | SERVES 12

2 cups sprouted rolled oats

¾ cup wheat bran

½ cup brown sugar

½ teaspoon salt

1 teaspoon cinnamon

½ cup unsweetened applesauce

2 eggs

¼ cup peanut butter

½ cup chocolate chips

Allergy-Free Option

If you or someone you know has a nut allergy, swap out the peanut butter for sunflower seed butter. It will give you the same great texture and will be a safe treat for everyone.

Preheat the oven to 350°F.

In a large bowl, stir together the oats, wheat bran, brown sugar, salt, and cinnamon.

In a separate bowl, whisk the applesauce, eggs, and peanut butter together.

Stir peanut butter mixture into the oats.

Fold the chocolate chips into the batter.

Pour batter into a greased 8" × 8" baking dish and spread until evenly distributed.

Bake for 25–30 minutes. Let cool for 5 minutes before cutting.

PER SERVING | Calories: 231 | Fat: 7 g | Protein: 8 g | Sodium: 112 mg | Fiber: 6 g | Carbohydrates: 35 g | Sugar: 12 g

Curried Oats with Tomatoes and Peas

Oat groats have a slightly sweet flavor of their own. Using the oat groats instead of rice adds another layer of flavor and texture to the curried tomatoes and peas.

INGREDIENTS | SERVES 4

1 cup sprouted oat groats
2 cups vegetable broth
1 teaspoon salt
1 tablespoon curry powder
1 teaspoon turmeric
1 cup frozen or fresh peas
1 cup tomatoes, diced
¼ cup chopped fresh parsley
¼ cup chopped green onions

Place oat groats, broth, salt, curry powder, and turmeric in a medium saucepan and bring to a boil.

Reduce heat and let the oat-groat mixture simmer, covered, for 30–40 minutes until the oat groats are cooked but still slightly chewy.

Add the peas to the pan with the oat groats and cover again, letting the peas cook for 5 minutes.

Once the peas are cooked and bright green, turn off the heat and stir in the tomatoes, parsley, and green onions. Serve immediately.

PER SERVING | Calories: 226 | Fat: 3 g | Protein: 11 g | Sodium: 902 mg | Fiber: 8 g | Carbohydrates: 38 g | Sugar: 4 g

Basic Sprouted Oatmeal Granola

This basic oatmeal can be eaten as-is, or you can use it as a base for your favorite granola flavors. Dried fruit, nuts, chocolate, and other spices would all be great additions.

INGREDIENTS | SERVES 4

1 cup sprouted rolled oats

1 tablespoon butter or neutral oil (like safflower or canola)

1 tablespoon maple syrup

1 teaspoon cinnamon

½ teaspoon salt

Granola Storage

After cooling completely, place the granola in a sealed container. It will keep for a week, covered. If you don't think you'll eat the batch before the end of the week, cut the recipe in half.

Place a skillet over medium heat and add oats.

Toast oats, stirring occasionally, for 5–7 minutes until they start to turn golden.

Remove the oats from the pan and set aside in a bowl. Add the butter or oil, maple syrup, cinnamon, and salt to the pan. Stir together and let cook for 1–2 minutes or until fragrant.

Place the oats back into the skillet and stir them into the maple syrup mixture. Let this cook together for 2–3 minutes, making sure all the oats are coated.

Pour the oats into a bowl or onto a plate to cool.

PER SERVING | Calories: 220 | Fat: 6 g | Protein: 7 g | Sodium: 310 mg | Fiber: 5 g | Carbohydrates: 34 g | Sugar: 4 g

Sprouted Oat Granola, Nut, and Fruit Yogurt Parfaits

If you want even more flavor or texture in your parfaits, add some extra nuts or fruit to your granola before layering everything together.

INGREDIENTS | SERVES 4

½ cup sliced almonds

2 peaches, diced and peeled (optional)

1 cup berries

¼ cup honey

1 batch Basic Sprouted Oatmeal Granola (see recipe in this chapter)

2 cups low-fat vanilla yogurt

Make Your Own Greek Yogurt

Greek yogurt has a much thicker texture and consistency than regular yogurt. To replicate that texture at home, place a colander over a bowl and line the colander with cheesecloth or paper towels. Pour your plain yogurt into the colander and let it drain, refrigerated, for a few hours or overnight. The yogurt left in the colander will be extra thick and creamy, and the whey in the bowl can be discarded or used in smoothies.

In a medium bowl, mix the almonds, peaches, berries, and honey together.

Take 4 glasses or bowls and place a spoonful of the Basic Sprouted Oatmeal Granola in the bottom of each dish.

Layer on ¼ cup of the yogurt into each dish.

Place a spoonful of the almond and fruit mixture on top of the yogurt.

Repeat the layers until all the yogurt, granola, and fruit mixture is gone.

PER SERVING | Calories: 473 | Fat: 14 g | Protein: 14 g | Sodium: 346 mg | Fiber: 8 g | Carbohydrates: 63 g | Sugar: 28 g

Maple Bacon and Egg Oats

Sweet and salty is a classic combination. Baking the bacon with the maple syrup gives it a crispy, almost candy-like flavor and texture. If you don't have maple syrup on hand, brown sugar works great, too.

INGREDIENTS | SERVES 4

4 slices bacon
¼ cup maple syrup
2 cups sprouted steel-cut oats
4 cups water
1 teaspoon salt
1 tablespoon olive oil
4 eggs
1 teaspoon salt
½ teaspoon pepper

Preheat the oven to 375°F.

Lay bacon flat on a foil-lined baking sheet and drizzle with the maple syrup.

Bake the bacon for 20–25 minutes or until it is fully cooked.

While the bacon is cooking, place the oats, water, and salt in a saucepan and bring to a boil. Simmer the oats until they are creamy and the liquid is absorbed, about 10–15 minutes.

Heat a skillet over medium heat and add olive oil.

Crack eggs into the skillet and sprinkle with salt and pepper. Cook on the first side for 2–3 minutes or until the whites are starting to set. Flip over and cook for 1–2 minutes, then remove from pan.

To serve, crumble the bacon and stir into the cooked oats. Divide the oat mixture into four bowls and top each with one egg.

PER SERVING | Calories: 540 | Fat: 17 g | Protein: 22 g | Sodium: 1,525 mg | Fiber: 9 g | Carbohydrates: 70 g | Sugar: 14 g

Smoky Black Bean Oat Cakes

These oat cakes make a great weeknight dinner and are even more delicious the day after you've made them. If you have leftovers, reheat them in the oven to keep them crisp around the edges.

INGREDIENTS | SERVES 6

2 (15-ounce) cans black beans, drained and rinsed

1 cup shredded carrots

3 scallions, chopped

½ cup cilantro, chopped

1 clove garlic, minced

1 tablespoon olive oil

1 tablespoon smoked paprika

1 tablespoon chili powder

1 tablespoon salt

1 teaspoon pepper

1 cup sprouted rolled oats

Smoked Paprika

Spanish smoked paprika has a very different taste than sweet Hungarian paprika. The smoked variety has been cooked over fire, giving it a roasted warmth that the sweet version doesn't offer.

Preheat the oven to 350°F.

Place the beans, carrots, scallions, cilantro, garlic, oil, spices, salt, and pepper in a food processor. Process the mixture until the beans are mostly broken down and the mixture is well blended.

Place the bean mixture into a large bowl and fold in the oats.

Form mixture into 6 patties and place on a parchment-lined baking sheet.

Bake the oat cakes for 20–30 minutes, carefully flipping them halfway through.

PER SERVING (1 oat cake) | Calories: 344 | Fat: 5 g | Protein: 18 g | Sodium: 601 mg | Fiber: 18 g | Carbohydrates: 58 g | Sugar: 3 g

Butternut Squash and Sweet Onion Risotto

The cubes of butternut squash in this risotto add a beautiful pop of color to the dish. If you'd like even more color, let the onions caramelize a bit on their own before adding the squash to the pan. Just make sure to cook the onions on low and keep an eye on them so they don't burn.

INGREDIENTS | SERVES 4

2 tablespoons olive oil

½ medium onion, diced

2 cups butternut squash, diced into 1" pieces

1 cup sprouted steel-cut oats

4 cups vegetable broth, simmering

½ cup Parmesan cheese, freshly grated

1 teaspoon dried sage

1 teaspoon dried rosemary

Place a large skillet over medium heat and add the olive oil.

Add the onion and butternut squash to the oil. Cook, stirring occasionally, for 8–10 minutes until butternut squash is beginning to soften.

Stir the steel-cut oats into the pan and cook for 2–3 minutes with the vegetables.

Pour 1 cup of the simmering broth into the pan, stirring, and let the mixture simmer until the broth is almost completely absorbed.

Add another ½–1 cup of the broth to the pan, stirring occasionally, and let the broth absorb into the oats. Once one batch of broth has been mostly absorbed, add another cup every 5 minutes or so, and mix until the oats are cooked and the mixture is creamy.

Once all the broth has been added and the oats are cooked and have released their starches, stir in the Parmesan, dried sage, and dried rosemary.

Serve warm or at room temperature.

PER SERVING | Calories: 342 | Fat: 13 g | Protein: 15 g | Sodium: 746 mg | Fiber: 5 g | Carbohydrates: 41 g | Sugar: 5 g

No-Bake Oatmeal, Chocolate Chip, and Almond Butter Bites

Having a few dessert options that don't require heating up the oven should be required in the summer. These snack bites come together in minutes and are a cool treat for a hot afternoon. Make sure to keep them refrigerated, as they stay together better when cooled.

INGREDIENTS | SERVES 20

2½ cups sprouted rolled oats

½ cup chocolate chips

½ cup shredded unsweetened coconut

⅓ cup sunflower seeds

2 tablespoons ground flaxseed

1 teaspoon salt

½ cup almond butter

¾ cup honey

¼ cup melted coconut oil, or neutral oil (like safflower or canola)

In a large bowl, mix the oats, chocolate chips, coconut, sunflower seeds, flaxseed, and salt together.

In a separate bowl, mix the almond butter, honey, and oil together.

Toss the almond butter mixture with the dry ingredients, and stir until combined and all of the oat mixture is coated.

Form into 1" rounds and place on a baking sheet or plate.

Place in the refrigerator to set.

PER SERVING (2 snack pieces) | Calories: 240 | Fat: 11 g | Protein: 5 g | Sodium: 128 mg | Fiber: 3 g | Carbohydrates: 31 g | Sugar: 14 g

Sprouted Oatmeal and Almond Brittle

"Brittle" isn't just meant for peanuts. This dessert is made in the microwave and makes a great holiday gift or topping for ice cream.

INGREDIENTS | SERVES 8

1½ cups chopped almonds
1 cup sugar
½ cup light corn syrup
1 teaspoon salt
1 tablespoon butter
1 teaspoon vanilla extract
1 teaspoon baking soda
½ cup sprouted oats

Homemade Holiday Gifts

This quick brittle is a great recipe to make to give to friends and family around the holidays. Once it's cooled, it will keep in a container or sealed bags for a few weeks. Make 1–2 big batches before your holiday party or keep extras on hand for unexpected guests.

Grease a baking sheet or line with parchment paper.

Stir together almonds, sugar, corn syrup, and salt in a large microwave-safe bowl.

Heat mixture in microwave on high for 6–7 minutes.

Remove bowl from the microwave and stir in the butter and vanilla.

Place back in the microwave and heat for 2–3 more minutes until mixture is bubbling and turning golden.

Carefully stir in the baking soda and oats, as the mixture will foam up from the baking soda.

Immediately pour the brittle mixture onto the baking sheet and spread out into an even layer. Let the mixture cool for at least 15 minutes until it has hardened. Break into pieces to serve.

PER SERVING | Calories: 315 | Fat: 11 g | Protein: 5 g | Sodium: 466 mg | Fiber: 3 g | Carbohydrates: 52 g | Sugar: 32 g

Banana Baked Oatmeal

Busy mornings call for easy breakfasts. You can throw this baked oatmeal together on the weekend, store what's left over in the refrigerator, and reheat portions later.

INGREDIENTS | SERVES 6

2 cups sprouted oats
½ cup brown sugar
1 teaspoon cinnamon
1 teaspoon baking soda
½ teaspoon salt
1 cup milk
1 egg
½ cup applesauce
1 large banana, diced

Cooking with Kids

Get your kids involved in the kitchen and let them help mix up this easy breakfast bake. Instead of folding in the diced bananas, kids can lay them on top of the batter in a smiley face, in the shape of their name, or in any other design they want before baking.

Preheat the oven to 350°F.

In a large bowl, mix together the oats, brown sugar, cinnamon, baking soda, and salt.

In a separate bowl, whisk the milk, egg, and applesauce. Stir the wet ingredients into the dry.

Fold in the diced banana.

Pour the batter into a greased 8" × 8" baking dish and bake for 20–25 minutes until the edges are golden and the center is set.

PER SERVING | Calories: 303 | Fat: 4 g | Protein: 10 g | Sodium: 405 mg | Fiber: 6 g | Carbohydrates: 55 g | Sugar: 18 g

No-Bake Cocoa Coconut Cookies

An easy no-bake cookie recipe is the perfect midweek treat. Kids love helping with these cookies, and everyone enjoys eating them. If you don't like coconut, you can leave it out and savor the pure cocoa flavor.

INGREDIENTS | YIELDS 3–4 DOZEN COOKIES

1 stick (½ cup) butter

½ cup milk

2 cups sugar

2 cups sprouted rolled oats

½ cup unsweetened baking cocoa

½ cup shredded coconut

1 teaspoon vanilla extract

¼ teaspoon salt

Place the butter, milk, and sugar in a medium saucepan and bring the mixture to a boil.

Cook at a rolling boil for 3 minutes.

Remove the pan from the heat and stir in the sprouted oats, cocoa, coconut, vanilla, and salt.

Drop the dough by the spoonful onto parchment paper.

Let the cookies sit until they have set and you can easily peel off the paper.

PER SERVING (2 cookies) | Calories: 173 | Fat: 6 g | Protein: 3 g | Sodium: 33 mg | Fiber: 2 g | Carbohydrates: 28 g | Sugar: 18 g

Peach and Raspberry Oatmeal Crisp

Peaches and raspberries are usually ripe at the same time, meaning this dessert is packed with bright summer flavor and perfectly ripe fruit. If you can't find one of them or would rather have a different mix, just make sure to use the same amount of total fruit in the crisp.

INGREDIENTS | SERVES 6

2½ cups raspberries

3 peaches, peeled and diced

1 tablespoon sugar

1 tablespoon plus ¼ cup whole-wheat flour, divided

⅔ cup sprouted rolled oats

¼ cup brown sugar

¼ cup canola or safflower oil

½ teaspoon salt

½ teaspoon cinnamon

Preheat the oven to 350°F.

Toss fruit with sugar and 1 tablespoon whole-wheat flour, and pour into a greased 8" × 8" baking dish.

In a separate bowl, mix ¼ cup whole-wheat flour, oats, brown sugar, oil, salt, and cinnamon together until combined. Spread mixture over the fruit.

Bake for 35–45 minutes or until the topping is browned and fruit is bubbling around the edges.

PER SERVING | Calories: 264 | Fat: 11 g | Protein: 5 g | Sodium: 3 mg | Fiber: 7 g | Carbohydrates: 39 g | Sugar: 16 g

Maple and Pumpkin Oatmeal Porridge

Nothing says fall like a warm bowl of tasty oatmeal on a chilly morning.
The mix of pumpkin, spices, and maple syrup put this breakfast over the top.

INGREDIENTS | SERVES 4

2 cups water

1 cup sprouted rolled oats

1 teaspoon salt

1 ripe banana, peeled and sliced

1 teaspoon cinnamon

½ cup pumpkin purée

2 tablespoons maple syrup

Bring water to a boil in a medium saucepan.

Add oats, salt, and banana to the pan and bring back to a boil.

Reduce heat and let the oats simmer for 5–10 minutes, stirring occasionally until the oats are cooked and the liquid has been absorbed.

Remove the oats from the heat and stir in the cinnamon and pumpkin purée.

Divide into 2 bowls. Top each serving with maple syrup and serve.

PER SERVING | Calories: 229 | Fat: 3 g | Protein: 7 g |
Sodium: 588 mg | Fiber: 6 g | Carbohydrates: 42 g | Sugar: 9 g

Sprouted Oat Milk

This milk is a good liquid base for smoothies, soups, and desserts. Some additional sweeteners that can be used include dates, raisins, apricots, agave nectar, honey, maple syrup, and berries.

INGREDIENTS | SERVES 2

1 cup oat groats, sprouted
2 cups water

Using the sprouted oat groats, make a seed milk by blending them on high speed with 2 cups of water. Pour through a nut milk bag and squeeze out the liquid.

Use on your favorite cereal or in smoothies.

PER SERVING | Calories: 320 | Fat: 6 g | Protein: 14 g | Sodium: 7 mg | Fiber: 8 g | Carbohydrates: 56 g | Sugar: 2 g

Banana Oat Milkshake

You can make this recipe in about 5 minutes, making it a perfect breakfast on busy mornings.

INGREDIENTS | SERVES 2

1 cup sprouted oat groats or soaked oats

2 cups water

¾ cup banana

2 tablespoons maple syrup

Blend the oats on high with 2 cups of water.

Add the banana and maple syrup and blend until combined.

PER SERVING | Calories: 422 | Fat: 6 g | Protein: 15 g | Sodium: 9 mg | Fiber: 10 g | Carbohydrates: 82 g | Sugar: 21 g

CHAPTER 9

Sprouted Quinoa Recipes

Mexican Quinoa Salad

The main flavors in this salad come from the salsa, chili powder, and cumin. If some salsas are too spicy for you, choose one that's more mild in flavor, but make sure to keep the seasonings for depth and color.

INGREDIENTS | SERVES 6

1½ cups sprouted quinoa

1 (15-ounce) can black beans, drained and rinsed

1 cup salsa

1 cup corn (thawed if frozen)

½ cup chopped scallions

1 teaspoon chili powder

1 teaspoon cumin

1 tablespoon olive oil

1 teaspoon salt

Place sprouted quinoa in a large bowl and gently fold in the beans, salsa, corn, and scallions.

In a separate bowl, mix the chili powder, cumin, olive oil, and salt together.

Pour the oil mixture over the quinoa and toss to coat.

Serve either warm, at room temperature, or cool.

PER SERVING | Calories: 203 | Fat: 4 g | Protein: 9 g | Sodium: 698 mg | Fiber: 9 g | Carbohydrates: 35 g | Sugar: 4 g

Thawing Frozen Vegetables

If you know ahead of time that you'll need frozen vegetables for dinner, you can put the bag in the fridge and let them thaw overnight. But if you need to have the vegetables thaw faster, pour them into a colander and run cold water over them until they are no longer frozen. Let them drain for a few minutes before adding to the dish.

Quinoa with Zucchini, Blueberries, and Feta

Blueberries aren't usually used in savory dishes, but the sweet berries balance well with the salty feta. If blueberries aren't your favorite, diced strawberries would be another tasty option.

INGREDIENTS | SERVES 6

1½ cups sprouted quinoa

1 cup blueberries (thawed if frozen)

1 cup chickpeas, drained and rinsed (or sprouted)

1 medium zucchini

¼ cup feta cheese

¼ cup olive oil

2 tablespoons fresh parsley, chopped

1 teaspoon Herbes de Provence

1 teaspoon salt

Place quinoa in a large bowl and toss gently with the blueberries and chickpeas.

Slice the zucchini lengthwise and dice into bite-sized pieces.

Stir the zucchini into the quinoa.

In a small bowl, crumble the feta cheese and stir together with the oil, parsley, Herbes de Provence, and salt.

Pour dressing over quinoa, toss to coat, and serve.

PER SERVING | Calories: 217 | Fat: 12 g | Protein: 6 g | Sodium: 468 mg | Fiber: 4 g | Carbohydrates: 22 g | Sugar: 4 g

Herbes de Provence

This mix of herbs is a combination of lavender, French, and Italian herbs that show the historical influence of the Roman culture on the food and flavors of the area. The most common herbs in this mix are rosemary, fennel, thyme, savory, basil, tarragon, and lavender, although the herbs mix can differ a little depending on the brand you buy.

Quinoa Summer Vegetable Salad

This protein-packed salad is a quick dinner option on a warm summer night. And since any vegetable would work in this, it's also a great way to clean out the fridge.

INGREDIENTS | SERVES 6

2½ cups sprouted red quinoa

1 cup chickpeas, drained and rinsed (or sprouted)

1 medium zucchini, sliced

1 medium yellow squash, sliced

1 cup cherry tomatoes, halved

¼ cup fresh parsley

¼ cup fresh mint

2 teaspoons salt

1 teaspoon pepper

1 tablespoon lemon juice

2 tablespoons olive oil

In a large bowl, stir together the quinoa, chickpeas, zucchini, squash, and tomatoes.

In a separate bowl, whisk together the parsley, mint, salt, pepper, lemon juice, and olive oil.

Pour dressing over quinoa and toss together.

Serve chilled or at room temperature.

PER SERVING | Calories: 188 | Fat: 7 g | Protein: 6 g | Sodium: 777 mg | Fiber: 5 g | Carbohydrates: 26 g | Sugar: 3 g

Main or Side Dish?

Because of the protein in both the quinoa and chickpeas, this salad is hearty enough to stand as the main dish for a light summer supper or quick lunch. But it's also delicious alongside grilled chicken, steak, or fish.

Roasted Butternut, Cranberry, and Walnut Quinoa Salad

If you're looking for a new dish to make for your holiday dinner, try this quinoa salad. The flavors are perfect in fall or winter, and the butternut squash and cranberries bring a splash of color to the salad.

INGREDIENTS | SERVES 4

2 cups butternut squash, diced

1 tablespoon coconut oil, melted

1 teaspoon salt

2 cups sprouted quinoa

½ cup dried cranberries

½ cup chopped walnuts

¼ cup chopped scallions

¼ cup chopped parsley

2 tablespoons maple syrup

Cut the Sugar

When choosing dried fruits at the store, check the nutritional information and ingredients to see if there are added sugars listed. Dried fruits are always sweeter than fresh because the flavors and natural sugars are concentrated in the drying process. If you can find dried fruits with no added sugar, they're a much healthier option.

Preheat the oven to 375°F.

Toss diced butternut squash with coconut oil and salt, and spread out in an even layer on a baking sheet or dish lined with parchment paper.

Roast for 20 minutes. Flip squash pieces, and roast for 15 more minutes or until the squash is cooked and browning on the outside.

Place roasted squash in a large bowl and stir in quinoa, cranberries, walnuts, scallions, parsley, and maple syrup. Toss together so everything is coated with the syrup.

Serve warm.

PER SERVING | Calories: 357 | Fat: 15 g | Protein: 8 g | Sodium: 597 mg | Fiber: 5 g | Carbohydrates: 53 g | Sugar: 21 g

Baked Zucchini, Tomato, and Quinoa Parmesan

Italian dishes don't always have to use pasta as the base.
For a gluten-free option, try this quinoa Parmesan casserole.

INGREDIENTS | SERVES 6

2 medium zucchini
4 medium tomatoes
4 teaspoons salt, divided
2 cups sprouted quinoa
1 cup tomato sauce
1 clove garlic, minced
1 tablespoon olive oil
1 tablespoon oregano
1 tablespoon basil
1 tablespoon parsley
1 teaspoon pepper
1 cup mozzarella cheese, shredded
½ cup Parmesan cheese, shredded

Slice the zucchini and tomatoes into ½" thick slices and place in a colander. Sprinkle them with 2 teaspoons of the salt and let them sit for 15 minutes to release some of their moisture.

Preheat the oven to 375°F.

In a large bowl, stir together the quinoa, tomato sauce, garlic, olive oil, oregano, basil, parsley, remaining 2 teaspoons of salt, and pepper.

Pour half of the quinoa mixture into a greased 9" × 13" baking dish, then top with half of the sliced zucchini and tomatoes. Sprinkle with ½ cup of the shredded mozzarella.

Repeat the layers, adding the rest of the quinoa mixture and the last of the zucchini and tomatoes, and top with the remaining mozzarella and the Parmesan cheese.

Bake for 30–35 minutes or until the cheese is melted and beginning to brown.

PER SERVING | Calories: 210 | Fat: 8 g | Protein: 12 g | Sodium: 1,623 mg | Fiber: 4 g | Carbohydrates: 23 g | Sugar: 5 g

Quinoa Banana Pecan Quick Bread

Everyone loves banana bread. This recipe is a good way to sneak in some whole grains without sacrificing texture or flavor.

INGREDIENTS | SERVES 12

1½ cups whole-wheat pastry flour

1 cup sprouted quinoa

½ cup sprouted (or nonsprouted) oats

1½ teaspoons baking powder

¼ teaspoon baking soda

½ teaspoon salt

1 teaspoon cinnamon

½ cup chopped pecans

2 ripe medium-sized bananas, mashed

1 cup buttermilk

¾ cup brown sugar

1 teaspoon vanilla extract

2 tablespoons oil or melted butter

Preheat the oven to 350°F.

Stir together the flour, quinoa, oats, baking powder, baking soda, salt, cinnamon, and pecans in a large bowl.

In a separate bowl, mix the mashed bananas with the buttermilk, brown sugar, vanilla, and oil or butter.

Add banana mixture into the flour mixture, and fold together until the batter is just combined.

Pour batter into a greased 9" × 5" loaf pan and bake for 50–55 minutes until the top is golden and a toothpick comes out clean when inserted into the center of the loaf.

PER SERVING | Calories: 225 | Fat: 7 g | Protein: 5 g | Sodium: 206 mg | Fiber: 4 g | Carbohydrates: 38 g | Sugar: 14 g

Baking Oil Options

For most baked goods that call for oil, make sure to choose neutral-flavored oils such as canola, safflower, or vegetable. Flaxseed oil has a nutty flavor that would be delicious in this bread. Just make sure to keep flaxseed oil in the refrigerator, as it can go rancid quickly if it's not kept cool.

Berry Nutty Quinoa Breakfast Porridge

The soft and fluffy texture of quinoa makes it a great option for breakfast. Since it has more protein than regular oats, it can also help fill you up and keep you satisfied throughout the morning.

INGREDIENTS | SERVES 4

2 cups sprouted red or black quinoa

1 cup water

1 cup milk

1 teaspoon salt

1 teaspoon cinnamon

1 cup berries

½ cup chopped walnuts, pecans, or almonds

2 tablespoons ground flaxseed

1 tablespoon honey

Place the quinoa, water, milk, and salt in a medium saucepan; bring to a simmer.

Let the quinoa cook, stirring occasionally, for 5–10 minutes until the milk and water are absorbed.

Stir in the cinnamon, berries, nuts, flaxseed, and honey.

Divide into 4 bowls and serve warm.

PER SERVING | Calories: 296 | Fat: 14 g | Protein: 9 g | Sodium: 615 mg | Fiber: 6 g | Carbohydrates: 36 g | Sugar: 11 g

Quinoa, Buckwheat, and Oatmeal Granola

The mix of grains, nuts, and fruit gives this granola a fantastic texture. If you like one texture more than another (such as buckwheat over oats), you can change up the measurements of the grains to your preference.

INGREDIENTS | YIELDS 4½ CUPS GRANOLA

¾ cup sprouted quinoa

¾ cup raw buckwheat groats

¾ cup old-fashioned oats

2 tablespoons ground flaxseed

½ cup chopped almonds

⅓ cup sunflower seeds

⅓ cup chopped walnuts

⅓ cup shredded coconut

½ cup dried cherries

2 teaspoons cinnamon

1 teaspoon salt

½ cup maple syrup

½ cup coconut oil, melted (or other neutral oil)

Preheat the oven to 250°F.

In a large bowl, mix together the quinoa, buckwheat groats, oats, flaxseed, almonds, sunflower seeds, walnuts, coconut, dried cherries, cinnamon, and salt.

Pour maple syrup and melted coconut oil over the granola mixture and toss together, completely coating all of the granola with the oil and syrup.

Pour granola onto a baking sheet lined with parchment paper and bake for 60 minutes.

Let the granola cool for 5 minutes before breaking into pieces.

PER SERVING (approximately ¼ cup) | Calories: 300 | Fat: 15 g | Protein: 7 g | Sodium: 239 mg | Fiber: 5 g | Carbohydrates: 35 g | Sugar: 10 g

Coconut Oil

Using coconut oil in baked goods and for cooking gives a slightly sweet flavor and just a hint of coconut in the final dish. At room temperature, coconut oil is solid, but it melts quickly when heated up.

Maple Pecan Quinoa Cookies

These fluffy, maple syrup–sweetened cookies are a nice contrast to regular oatmeal-type cookies.

INGREDIENTS | YIELDS 3½ DOZEN COOKIES

1 cup (2 sticks) butter, softened to room temperature

2 eggs

1 teaspoon vanilla extract

1 cup maple syrup

1 cup white whole-wheat flour

1½ cups all-purpose flour

1 teaspoon baking soda

1 teaspoon cinnamon

½ teaspoon salt

2 cups oats

1 cup sprouted quinoa

1 cup chopped pecans

Preheat the oven to 350°F.

Beat the softened butter until light and creamy, 3–4 minutes.

Add the eggs, one at a time, to the butter and mix until combined.

Mix in the vanilla and maple syrup.

In a separate bowl, mix the flours, baking soda, cinnamon, and salt. Add half of the flour mixture to the butter, mixing until the flour is incorporated. Add the remaining flour mixture and mix in.

Slowly mix in the oats, quinoa, and chopped pecans until the nuts are evenly distributed in the dough.

Drop dough by rounded tablespoons 1"–2" apart on a baking sheet and bake at 350°F for 10–12 minutes until golden around the edges.

Cool for 1 minute before moving to a cooling rack.

PER SERVING (1 cookie) | Calories: 139 | Fat: 7 g | Protein: 3 g | Sodium: 62 mg | Fiber: 1 g | Carbohydrates: 17 g | Sugar: 5 g

Southwestern Bean and Quinoa Cakes

Using both the quinoa and beans gives these cakes a nice punch of protein. Serve these cakes on buns or on top of salad. They can also be made into smaller patties and served as an appetizer with a dip or salsa.

INGREDIENTS | SERVES 6

1 (15-ounce) can pinto beans, drained and rinsed

1 (15-ounce) can black beans, drained and rinsed

½ cup shredded carrots

½ cup scallions, chopped

1 chipotle in adobo sauce, chopped

1 garlic clove, chopped

1 tablespoon ground flaxseed

1 teaspoon salt

1 teaspoon cumin

1 teaspoon coriander

1 cup sprouted quinoa

Preheat the oven to 350°F.

Place all ingredients except quinoa in the bowl of a food processor.

Pulse the bean mixture until the vegetables are chopped and the beans are broken down.

Move bean mixture into a large bowl and mix in the quinoa.

Shape into 6 patties and place on a parchment paper–lined baking sheet.

Bake for 15–20 minutes. Serve warm.

PER SERVING (1 cake) | Calories: 264 | Fat: 2 g | Protein: 15 g | Sodium: 482 mg | Fiber: 14 g | Carbohydrates: 48 g | Sugar: <1 g

Chipotle in Adobo Sauce

These sweet and spicy peppers are red jalapeños that have been dried, smoked, and canned in a thin and spicy tomato sauce. Depending on the brand, chipotles in adobo sauce can be very spicy, so be cautious when adding it to a recipe until after you've tasted the sauce and a bit of the pepper.

Quick Quinoa Primavera

Quinoa has a soft and fluffy texture when it's sprouted or cooked. The addition of the wine, broth, and cream gives this primavera a rich but delicate touch.

1 pound fresh asparagus
1 tablespoon olive oil
1 cup fresh green peas
1 cup carrots, shredded
½ cup vegetable broth
½ cup white wine
2 tablespoons cream or half and half
1½ cups sprouted quinoa
1 teaspoon salt
1 tablespoon fresh lemon juice
¼ cup fresh parsley, chopped

Versatile Primavera

Typical primavera pasta dishes are full of fresh vegetables, but they can also include lean proteins and more robust flavors, such as seasonal herbs like mint and rosemary or the smoky hint of bacon, depending on your preferences. Add in one new ingredient every time you make this dish to keep it new and fresh.

Trim the ends of the asparagus and chop into 1" pieces.

Heat a large skillet over medium heat and add the olive oil to the pan.

Sauté the asparagus, peas, and carrots in oil for 5–8 minutes, stirring occasionally, until the vegetables are crisp-tender.

Stir in the broth and wine; let the mixture simmer for 1–2 minutes.

Add the cream, quinoa, salt, and lemon juice; cook for 3–4 minutes or until the liquid has absorbed into the quinoa.

Remove the pan from the heat and sprinkle with the parsley before serving.

PER SERVING | Calories: 197 | Fat: 6 g | Protein: 8 g | Sodium: 591 mg | Fiber: 6 g | Carbohydrates: 26 g | Sugar: 5 g

Roasted Vegetable and Quinoa Meatloaf

Instead of using the typical oatmeal or bread crumbs in your meatloaf, toss in some sprouted quinoa for a slightly different texture and even more protein.

INGREDIENTS | SERVES 8

1 onion, finely diced
2 carrots, finely diced
1 red pepper, finely diced
1 tablespoon olive oil
2 teaspoons salt, divided
1 teaspoon pepper, divided
¾ cup sprouted quinoa
1½ pounds lean ground beef
1 egg
1 teaspoon oregano
1 clove garlic, minced
¼ cup ketchup
1 tablespoon Dijon mustard
1 tablespoon maple syrup

Preheat the oven to 375°F.

Toss the onion, carrots, and red pepper with the olive oil, 1 teaspoon of the salt, and ½ teaspoon of the pepper, and place on a baking sheet. Roast for 25–30 minutes until the vegetables are cooked.

In a large bowl, mix the quinoa, ground beef, egg, 1 teaspoon salt, ½ teaspoon pepper, oregano, and garlic together. Gently mix in the roasted vegetables.

Press meatloaf mixture into a greased 9" × 5" loaf pan or hand-form into a loaf shape in a baking dish.

In a small bowl, mix the ketchup, Dijon mustard, and maple syrup together. Brush over the top of the meatloaf.

Bake meatloaf for 40–50 minutes or until a meat thermometer reads 170°F.

PER SERVING | Calories: 184 | Fat: 7 g | Protein: 20 g | Sodium: 749 mg | Fiber: 1 g | Carbohydrates: 10 g | Sugar: 4 g

Quinoa Stuffed Peppers

If you're looking to add new grains into your diet, making the switch from rice to quinoa in stuffed peppers is an easy way to try a delicious new option.

INGREDIENTS | SERVES 4

4 bell peppers, any color
1 pound spicy Italian sausage
1 medium onion, diced
1 clove garlic, minced
1 cup sprouted quinoa
1 cup crushed tomatoes
1 teaspoon salt
½ teaspoon pepper
1 teaspoon oregano
½ cup mozzarella cheese, shredded

Did You Know?

Bell peppers, no matter what color, are high in many vitamins and minerals including vitamins C and A. Bell peppers range in color from yellow to red to green to purple. Try finding some new varieties at your local farmers' market to use as the base for this stuffed pepper recipe.

Preheat the oven to 375°F.

Cut each pepper in half lengthwise (from top to bottom), and remove the seeds and ribs. Place cut side up in a baking dish.

Place a skillet over medium heat and brown the sausage, breaking it up with a spoon as it cooks.

Once the sausage is browned, add the onion and garlic, and cook for 2–3 minutes until fragrant.

Remove the pan from heat and stir in the quinoa, tomatoes, salt, pepper, and oregano.

Spoon the quinoa into the pepper halves and top each with some shredded mozzarella cheese.

Bake for 35–40 minutes until the peppers have softened and the cheese is melted.

PER SERVING | Calories: 467 | Fat: 28 g | Protein: 26 g | Sodium: 1,905 mg | Fiber: 6 g | Carbohydrates: 28 g | Sugar: 5 g

Cheesy Quinoa

A whole-grain twist on macaroni and cheese, this quinoa dish offers the same soft texture as mac 'n cheese but with even more nutritional punch and flavor.

INGREDIENTS | SERVES 4

1 cup sprouted quinoa
2 cups chicken broth
1 teaspoon garlic salt
1 teaspoon dry mustard
1 cup Cheddar cheese, shredded
1 tablespoon butter

Decadent Dinner

While this twist on mac 'n cheese is a little healthier than a typical macaroni recipe, you can add some familiarity back with a bread crumb or cheesy crust on the top, and bake the casserole before serving.

Mix the quinoa, broth, garlic salt, and dry mustard in a saucepan. Bring to a boil and stir the mixture together.

Cover the pan and reduce the heat to low. Let the quinoa simmer on low for 10–15 minutes until the majority of the liquid has been absorbed.

Turn off the heat and stir in the Cheddar and butter.

Serve warm.

PER SERVING | Calories: 207 | Fat: 13 g | Protein: 11 g | Sodium: 777 mg | Fiber: 1 g | Carbohydrates: 11 g | Sugar: <1 g

Whole-Grain Breakfast Cookies

Grab-and-go breakfasts make weekday mornings easy. These breakfast cookies are full of whole grains, fruit, and nuts that can be changed with the mix-ins you like the most. Make a batch on the weekends and freeze any extras for later.

INGREDIENTS | YIELDS 2 DOZEN

1 cup whole-wheat pastry flour
¼ cup all-purpose flour
½ teaspoon baking soda
1 teaspoon cinnamon
½ teaspoon salt
2 tablespoons butter, softened
¼ cup safflower oil or other neutral oil
½ cup brown sugar
1 egg
¼ cup unsweetened applesauce
1 teaspoon vanilla extract
½ cup oats
½ cup sprouted quinoa
½ cup dried cherries
½ cup chopped walnuts

Going Gluten Free?

Swapping out the wheat flours for a gluten-free flour like oat, quinoa, buckwheat, or a mix of those and some almond meal will keep these treats free of gluten. Try a few different mixes of flours to figure out what balance you like the best.

Preheat the oven to 350°F.

Whisk the flours, baking soda, cinnamon, and salt together in a medium bowl.

In a large bowl, beat the butter together with the oil and brown sugar until creamy. Add the egg, applesauce, and vanilla, and mix for another minute.

Pour the flour mixture into the butter mixture and mix for 1–2 minutes until the flour is combined.

Slowly mix in the oats, quinoa, dried cherries, and walnuts until they are evenly distributed in the dough.

Taking 2 tablespoons of dough at a time, roll the dough into rounds and place 3" apart on a parchment paper–lined baking sheet. Flatten each cookie with your hand until it is ¼" thick.

Bake cookies for 12 minutes until they're starting to turn golden but are still soft. Let the cookies cool for 1–2 minutes on the baking sheet before moving to a cooling rack to cool completely.

PER SERVING (1 cookie) | Calories: 101 | Fat: 5 g | Protein: 2 g | Sodium: 76 mg | Fiber: 1 g | Carbohydrates: 12 g | Sugar: 4 g

Quinoa, Nut, and Fruit Snack Bars

You can have granola bars without high-fructose corn syrup or other ingredients that you can't pronounce. Eaten alone or crumbled on yogurt, these bars are a nice option to have in the house for a quick breakfast or a filling afternoon snack.

INGREDIENTS | SERVES 18

1 cup dried fruit mix

¼ cup fresh orange juice

1 teaspoon vanilla extract

2 eggs, beaten

2 cups oats

1 cup sprouted quinoa

½ cup chopped pecans

½ cup brown sugar

1 teaspoon cinnamon

½ teaspoon salt

¼ cup coconut oil or butter, melted

Prepping Ahead

Anytime you find yourself making a batch of these bars, double the recipe and make two pans. Once the bars are completely cooled, wrap each bar in plastic wrap and place into a bag in the freezer. The bars don't take long to thaw, and you'll be stocked up on healthy snacks or quick breakfast options for months to come.

Preheat the oven to 325°F.

In a small bowl, mix the dried fruit, orange juice, vanilla, and beaten eggs; set aside.

In a large bowl, mix the oats, quinoa, pecans, brown sugar, cinnamon, and salt. Pour the melted coconut oil over the oat mixture and toss to combine.

Stir in the dried fruit mixture.

Press dough into an even layer in a greased 9" × 13" baking dish.

Bake for 15–20 minutes until the edges are golden. Let cool before cutting.

PER SERVING | Calories: 161 | Fat: 7 g | Protein: 4 g | Sodium: 72 mg | Fiber: 3 g | Carbohydrates: 22 g | Sugar: 4 g

Triple Coconut Quinoa

This triple use of coconut gives the fluffy quinoa an irresistible flavor. Try this under your favorite curry or stir-fry dish, or add some fresh fruit and serve it up for breakfast.

INGREDIENTS | SERVES 4

1 tablespoon coconut oil
1 cup sprouted quinoa
½ cup light coconut milk
½ cup water
1 teaspoon salt
¼ cup shredded coconut

Sweet and Spicy

Want a little more heat with your sweet? Add a pinch or two of crushed red pepper or cayenne to the quinoa for a kick of spice that will balance with the sweetness of the coconut.

Melt the coconut oil in a medium saucepan. Stir in the sprouted quinoa and let it cook in the oil for 2–3 minutes, stirring occasionally.

Pour the coconut milk, water, and salt into the quinoa and bring the mixture to a simmer.

Let the quinoa cook for 5–10 minutes until the liquid has been absorbed.

Fluff the quinoa with a fork and gently fold in the shredded coconut.

Serve warm.

PER SERVING | Calories: 159 | Fat: 12 g | Protein: 3 g | Sodium: 587 mg | Fiber: 2 g | Carbohydrates: 11 g | Sugar: <1 g

Bacon and Poblano Quinoa Salad

*Quick and easy, this quinoa salad can serve as a side dish to your
favorite protein or stand alone as the main meal with a nice salad on the side.
It's a great dish for summer when the corn is sweet and the peppers are abundant.*

INGREDIENTS | SERVES 4

¼ pound bacon, diced

2 poblano peppers, seeded and diced

1 cup fresh corn kernels

1 teaspoon salt

½ teaspoon pepper

1½ cups sprouted red quinoa

2 tablespoons olive oil

¼ cup fresh cilantro

1 teaspoon lime zest

Cutting Kernels from the Cob

The easiest way to get fresh kernels from the cob is to shuck the corn (remove the silks, leaves, and root end) and stand it up on the root end in a medium bowl. Holding the corn cob upright, run your knife down each side of the cob, cutting the kernels on the way down so they land in the bowl. Once you have cut all the way around the cob, discard the cob.

Place a skillet over medium heat and add the diced bacon. Cook, stirring occasionally, until the bacon begins to crisp. Remove the bacon from the pan and set aside.

Add the poblano peppers and corn kernels to the bacon fat in the pan and cook for 5–6 minutes, until the vegetables are browning and beginning to soften.

Remove the pan from the heat and stir in the salt, pepper, and quinoa. Toss everything together and pour into a large bowl.

Stir the crumbled bacon into the quinoa mixture and add the olive oil, cilantro, and lime zest.

Serve warm or at room temperature.

PER SERVING | Calories: 347 | Fat: 20 g | Protein: 15 g |
Sodium: 1,376 mg | Fiber: 4 g | Carbohydrates: 27 g | Sugar: 3 g

Chinese Kung Pao Almonds and Cashews with Sprouted Quinoa

Dinner in 30 minutes? You got it. This is essentially a mock stir-fry, a delicious, spicy dish seasoned with a homemade version of traditional hoisin sauce. It's best served with a fluffy grain like quinoa, steamed vegetables, and a sprinkling of sliced scallions.

INGREDIENTS | SERVES 4

½ cup almonds

½ cup cashews

¼ cup nama shoyu

¼ cup sesame oil

4 tablespoons maple syrup

1 tablespoon chopped fresh hot peppers (cayenne, jalapeño, chili)

½ clove garlic

1 tablespoon grated ginger

1 cup mung bean sprouts

1 cup additional chopped veggies (asparagus tips, chopped green or red bell peppers, celery, and cherry tomatoes)

2 cups red quinoa, sprouted

Soak the almonds and cashews for 8–12 hours in 4 cups of water. Drain and rinse.

Using a blender, prepare the hoisin sauce by blending together nama shoyu, sesame oil, maple syrup, hot peppers, garlic, and ginger.

Using a food processor with an S blade, pulse the almonds and cashews until chunky.

In a bowl, stir together the almond mixture, mung bean sprouts, assorted veggies, and prepared sauce.

Divide the quinoa between four bowls and top with the almond mixture.

PER SERVING | Calories: 694 | Fat: 33 g | Protein: 18 g | Sodium: 957 mg | Fiber: 9 g | Carbohydrates: 87 g | Sugar: 15 g

Almonds

Almonds are rich in protein, healthy fats, vitamin E, magnesium, and calcium. California is the world's largest producer of almonds. The almond skin contains a bitter tannin, which is removed by soaking the almond in water. You can speed up the process of removing the tannins by soaking the almonds in warm water for one hour.

Chipotle Sprout Wrap

This is a great recipe that can be made in less than 30 minutes.
It is a delicious wrap served with guacamole and salsa.

INGREDIENTS | SERVES 4

1 cup cashews

2 tablespoons olive oil

1 tablespoon fresh chipotle pepper,
   or 1 teaspoon chipotle powder

2 tablespoons lemon juice

Water for blending

4 collard leaves, stemmed

½ cup mung bean sprouts

½ cup red quinoa, sprouted

1 cup red bell pepper, sliced into strips

½ cup scallions, chopped

2 tablespoons minced fresh cilantro, for
   garnish

Blend the cashews, olive oil, chipotle, and lemon juice together. Slowly add a little water until it blends into a creamy sauce.

To assemble the wrap, lay the collard leaves flat. Spread a layer of cashew cream onto the leaves. Place some sprouts, quinoa, scallions, red bell pepper, and cilantro on one end of the leaves and roll tightly.

PER SERVING | Calories: 360 | Fat: 24 g | Protein: 10 g | Sodium: 25 mg | Fiber: 4 g | Carbohydrates: 31 g | Sugar: 3 g

Mung Bean Sprouts

Also called Chinese bean sprouts, these are the most popular sprouts in the world. They are readily available in most grocery stores. Mung beans are a protein-rich legume high in the minerals zinc, calcium, iron, magnesium, and potassium, and in vitamins A, B, C, and E. Mung sprouts can also be grown at home right in your kitchen.

Raw Sushi Nori Rolls

These nori rolls are delicious dipped into a soy and wasabi mix or hot chile paste for even more of a kick. Serve alongside a vegetable salad and miso soup for a complete meal.

INGREDIENTS | SERVES 2

2 sheets raw or roasted nori

¼ cup Nutty Garlic Spread for each sheet (see recipe in sidebar)

2 tablespoons microgreen sprouts (alfalfa, sunflower, clover, or radish) per sheet

2 tablespoons sprouted quinoa per sheet

2 tablespoons finely grated carrot per sheet or more

½ avocado, sliced

Nutty Garlic Spread

To make Nutty Garlic Spread, you will need 2 cups almonds, soaked; 1 cup cashews, soaked but crispy; ¼ cup celery hearts, chopped; 4 tablespoons red or white onion, chopped; 2 tablespoons lemon juice; 2 cloves garlic; and ¼ teaspoon salt. Then you just need to soak the almonds and cashews in water for 8–12 hours. Next, blend all the ingredients together in a food processor using the S blade, and you have a delicious spread that serves about 2–4 poeple.

Lay one nori sheet flat on a sushi mat. Spread about ¼ cup of the spread across one end of the nori. Add a layer of sprouts and top with the carrot and avocado.

Roll up the nori sheets tightly using the sushi mat. Just before the completing the roll, dip your finger in water and run it along the edge of the nori sheet to create a seal.

Cut the sushi rolls into six round pieces with a sharp knife (ideally with saw teeth) using a gentle see-saw motion. Repeat the process with the remaining nori sheet.

PER SERVING | Calories: 412 | Fat: 29 g | Protein: 13 g | Sodium: 100 mg | Fiber: 11 g | Carbohydrates: 31 g | Sugar: 3 g

CHAPTER 10

Sprouted Barley Recipes

Cinnamon Vanilla Breakfast Barley

Barley isn't meant just for soups and stews. The soft and puffy texture of the grain makes it a great option for breakfast—especially when it's cooked with cinnamon and vanilla.

INGREDIENTS | SERVES 2

1 cup sprouted barley

1 cup water

½ cup milk

1 teaspoon vanilla extract

1 teaspoon cinnamon

½ teaspoon salt

Cinnamon Kick

Did you know there are different types of cinnamon? One of the most flavorful choices on the market is Saigon cinnamon, which has a deeper and more robust flavor. You can also find roasted cinnamon that has a mild smoky taste.

In a small saucepan, bring sprouted barley, water, and milk to a boil over medium heat.

Lower the heat and simmer for 10–15 minutes until the barley has absorbed the liquid.

Remove the pan from the heat and stir in the vanilla, cinnamon, and salt.

Divide the mixture into two bowls and serve warm.

PER SERVING | Calories: 149 | Fat: 1 g | Protein: 4 g | Sodium: 697 mg | Fiber: 4 g | Carbohydrates: 30 g | Sugar: 4 g

Barley with Butternut Squash, Apples, and Swiss Chard

*Because of its mild flavor, barley can be used in sweet and savory dishes.
It easily takes on whatever flavor you want to have shine in your dish.*

INGREDIENTS | SERVES 4

2 cups butternut squash, diced into 1" pieces

¼ pound bacon, diced

1 clove garlic, minced

¼ cup scallions, sliced

1 medium apple, diced

3 cups Swiss chard, chopped

1 teaspoon olive oil

1½ cups sprouted barley

2 teaspoons honey

2 teaspoons fresh rosemary

1 teaspoon salt

½ teaspoon pepper

How to Dice a Butternut Squash

The easiest way to dice a butternut squash is to start by cutting the top and bottom off the squash so it can sit flat on a cutting board. Cut the squash in half right above where the squash bottom starts and the neck ends. Working with one piece at a time, set the squash on one of the cut ends and run your knife from top to bottom along the side, taking the peel off the squash. Once the peel has been trimmed, cut the squash in half lengthwise and dice.

Place diced butternut squash in a large microwave-safe bowl and cover with plastic wrap. Cook in the microwave on high for 5 minutes to steam the squash until it's just tender.

Cook diced bacon in a large skillet over medium heat, stirring frequently, until crisp. Remove from pan.

Add garlic, scallions, and steamed butternut squash to the bacon fat in the pan, and cook the vegetables until the mixture is fragrant and the squash starts to brown. Place vegetables in a large bowl.

Add diced apple to the hot skillet and cook for 2–3 minutes. Remove from the pan and add to the squash mixture.

Toss the chopped Swiss chard into the hot skillet with the olive oil. Cook for 2–3 minutes until the greens wilt down. Add greens to the squash and apples.

Stir barley, honey, rosemary, salt, and pepper into the squash mixture. Serve warm.

PER SERVING | Calories: 215 | Fat: 4 g | Protein: 10 g | Sodium: 1,085 mg | Fiber: 3 g | Carbohydrates: 38 g | Sugar: 9 g

Ham, Mushroom, Broccoli, and Barley Casserole

A twist on a white rice–based casserole, this barley-based dish tastes like something your mom would have made—with a healthier twist.

INGREDIENTS | SERVES 6

1 tablespoon olive oil

8 ounces cremini mushrooms, sliced

1 medium onion, diced

2 cloves garlic, minced

12 ounces frozen chopped broccoli, thawed

½ cup sour cream

2 cups cottage cheese

2 eggs, beaten

8 ounces lean ham, diced

2 cups sprouted barley

½ cup Parmesan cheese, grated

Get Your Greens

Not a fan of broccoli? Frozen (and thawed) chopped spinach or peas are other options for this casserole. They still give you the pop of color from the green and some added benefits from the vitamins and fiber.

Preheat the oven to 350°F.

Heat olive oil in a large skillet over medium heat and add sliced mushrooms. Cook the mushrooms until they are browned and tender, 5–7 minutes. Remove mushrooms from the pan and place them in a large bowl.

Add onion and garlic to the pan and cook for 2–3 minutes until the onion is softened.

Add onion and garlic to the mushrooms. Stir in the thawed chopped broccoli.

In a medium bowl, beat the sour cream, cottage cheese, and eggs together. Pour the cottage cheese mixture over the vegetables. Add the diced ham and the barley. Stir everything together until all of the vegetables and barley are coated.

Pour barley mixture into a greased 9" × 13" pan and sprinkle with the Parmesan. Cover the dish with foil and bake for 30 minutes.

Remove the foil and bake for another 10 minutes. Let the casserole cool for 10 minutes before serving.

PER SERVING | Calories: 329 | Fat: 15 g | Protein: 25 g | Sodium: 848 mg | Fiber: 4 g | Carbohydrates: 25 g | Sugar: 5 g

Veggie Barley Chili

Using barley thickens the chili, and the grains soak up the flavorful cooking liquid. Feel free to add your favorite meat if you'd rather have a nonvegetable-based meal.

INGREDIENTS | SERVES 8

3 cups water

1½ cups sprouted barley

1 (10-ounce) can Ro*tel brand diced tomatoes and green chiles

1 (15-ounce) can kidney beans, drained and rinsed

1 (15-ounce) can pinto beans, drained and rinsed

1 cup frozen corn

1 tablespoon chili powder

1 tablespoon cumin

1 teaspoon paprika

2 teaspoons salt

1 teaspoon pepper

Bring water to a boil in a large pot. Stir in barley and lower the heat to medium. Let the barley simmer for 5–7 minutes.

Stir the remaining ingredients into the barley and let the chili simmer for 10–15 more minutes. Serve hot.

PER SERVING | Calories: 214 | Fat: 1 g | Protein: 11 g | Sodium: 644 mg | Fiber: 11 g | Carbohydrates: 42 g | Sugar: 1 g

Ro*tel

Ro*tel is a brand of diced tomatoes and green chiles that add a nice kick of heat to this chili. You can leave it out if you don't want the chiles—just use a regular can of diced tomatoes.

Pork and Poblano Pot

Similar to rice in consistency, barley gives a great texture contrast in this dish when paired with the cooked pork and vegetables.

INGREDIENTS | SERVES 4

1 tablespoon olive oil, divided
1 medium zucchini, diced
8 ounces mushrooms, sliced
1 clove garlic, minced
2 poblano peppers, diced
1 pound pork loin, diced
1 cup diced tomatoes
1 (15-ounce) can pinto beans, drained and rinsed
1 cup water
1 cup sprouted barley
1 tablespoon cumin
1 tablespoon chili powder
1 tablespoon oregano
2 teaspoons salt

A Mild Heat

Poblano peppers have a mild flavor that makes this dish a good choice for anyone, kids included. If you want a little more heat in the pilaf, add one diced jalapeño with your poblano peppers.

Heat 1 teaspoon of the olive oil in a large skillet over medium heat. Add zucchini and cook for 3–5 minutes, stirring occasionally, until it starts to brown and soften. Remove from pan and set aside.

Add another 1 teaspoon of olive oil to the pan and toss in the sliced mushrooms. Cook for 3–4 minutes until the mushrooms have browned. Remove from pan and set aside.

Add another 1 teaspoon olive oil to the pan and add garlic and poblano peppers. Cook for 3–4 minutes, stirring occasionally, until the peppers have softened.

Add the diced pork loin to the pan and brown the pork on all sides.

Once the pork is browned, stir in the remaining ingredients. Bring mixture to a boil. Lower the heat and let the mixture simmer for 10–15 minutes until the pork is cooked through.

PER SERVING | Calories: 406 | Fat: 8 g | Protein: 38 g | Sodium: 1,451 mg | Fiber: 13 g | Carbohydrates: 48 g | Sugar: 4 g

Spring Vegetable Barley Risotto

While barley won't release starches as well as rice or steel-cut oats, it is still a nice option to use in a simple risotto. The consistency will be a bit different than a typical risotto, but the barley offers a nutty flavor and fluffy texture with the cooked vegetables.

INGREDIENTS | SERVES 4

4 cups vegetable broth

1 tablespoon olive oil

1 pound asparagus, chopped into 1" pieces

1 medium carrot, diced

1 cup fresh peas

1 clove garlic, minced

1 cup sprouted barley

½ cup white wine

¼ cup fresh parsley, chopped

1 teaspoon salt

½ cup Parmesan cheese, grated

Cooking with Alcohol

Using wine in this risotto adds another layer of flavor to the final dish. Since the alcohol burns off, you don't have to worry about any remaining in the risotto. Another option would be to use extra broth in place of the wine. It won't have the same flavor, but it will still be delicious.

Heat broth in a medium saucepan and simmer on low.

Place a large skillet over medium heat and add olive oil. Sauté the chopped asparagus, carrot, and peas for 5–7 minutes until the vegetables are crisp-tender.

Add garlic and barley to the skillet and cook for another 1–2 minutes.

Pour the wine in the pan and bring the mixture to a simmer. Let the vegetables and barley cook in the pan until the wine has been absorbed into the barley.

Add ¾ cup of the broth, stirring occasionally, until the broth has been absorbed. Keep adding the broth ¾ cup at a time until the barley has released some its starches and the liquid has been absorbed.

Once the barley is tender, remove from heat and stir in the parsley, salt, and Parmesan.

PER SERVING | Calories: 220 | Fat: 8 g | Protein: 14 g | Sodium: 1,338 mg | Fiber: 5 g | Carbohydrates: 20 g | Sugar: 3 g

Shrimp, Sausage, and Barley Gumbo

Gumbo is traditionally a stew with stock, meat, or shellfish; some type of thickener;
and the classic mix of celery, bell peppers, and onions.
This twist on gumbo keeps the same basic flavors but adds barley for extra texture.

INGREDIENTS | SERVES 4

2 links chicken sausage, diced

1 bell pepper, diced

3 celery stalks, diced

1 medium onion, diced

2 cloves garlic, minced

1 cup fresh or frozen okra, sliced

1 cup sprouted barley

1 cup water

1 (15-ounce) can crushed tomatoes

1 teaspoon paprika

1 teaspoon cayenne pepper

1 teaspoon oregano

1 teaspoon dried thyme

1 tablespoon olive oil

1 pound shrimp, peeled and deveined

1 teaspoon salt

½ teaspoon pepper

Heat a large pot over medium heat and add the diced chicken sausage. Cook the sausage, stirring occasionally, until the pieces are browned.

Stir in the bell pepper, celery, onion, garlic, and okra. Sauté the vegetables until they start to brown and have softened.

Add the barley, water, tomatoes, paprika, cayenne pepper, oregano, and thyme. Bring mixture to a boil, reduce the heat, and simmer for 10–15 minutes.

While the barley mixture is simmering, heat a large skillet over medium heat and add olive oil.

Add the shrimp to the skillet, sprinkle with salt and pepper, and cook for 3–4 minutes, flipping once, until the shrimp are pink and just cooked through; do not overcook.

Dish barley mixture into bowls and top with shrimp.

PER SERVING | Calories: 345 | Fat: 11 g | Protein: 34 g | Sodium: 1,436 mg | Fiber: 6 g | Carbohydrates: 29 g | Sugar: 4 g

Chicken Sausage

Pork is the meat typically associated with sausage, but many butcher shops and markets now offer both turkey and chicken sausages, which are usually lower in calories and fat. Most chicken sausages you can find will also be precooked, saving you an extra step and cooking time.

Green Chile Chicken and Barley Casserole

This casserole resembles a chili verde in that almost every ingredient is green. You can substitute your favorite salsa for the diced chiles for a different twist of flavors and colors.

INGREDIENTS | SERVES 6

2 cups cooked chicken, diced into 1" pieces

½ cup scallions, chopped

1 cup Monterey jack or white Cheddar cheese, shredded

2 teaspoons chili powder

1 teaspoon salt

½ teaspoon pepper

½ cup milk

½ cup fresh cilantro

8 ounces canned diced green chiles

1 cup sprouted barley

Preheat the oven to 375°F.

In a large bowl, mix together diced chicken, scallions, ½ cup of the shredded cheese, chili powder, salt, pepper, milk, cilantro, green chiles, and barley.

Pour mixture into a greased 2-quart casserole dish.

Top with remaining ½ cup of shredded cheese.

Bake for 25–35 minutes until the cheese is melted and browned and the casserole is heated through.

PER SERVING | Calories: 177 | Fat: 7 g | Protein: 17 g | Sodium: 856 mg | Fiber: 3 g | Carbohydrates: 12 g | Sugar: 3 g

Mexican Chopped Salad

This salad is full of fresh vegetables and is a delicious and light side dish for this cheesy casserole. Finely chop 1 head of romaine lettuce, ½ a small head of cabbage, ½ a medium red onion, 2 medium tomatoes, 4 scallions, and 1 bell pepper. Toss the ingredients together in a large bowl and stir in 1 cup of black beans (drained and rinsed), 1 cup of corn, 2 tablespoons olive oil, 2 tablespoons lime juice, 1 teaspoon salt, and ½ teaspoon pepper. Toss everything together and let the salad sit at room temperature for 30 minutes before serving.

(Serves 6. Per Serving: Calories: 180; Fat: 5 g; Protein: 7 g; Sodium: 419 mg; Fiber: 9 g; Carbohydrates: 30 g; Sugar: 9 g)

Almond Joy Barley Bowl

Chocolate isn't just for dessert anymore. The mix of cocoa powder and coconut milk makes this breakfast a rich and healthy way to start the day.

INGREDIENTS | SERVES 2

1 cup sprouted barley

1 cup coconut milk

1 teaspoon salt

½ cup water

1 teaspoon vanilla extract

1 tablespoon cocoa powder

2 tablespoons shredded coconut

2 tablespoons chopped almonds

In a medium saucepan, mix the barley, coconut milk, salt, water, vanilla, and cocoa powder.

Bring mixture to a boil, reduce the heat, and simmer for 10–15 minutes until the liquid is absorbed into the barley.

Divide barley into 2 bowls and top with shredded coconut and almonds.

PER SERVING | Calories: 473 | Fat: 38 g | Protein: 11 g | Sodium: 821 mg | Fiber: 7 g | Carbohydrates: 27 g | Sugar: 2 g

Coconut Milk

Canned coconut milk is the liquid from inside the shell of a coconut. Because coconuts are high in oil and fat, coconut milk is a thick and rich ingredient. If you'd like a lighter flavor in your dish, light canned coconut milks are also available.

Barley Rum Raisin Pudding

Soaking raisins in rum helps to soften the dried fruit and gives them a punch of flavor in this comforting dessert.

INGREDIENTS | SERVES 4

½ cup raisins

¼ cup dark rum

1 cup sprouted barley

½ teaspoon salt

2 cups milk

½ cup half and half

½ cup sugar

1 egg, beaten

1 teaspoon vanilla extract

Rice for Breakfast?

While rice pudding is typically served for dessert, leftover rice pudding also makes a delicious breakfast. It can be served warm or cold and is especially delicious alongside some fresh fruit and coffee.

In a small bowl, stir the raisins and rum together. Set aside to let the raisins soak and plump up.

In a large saucepan, mix together the barley, salt, milk, half and half, and sugar. Bring mixture to a simmer and cook for 20–30 minutes, stirring frequently, until the barley is tender and the mixture is creamy.

Slowly stir the beaten egg into the barley mixture, stirring constantly. Continue to cook for 1–2 more minutes.

Remove the pan from heat and stir in the vanilla and rum-soaked raisins.

Pour pudding into a dish and place a piece of plastic wrap directly on top of the pudding to keep it from forming a skin. Chill until ready to serve.

PER SERVING | Calories: 281 | Fat: 3 g | Protein: 7 g | Sodium: 369 mg | Fiber: 2 g | Carbohydrates: 57 g | Sugar: 42 g

Mushroom and Barley Soup

Mushroom and barley soup is nothing new, but using a mix of mushrooms and mushroom broth (if you can find it) helps bring this soup to a new level.

INGREDIENTS | SERVES 6–8

1 tablespoon olive oil

1 medium onion, diced

8 ounces cremini mushrooms, sliced

4 ounces portobello mushroom caps, diced

2 cloves garlic, minced

4 cups beef or mushroom broth

2 cups water

1½ cups sprouted barley

¼ cup fresh parsley

2 teaspoons dried thyme

1 teaspoon salt

½ teaspoon pepper

Heat olive oil in a large pot and add diced onion. Cook for 4–5 minutes, stirring occasionally, until the onions have softened and are translucent.

Add all of the mushrooms to the pot. Brown the mushrooms with the onions, 5–7 minutes.

Stir in the minced garlic and cook for 1 minute until fragrant.

Add remaining ingredients. Bring mixture to a boil and let the soup simmer on low for 20 minutes.

Serve with extra parsley.

PER SERVING | Calories: 98 | Fat: 3 g | Protein: 4 g | Sodium: 914 mg | Fiber: 3 g | Carbohydrates: 15 g | Sugar: 1 g

Cremini Mushrooms

Many people think that cremini mushrooms are a completely different variety of fungus, but creminis are actually just a more mature version of the button mushrooms you see in the market and a younger version of the giant portobello mushrooms used for stuffing and grilling.

Stuffed Cabbage Casserole with Barley and Sausage

Traditional stuffed cabbage is a dish that takes a long time to put together. Layering the ingredients in a casserole gives you the same great flavor but takes much less time to prepare.

INGREDIENTS | SERVES 6

½ pound lean ground beef

½ pound spicy Italian sausage (pork or turkey)

½ medium onion, diced

2 cloves garlic, minced

2 tablespoons tomato paste

4 cups chopped cabbage

1 cup sprouted barley

1 cup beef broth

1 cup diced tomatoes

Tomato Paste in a Tube

The majority of recipes that call for tomato paste only need 1–2 tablespoons at a time. Instead of opening a can for one spoonful, look for concentrated tomato paste in a tube at your local market. It keeps in the refrigerator for months and you can squeeze out exactly what you need. If you can't find it, you can always freeze extra tomato paste in an ice cube tray and place in a plastic bag to use later.

Preheat the oven to 375°F.

Heat a large skillet over medium heat and add ground beef and sausage. Brown the meat, stirring to break apart.

Add onion and garlic to the meat and cook for 2–3 more minutes until fragrant. Stir in the tomato paste and cook for another minute.

Remove from heat and place the meat mixture in a large bowl. Stir together with the chopped cabbage and barley.

Place cabbage mixture into a 9" × 13" baking dish, and pour the broth and diced tomatoes on top of the casserole.

Bake for 35–45 minutes until the cabbage is cooked and the casserole is heated through.

PER SERVING | Calories: 257 | Fat: 14 g | Protein: 17 g | Sodium: 629 mg | Fiber: 3 g | Carbohydrates: 15 g | Sugar: 4 g

Fruit and Nut Barley Salad

*Looking for a new weekday lunch? This barley salad is filling and healthy,
full of fruit, nuts, and a yogurt-based dressing.*

INGREDIENTS | SERVES 4

2 cups sprouted barley

1 medium apple, cored and diced

½ cup dried cranberries

½ cup chopped walnuts

½ cup diced celery

¾ cup plain yogurt

1 teaspoon apple cider vinegar

1 teaspoon Dijon mustard

2 teaspoons fresh orange zest

1 teaspoon salt

½ teaspoon pepper

In a large bowl, mix together the barley, apple, dried cranberries, walnuts, and celery.

Whisk the yogurt, apple cider vinegar, Dijon mustard, orange zest, salt, and pepper together in a small bowl.

Pour yogurt mixture over barley and toss the ingredients together until the fruit and barley are covered with the yogurt.

Serve chilled.

PER SERVING | Calories: 345 | Fat: 11 g | Protein: 6 g | Sodium: 625 mg | Fiber: 6 g | Carbohydrates: 54 g | Sugar: 23 g

Apple Cider Vinegar

Also known as the Mother, apple cider vinegar has many benefits and is touted as a remedy for a variety of health issues. It is rich in enzymes and potassium, helps to support a healthy immune system, and promotes good digestion.

Triple Bean and Barley Salad

Bring this three-bean salad to your next picnic, and it will be the hit of the meal. Bean salads aren't meant to always be the same—using a different mix of beans as well as the barley brings a new dimension to this classic dish.

INGREDIENTS | SERVES 6

1½ cups water

1 cup fresh green beans, trimmed

1 cup frozen edamame (soybeans)

1 cup cannellini beans, drained and rinsed

1 cup sprouted barley

1 teaspoon salt

½ teaspoon pepper

1 tablespoon apple cider vinegar

1 tablespoon sugar

¼ cup scallions, chopped

Bring water to a boil in a medium saucepan.

Add green beans and edamame to the water and cook for 5–7 minutes until the green beans are bright green and the edamame is thawed.

Remove the beans from the pan and place in a bowl.

Add the cannellini beans, barley, salt, pepper, apple cider vinegar, sugar, and scallions, and toss to mix.

Serve at room temperature or chilled.

PER SERVING | Calories: 121 | Fat: 2 g | Protein: 6 g | Sodium: 389 mg | Fiber: 5 g | Carbohydrates: 21 g | Sugar: 3 g

What Is Edamame?

Edamame are young soybeans and are traditionally served steamed in the pods. They have a firm, yet creamy texture and are delicious as a snack, or shelled and added to salads and stir-frys.

Spiced Chicken and Barley

Chicken thighs give a deeper and richer flavor to this dish,
but you can use any cut of chicken that you'd like.

INGREDIENTS | SERVES 4

1 pound boneless, skinless chicken thighs

1 tablespoon cumin

1 teaspoon garlic powder

1 teaspoon ground ginger

1 teaspoon curry powder

1 teaspoon ground coriander

1 teaspoon paprika

2 teaspoons salt

1 teaspoon pepper

1 tablespoon olive oil

1 onion, thinly sliced

1 red pepper, diced

2 tablespoons tomato paste

1 cup sprouted barley

1 cup chicken broth

¼ cup half and half

¼ cup fresh cilantro, chopped

Dice the chicken into bite-sized pieces. Toss the chicken with the cumin, garlic powder, ground ginger, curry powder, ground coriander, paprika, salt, and pepper.

Heat a large skillet over medium heat and add the olive oil and the chicken. Brown each side, then remove the chicken from the pan and set aside.

Add the onion and pepper to the pan and cook for 3–4 minutes until the vegetables have softened.

Stir the tomato paste into the vegetables and cook for another minute.

Add the barley and broth, and bring to a simmer. Cook for 10 minutes, then add diced chicken and the half and half to the pan.

Remove from heat and stir in chopped cilantro before serving.

PER SERVING | Calories: 290 | Fat: 11 g | Protein: 26 g | Sodium: 1,442 mg | Fiber: 4 g | Carbohydrates: 22 g | Sugar: 4 g

Coriander

The spice known as coriander is actually the seeds of the cilantro plant. If you're not a fan of fresh cilantro, you can leave that out of the dish, but make sure to keep the ground coriander in the spice mixture. It has a different and less pungent flavor than fresh cilantro.

Barley, Red Lentil, and Couscous Pilaf

This mix of whole grains, protein, and whole-wheat pasta can serve as the base for almost any main dish or vegetable. The different textures keep this pilaf interesting, while the light flavor can pair with anything else you're serving.

INGREDIENTS | SERVES 6

1 tablespoon olive oil

1 medium onion, diced

1 carrot, diced

1 clove garlic, minced

1 cup sprouted barley

1 cup sprouted (or nonsprouted) red lentils

1 cup dry whole-wheat couscous

6 cups vegetable broth

¼ cup fresh parsley, chopped

1 teaspoon salt

½ teaspoon pepper

Whole-Wheat Couscous

Couscous is made from semolina flour and is actually a tiny pasta. Since the texture is closer to that of a grain, couscous is used more often in ways where you would find whole grains rather than pasta. The fluffy texture of couscous is perfect for a side dish or to add into soups and stews.

Heat oil in a large saucepan and add the diced onion and carrot. Let the vegetables cook for 5–7 minutes, stirring occasionally, until softened.

Stir the minced garlic into the pot and cook for 1–2 minutes until the garlic is fragrant.

Add the barley, red lentils, and couscous to the vegetables and stir together.

Pour the broth into the barley mixture and bring it to a boil.

Lower the heat to a simmer, cover the pot, and let the mixture simmer for 20–25 minutes, until the lentils have broken down, the barley and couscous are tender, and the liquid has been absorbed.

Remove the pot from heat and stir in the parsley, salt, and pepper before serving.

PER SERVING | Calories: 276 | Fat: 5 g | Protein: 13 g | Sodium: 596 mg | Fiber: 3 g | Carbohydrates: 46 g | Sugar: 1 g

CHAPTER 11

Sprouted Wheat and Buckwheat Recipes

Wheatberry and White Bean Salad

The mix of Italian herbs and flavors in this salad strikes a nice balance with the chewy wheatberries. Swapping out the pasta for a nutty whole grain gives a new flavor to this dish.

INGREDIENTS | SERVES 4

1 cup sprouted wheatberries

2 cups water

1 teaspoon salt

1 (15-ounce) can cannellini beans, drained and rinsed

½ cup sun-dried tomatoes

¼ cup fresh parsley, chopped

2 tablespoons fresh rosemary, chopped

2 tablespoons olive oil

1 teaspoon salt

Sun-Dried or Oven-Roasted Tomatoes

Because tomato season doesn't last very long in the summer, sun-dried tomatoes are a great option to use in this dish year-round. If you find yourself making this in the summer, try slow-roasting tomatoes to toss in the salad instead. For the slow-roasted tomatoes, slice some Romas in half lengthwise and place cut side up on a baking sheet. Drizzle with olive oil, sprinkle with salt and pepper, and roast at 225°F for 4–5 hours until the tomatoes have shrunk but are still juicy.

In a medium saucepan, bring wheatberries, water, and salt to a boil over medium heat. Simmer the wheatberries for 15 minutes.

Drain wheatberries and in a medium bowl, mix together with the cannellini beans and sun-dried tomatoes.

Stir in the chopped parsley, rosemary, olive oil, and salt.

Serve warm or at room temperature.

PER SERVING | Calories: 387 | Fat: 8 g | Protein: 18 g | Sodium: 1,021 mg | Fiber: 18 g | Carbohydrates: 64 g | Sugar: 3 g

Strawberry Wheatberry Salad

Fresh strawberries are one of the best things about early summer. The red, juicy fruits go well with just about everything, and pairing them with a mix of fresh herbs is one way to really show them off.

INGREDIENTS | SERVES 4

1½ cups sprouted wheatberries

3 cups water

1 teaspoon salt

1 cup chopped strawberries

¼ cup fresh basil, chopped

¼ cup fresh mint, chopped

¼ cup fresh chives, chopped

¼ cup radishes, sliced

¼ cup olive oil

2 teaspoons Dijon mustard

2 teaspoons orange zest

¼ cup fresh orange juice

1 teaspoon salt

½ teaspoon pepper

In a medium saucepan, bring wheatberries, water, and salt to a boil. Cook, simmering, for 15 minutes.

Drain wheatberries and pour them into a large bowl.

Add strawberries, basil, mint, chives, and radishes to the wheatberries and toss them all together.

In a small bowl, mix together the olive oil, Dijon mustard, orange zest, orange juice, salt, and pepper.

Pour dressing over salad and toss to coat.

PER SERVING | Calories: 378 | Fat: 15 g | Protein: 12 g | Sodium: 910 mg | Fiber: 10 g | Carbohydrates: 54 g | Sugar: 4 g

How to Zest Citrus

If you've never zested fruit before, it may sound intimidating, but it's one of the easiest things to do. You'll need a microplane or zester tool and your citrus—lemon, lime, orange, or grapefruit. Run the zester over the peel of the citrus, removing the bright-colored zest from the fruit and stopping when you get to the lighter, white pith. The pith is bitter, which you don't want, but the zest is full of essential oils and flavor to add to your dish.

Honey Wheatberry Bread

There aren't many things better than the smell of freshly baked bread. While yeast recipes can sometimes be intimidating, this recipe is basically foolproof. Try it, and you'll find yourself hooked on fresh bread.

INGREDIENTS | SERVES 12

3 cups bread flour

4½ teaspoons active dry yeast

½ cup honey

⅓ cup plus 1 tablespoon olive oil, divided

2½ cups warm water

3 cups white whole-wheat flour

¾ cup sprouted wheatberries

1 tablespoon olive oil

In the bowl of a stand mixer (or other large bowl), mix together the bread flour, yeast, honey, and ⅓ cup of the olive oil.

Slowly mix the water into the flour mixture until all of the flour is incorporated.

Add the flour, 1 cup at a time, and sprouted wheatberries until the dough is still a little sticky but easy to handle. Knead dough (with a dough hook or by hand) for 5 minutes until it is smooth and springs back when you touch it.

Pour 1 tablespoon of olive oil into a large bowl and add the dough. Cover the bowl and let it rest in a warm place for 1–1½ hours or until the dough has doubled in size.

Punch the dough down and divide it into two pieces. Roll out each piece into a rectangle, about ½" thick, and roll it back up lengthwise before placing each one in a greased 9" × 5" loaf pan. Cover the loaf pans and let the dough rise again, covered, for 40–50 minutes until the dough has doubled in size.

While dough is rising in the loaf pans, preheat the oven to 375°F.

Bake loaves for 40–50 minutes until the loaves are golden and sound hollow when you tap the tops.

PER SERVING | Calories: 374 | Fat: 8 g | Protein: 9 g | Sodium: 3 mg | Fiber: 3 g | Carbohydrates: 66 g | Sugar: 11 g

Wheatberry Cranberry Salad

Cranberries aren't just meant to be the garnish at your holiday table. The tart berries are bursting with flavor in this salad, and the bright fuchsia color makes this dish stand out from the rest.

INGREDIENTS | SERVES 6

1½ cups fresh cranberries

2 tablespoons maple syrup

1 tablespoon orange zest

1½ cups sprouted wheatberries

2 medium zucchini, diced

1 cup chickpeas, drained and rinsed

½ cup feta cheese, crumbled

2 tablespoons olive oil

1 tablespoon apple cider vinegar

1 teaspoon Dijon mustard

1 teaspoon salt

½ teaspoon pepper

Fresh Cranberries

Typically, fresh cranberries start showing up in markets and stores just before Thanksgiving and are available through the holiday season. If you want to make this and can't find fresh cranberries, substitute dried cranberries. You won't need to cook them until they burst, but definitely still heat them up with the orange juice and maple syrup to infuse some flavor and soften them before adding them to the salad.

Mix the cranberries, maple syrup, and orange zest in a small saucepan. Bring the mixture to a boil and simmer for 5–10 minutes or until most of the cranberries have popped. Remove mixture from heat and let it cool while you mix the rest of the salad.

In a large bowl, mix together the wheatberries, zucchini, chickpeas, and feta cheese.

In a small bowl, mix the olive oil, apple cider vinegar, Dijon mustard, salt, and pepper, and pour over the wheatberry mixture.

Pour the cooled cranberries into the wheatberries and toss together.

Serve warm or at room temperature.

PER SERVING | Calories: 317 | Fat: 9 g | Protein: 12 g | Sodium: 536 mg | Fiber: 10 g | Carbohydrates: 50 g | Sugar: 8 g

Roasted Peach and Wheatberry Breakfast Parfaits

*This layered breakfast takes a bit more time than pouring a bowl of cereal,
but it's the perfect way to start the day on a lazy Saturday morning.*

INGREDIENTS | SERVES 4

1 cup sprouted wheatberries
2 tablespoons honey
1 teaspoon cinnamon
4 medium peaches, halved and pitted
¼ cup light brown sugar
2 cups plain yogurt

Sweetener Substitutes

While this recipe calls for honey and brown sugar, you can substitute your favorite sweeteners for these. Agave nectar, maple syrup, and Sucanat will also be great in this dish.

In a medium bowl, stir the wheatberries, honey, and cinnamon together. Set aside.

Preheat the oven to 375°F.

Place peach halves, cut side up, on a greased or parchment paper or foil-lined baking sheet. Sprinkle each peach half with some brown sugar.

Roast the peaches for 8–10 minutes until they have softened and the sugar has melted. Remove from the oven and let the peaches cool for 5 minutes.

Dice the peaches. Add a palmful of peaches to the bottom of four glasses or dishes.

Layer some yogurt and wheatberries on top, then repeat the layers until all of the ingredients have been used. Serve immediately.

PER SERVING | Calories: 358 | Fat: 5 g | Protein: 13 g |
Sodium: 60 mg | Fiber: 8 g | Carbohydrates: 70 g | Sugar: 35 g

Black Bean, Balsamic, Wheatberry, and Feta Salad

Next time you're invited to a summer potluck, toss this easy salad together and get ready to hand out the recipe. It's as delicious cold as it is warm temperature, and it's even better the day after you make it.

INGREDIENTS | SERVES 8

2 cups sprouted wheatberries

2 medium zucchini, diced

1 medium yellow squash, diced

1 large tomato, diced

2 (15-ounce) cans black beans, drained and rinsed

½ red onion, diced

½ cup feta, crumbled

¼ cup fresh basil, chopped

¼ cup fresh parsley, chopped

1 teaspoon salt

½ teaspoon pepper

¼ cup balsamic vinegar

¼ cup olive oil

In a large bowl, mix together the wheatberries, zucchini, yellow squash, tomato, black beans, red onion, and feta.

Stir in the basil, parsley, salt, and pepper.

Pour balsamic vinegar and olive oil over the salad and toss together.

Serve cold or at room temperature.

PER SERVING | Calories: 380 | Fat: 9 g | Protein: 18 g | Sodium: 378 mg | Fiber: 15 g | Carbohydrates: 59 g | Sugar: 4 g

Baked Italian Bulgur Casserole

This baked casserole tastes like it has been cooking all day, but it's quick enough to throw together after a full day's work and still have dinner at a reasonable hour.

INGREDIENTS | SERVES 6

1 pound lean ground beef

1 onion, diced

2 cloves garlic, minced

1½ cups beef broth

1 (15-ounce) can diced tomatoes, drained

1 cup sprouted bulgur

1 tablespoon parsley

1 tablespoon oregano

1 teaspoon salt

½ teaspoon pepper

½ cup Parmesan cheese, grated

Not a Fan of Ground Meat?

Any ground meat (beef, pork, buffalo, turkey, chicken) could be used in this recipe, but if you'd rather have a different cut, use your favorite protein and make sure to brown the meat and cook it until it's almost done before letting it finish cooking in the oven.

Preheat the oven to 350°F.

Cook ground beef, onion, and garlic in a large skillet, stirring frequently to break up the meat, until the beef is browned and cooked through.

Stir the broth, tomatoes, bulgur, parsley, oregano, salt, and pepper into the beef mixture and pour into a 3-quart casserole dish.

Cover and bake for 35–45 minutes until the liquid has been absorbed.

Stir the cheese into the casserole and serve.

PER SERVING | Calories: 218 | Fat: 10 g | Protein: 21 g | Sodium: 1,042 mg | Fiber: 2 g | Carbohydrates: 11 g | Sugar: <1 g

Roasted Chicken Tabbouleh

Tabbouleh is a traditional Arab salad made of bulgur, tomato, cucumber, parsley, mint, olive oil, and lemon juice. Often served as a garnish or side salad, tabbouleh can also stand as a main dish when you add in roasted chicken.

INGREDIENTS | SERVES 4

2 bone-in, skin-on chicken breasts

3 tablespoons olive oil, divided

3 teaspoons salt, divided

1½ teaspoons pepper, divided

1 cup sprouted bulgur

1½ cups water

2 medium tomatoes, chopped

½ medium cucumber, diced

¼ cup fresh mint, chopped

¼ cup fresh parsley

1 tablespoon lemon juice

Bone-In, Skin-On

If you're ever roasting chicken, make sure to select pieces that are still bone-in, skin-on. They will take a bit longer to cook, but the skin keeps the moisture inside the meat and the bones add a depth of flavor that you can't get from boneless chicken.

Preheat the oven to 375°F. Brush chicken with 1 tablespoon olive oil and season with 2 teaspoons salt and 1 teaspoon pepper.

Roast chicken for 40–45 minutes until the juices run clear. Remove from the oven and let the chicken cool for 10 minutes.

While the chicken is cooking, pour the bulgur into a heat-proof bowl and bring water to a boil on the stovetop. Pour the boiling water over the bulgur, cover the bowl, and let the bulgur steam for 20 minutes.

Remove the skin from the chicken and dice the meat into bite-sized pieces.

Stir the diced chicken, tomatoes, cucumber, mint, parsley, 2 tablespoons olive oil, lemon juice, 1 teaspoon salt, and ½ teaspoon pepper into the cooked bulgur.

PER SERVING | Calories: 369 | Fat: 19 g | Protein: 28 g | Sodium: 1,966 mg | Fiber: 4 g | Carbohydrates: 13 g | Sugar: 3 g

Brown Sugar and Banana Bulgur Muffins

A different twist on banana bread, these muffins are the perfect snack to grab and go.

INGREDIENTS | SERVES 12

3 ripe medium bananas
⅓ cup coconut oil, melted
⅓ cup unsweetened applesauce
1 teaspoon vanilla extract
½ cup brown sugar
2 cups whole-wheat pastry flour
½ cup sprouted bulgur
1 teaspoon baking soda
½ teaspoon baking powder
½ teaspoon salt

Preheat the oven to 350°F.

Mash the bananas in a large bowl. Stir in the melted coconut oil, applesauce, vanilla, and brown sugar.

Stir the flour, bulgur, baking soda, baking powder, and salt into the banana mixture.

Pour the batter ¾ of the way full into each cup in a greased muffin tin.

Bake for 20–25 minutes until the muffins are golden and spring back when you tap the tops.

PER 1 MUFFIN WITHOUT FROSTING | Calories: 183 | Fat: 6 g | Protein: 2 g | Sodium: 203 mg | Fiber: 4 g | Carbohydrates: 30 g | Sugar: 10 g

Want a Little Frosting?

If you want to transition these muffins into more of a sweet treat, whip 4 ounces of softened cream cheese with 1 stick of softened butter, 1 teaspoon vanilla extract, and 1½ cups of powdered sugar. Add a dollop of the cream cheese frosting to each muffin for a sweet and tangy topping.

(Serves 12. Per Serving (frosting only): Calories: 147; Fat: 10 g; Protein: <1 g; Sodium: 31 mg; Fiber: 0 g; Carbohydrates: 13 g; Sugar: 12 g)

Spiced Beef and Bulgur Stuffed Tomatoes

When choosing tomatoes for this dish, make sure to get ones that are large enough to hold the filling and ones that can stand up in the pan. If the tomato won't sit evenly, slice a bit of the tomato off the bottom until it has an even bottom surface.

INGREDIENTS | SERVES 4

4 large tomatoes
½ pound lean ground beef
½ medium onion, diced
1 clove garlic, minced
¾ cup sprouted bulgur
¼ cup water
1 teaspoon cumin
1 teaspoon ground coriander
1 teaspoon salt
½ teaspoon pepper
½ cup Parmesan cheese

Preheat the oven to 375°F.

Trim the bottom of each tomato so it can sit upright in a baking dish. Remove the top of each tomato and take out the core and most of the seeds. Place the cored tomatoes in an 8" × 8" baking dish.

Cook the ground beef, onion, and garlic in a large skillet, stirring frequently, until the beef is browned and cooked.

Stir the bulgur, water, cumin, coriander, salt, and pepper into the beef mixture.

Divide the bulgur mixture between the four tomatoes, filling each one to the top.

Sprinkle the top of each tomato with Parmesan and bake for 25–35 minutes until the tomatoes have softened and the cheese is melted.

PER SERVING | Calories: 219 | Fat: 10 g | Protein: 19 g | Sodium: 823 mg | Fiber: 4 g | Carbohydrates: 15 g | Sugar: 5 g

Stuffed Pepper Casserole

Rather than taking the time to stuff individual peppers, this casserole takes all the great flavors from a traditional stuffed pepper and mixes them together into one cheesy-topped dish.

INGREDIENTS | SERVES 6

1 pound spicy Italian sausage

3 bell peppers, chopped

1 onion, chopped

2 cups sprouted bulgur

2 cups crushed tomatoes

1 tablespoon oregano

1 tablespoon parsley

1 tablespoon basil

1 teaspoon salt

½ teaspoon pepper

1½ cups mozzarella cheese, shredded

Season It Your Way

Feeling zesty? Trade out the oregano, parsley, and basil for Mexican oregano, chili powder, and cumin for a spicy twist on this casserole.

Preheat the oven to 350°F.

Brown the sausage with the peppers and onion, stirring to break up the meat while it cooks.

Stir the bulgur, tomatoes, oregano, parsley, basil, salt, and pepper into the sausage mixture.

Pour half of the pepper mixture into a greased 2-quart casserole dish and top with ¾ cup of the mozzarella. Layer the remaining pepper mixture and then top with the rest of the mozzarella.

Bake for 25–30 minutes until the cheese is melted and beginning to brown.

PER SERVING | Calories: 437 | Fat: 29 g | Protein: 21 g | Sodium: 1,219 mg | Fiber: 5 g | Carbohydrates: 25 g | Sugar: 2 g

Tuna and Olive Salad over Bulgur with Feta Dressing

Most tuna salads are served in between bread or on a green salad. This take on tuna salad gets spooned over fluffy bulgur and topped with a feta-filled dressing.

INGREDIENTS | SERVES 4

8 ounces albacore tuna packed in olive oil

4 ounces pitted green and kalamata olives, chopped

¼ cup scallions, sliced

¼ cup sun-dried tomatoes, chopped

1 cup sprouted bulgur

1½ cups water

½ cup olive oil

¼ cup red wine vinegar

1 teaspoon salt

½ teaspoon pepper

½ teaspoon dried oregano

¼ cup feta cheese, crumbled

In a medium bowl, flake the tuna into pieces with a fork.

Stir the chopped olives, scallions, and sun-dried tomatoes with the tuna and set aside.

Place bulgur in a heatproof bowl and bring the water to a boil. Pour the water over the bulgur and cover the bowl. Let the bulgur steam for 15–20 minutes.

In a small bowl, mix the olive oil, red wine vinegar, salt, pepper, oregano, and feta cheese together.

To serve, divide the bulgur onto four plates, top with some of the tuna mixture, and drizzle with the dressing.

PER SERVING | Calories: 453 | Fat: 36 g | Protein: 18 g | Sodium: 1,237 mg | Fiber: 3 g | Carbohydrates: 13 g | Sugar: 2 g

Mini Buffalo Meatloaves

Everyone loves the crispy edges of the meatloaf. Making mini versions for everyone to have gives your dinner guests the best parts of the meatloaf on each plate.

INGREDIENTS | SERVES 6

1½ pounds ground buffalo
1 small onion, diced
1 clove garlic, minced
1 teaspoon salt
½ teaspoon pepper
1 egg
½ cup sprouted bulgur
1 tablespoon parsley
½ cup tomato sauce
2 tablespoons maple syrup
1 tablespoon Dijon mustard

Preheat the oven to 350°F.

In a large bowl, mix the ground buffalo with onion, garlic, salt, pepper, egg, bulgur, and parsley. Form into six mini loaves and place on a greased or parchment paper–lined baking sheet.

Mix the tomato sauce, maple syrup, and Dijon mustard together. Brush the tomato mixture on top of each meatloaf.

Bake meatloaves for 35–45 minutes until a meat thermometer reads 165–170°F.

PER SERVING | Calories: 146 | Fat: 2 g | Protein: 24 g | Sodium: 526 mg | Fiber: 1 g | Carbohydrates: 8 g | Sugar: 4 g

Buttermilk Mashed Potatoes

Meatloaf calls for mashed potatoes. For an easy side, place 2 pounds of peeled and diced Yukon Gold potatoes in a large pot. Add cold water that fills up to 3" above the potatoes and bring them to a boil. Let the potatoes simmer for 10–15 minutes or until you can easily pierce them with a fork. Drain the potatoes and return them to the pot. Mash them and add in 1 cup of buttermilk, 2 teaspoons salt, and 1 teaspoon pepper. Stir together, adding more buttermilk until you reach your desired consistency.

(Serves 6. Per Serving: Calories: 147; Fat: <1 g; Protein: 4 g; Sodium: 825 mg; Fiber: 3 g; Carbohydrates: 32 g; Sugar: 3 g)

Apple, Walnut, and Bulgur Breakfast Bake

Running short on time in the morning?
Put this breakfast together the night before and refrigerate it until you're ready to bake.

INGREDIENTS | SERVES 6

2 cups sprouted bulgur

½ cup brown sugar

1 teaspoon cinnamon

1 teaspoon baking soda

1 teaspoon salt

1 egg

½ cup applesauce

1 cup milk

½ cup chopped walnuts

1 large apple, diced

Hot and Cold

This breakfast bake is delicious when it's warm right out of the oven with a scoop of yogurt or a pat of butter. But it's just as tasty eaten the next morning, cold with milk or reheated for a quick morning meal.

Preheat the oven 350°F.

In a large bowl, mix bulgur, brown sugar, cinnamon, baking soda, and salt.

In a separate bowl, mix the egg, applesauce, and milk together and pour into the bulgur mixture. Stir together until all of the bulgur is incorporated.

Fold the walnuts and diced apple into the batter.

Pour batter into a greased 8" × 8" baking dish.

Bake for 20–25 minutes until the edges are golden and the center is set.

PER SERVING | Calories: 210 | Fat: 7 g | Protein: 6 g | Sodium: 633 mg | Fiber: 4 g | Carbohydrates: 33 g | Sugar: 19 g

Pesto, Pea, and Wheatberry Salad

*Pesto is typically paired with pasta or tomatoes and mozzarella,
but this salad pairs the bright pesto with nutty wheatberries and sweet spring peas.
To add even more green to this salad, toss in a few cups of baby spinach or arugula.*

INGREDIENTS | SERVES 4

2 cups basil
¼ cup chopped walnuts
¼ cup Parmesan cheese, grated
1 clove garlic, chopped
1 teaspoon salt
⅓ cup olive oil
1½ cups sprouted wheatberries
3 cups water
1½ cups fresh peas

Place the basil, walnuts, Parmesan, garlic, and salt in the bowl of a food processor. Pulse until the nuts, garlic, and basil are chopped and mixed together but not completely smooth.

Drizzle in the olive oil, slowly, while the food processor is running. Set aside.

In a medium saucepan, bring wheatberries and water to a boil. Let the wheatberries simmer for 15 minutes, then add the fresh peas to the wheatberries. Let them cook together for 5 minutes until the peas are cooked and bright green.

Drain the wheatberries and peas, and pour into a large bowl.

Pour the pesto over the wheatberries and peas, and toss together. Serve with extra Parmesan on top.

PER SERVING | Calories: 482 | Fat: 25 g | Protein: 11 g | Sodium: 930 mg | Fiber: 10 g | Carbohydrates: 52 g | Sugar: 3 g

Cocoa Chipotle Wheatberry Chili

*A simmering pot of chili is one of the best savory meals on a cold winter evening.
Adding just a spoonful of cocoa powder adds a depth and slight sweetness that creates the perfect
balance with the heat from the pepper and spices.*

INGREDIENTS | SERVES 8

1 pound ground buffalo

1 onion, diced

1 clove garlic, minced

1 carrot, peeled and diced

1 (15-ounce) can black beans, drained
and rinsed

1 (15-ounce) can pinto beans, drained
and rinsed

1 (15-ounce) can kidney beans, drained
and rinsed

1 cup sprouted wheatberries

1 (15-ounce) can crushed tomatoes

2 tablespoons tomato paste

2 chipotle peppers in adobo sauce,
chopped

1 tablespoon cocoa powder

1 tablespoon cumin

1 tablespoon smoked paprika

2 teaspoons salt

Brown the ground buffalo in a large pot over medium heat, stirring to break up the meat as it cooks.

Add the onion, garlic, and carrot, and cook for 5–7 minutes until softened.

Stir remaining ingredients into the meat.

Bring mixture to a boil, lower the heat, and let the chili simmer for 20–30 minutes to let the flavors develop.

Serve warm with your favorite chili toppings.

PER SERVING | Calories: 255 | Fat: 2 g | Protein: 23 g |
Sodium: 508 mg | Fiber: 11 g | Carbohydrates: 38 g | Sugar: 1 g

The Right Cocoa

Unsweetened cocoa powder, which is usually used for baking, will add that rich cocoa flavor without any additional sweetness. You could also use the same amount of a sweetened cocoa powder or chopped bitter or semisweet chocolate. If you use actual chocolate, just make sure to let the chocolate fully melt so it can be evenly distributed into the chili.

Buckwheat Overnight Breakfast Bowl

Rushed Monday mornings won't be a problem anymore.
This buckwheat bowl sits and soaks overnight, leaving no work for you in the morning.

INGREDIENTS | SERVES 4

2 cups sprouted buckwheat groats

1½ cups milk

2 tablespoons ground flaxseed

¼ cup agave nectar or maple syrup

1 teaspoon salt

1 teaspoon vanilla extract

1 teaspoon cinnamon

¼ cup chopped pecans

½ cup dried fruit

2 medium bananas or fresh berries, for topping

Pour buckwheat groats and milk into a bowl and let them soak, covered, overnight in the fridge.

In the morning, pour the soaked buckwheat and milk mixture into the blender. Add the flaxseed, agave, salt, vanilla, and cinnamon. Blend mixture until smooth.

Divide mixture into four bowls and top with chopped pecans, dried fruit, and fresh fruit before serving.

PER SERVING | Calories: 344 | Fat: 9 g | Protein: 8 g | Sodium: 630 mg | Fiber: 7 g | Carbohydrates: 60 g | Sugar: 25 g

Sprouted Buckwheat Herb Summer Salad

Summer is the season for fresh herbs, crisp vegetables, and bright flavors. This buckwheat salad is the perfect example of an easy summer dish that can be spiced up with whatever you have in the fridge.

INGREDIENTS | SERVES 6

2 cups sprouted buckwheat groats

1 cup fresh parsley, chopped

1 cup fresh basil, chopped

½ cup fresh mint, chopped

2 medium tomatoes, diced

½ large cucumber, diced

1 medium carrot, thinly sliced

½ cup scallions, sliced

2 cloves garlic, minced

½ cup fresh lemon juice

½ cup olive oil

2 teaspoons salt

½ teaspoon pepper

In a large bowl, toss sprouted buckwheat groats with the parsley, basil, mint, tomatoes, cucumber, carrot, scallions, and garlic.

Pour lemon juice and olive oil over the salad and mix together.

Season with salt and pepper. Serve chilled or at room temperature.

PER SERVING | Calories: 235 | Fat: 18 g | Protein: 3 g | Sodium: 739 mg | Fiber: 3 g | Carbohydrates: 16 g | Sugar: 3 g

Side or Salad?

To make this buckwheat dish an even bigger salad to serve as a main meal, toss in some baby spinach or mixed greens and some type of beans for protein. You could also serve this as-is with grilled chicken or fish seasoned with the same herbs found in the salad.

Pumpkin Spice Buckwheat Porridge

Most dishes that have this mix of spices and pumpkin purée are served warm. This buckwheat porridge, meant to be served chilled, has the texture and flavor of a thick pumpkin smoothie. If you'd rather have it as a warm breakfast, gently heat it on low on your stovetop until it is warmed through.

INGREDIENTS | SERVES 4

2 cups sprouted buckwheat groats

1 cup milk

½ cup pumpkin purée

½ cup maple syrup

1 teaspoon salt

1 teaspoon vanilla extract

1 teaspoon cinnamon

½ teaspoon ground ginger

½ teaspoon nutmeg

Canned or Fresh?

Pumpkin purée can usually be found in any grocery store, but if you can't find any, it can easily be made at home. To make your own, take 1 or 2 small pumpkins, cut them in half, and scoop out the seeds. Slice the pumpkin halves into quarters and roast at 350°F for 40–45 minutes or until the pumpkin is fork-tender. Let the pumpkin cool, then peel the skin off and place the pumpkin flesh in the food processor. Let the food processor run until the pumpkin is smooth.

Place sprouted buckwheat groats, milk, pumpkin purée, and maple syrup in a blender.

Process until the mixture is smooth.

Add the salt, vanilla, cinnamon, ground ginger, and nutmeg to the blender, and blend again until everything is smooth and mixed together.

Divide into four bowls. Top with an extra drizzle of maple syrup, if desired.

PER SERVING | Calories: 225 | Fat: 1 g | Protein: 5 g | Sodium: 617 mg | Fiber: 4 g | Carbohydrates: 50 g | Sugar: 29 g

Harvest Buckwheat Salad

The familiar flavors of maple and cranberries are staples in fall dishes. The kale provides volume and color to this salad, while the buckwheat and pecans give it some crunch.

INGREDIENTS | SERVES 6

1½ cups sprouted buckwheat groats
1½ cups kale, finely chopped
½ cup dried cranberries
½ cup chopped pecans
¼ cup olive oil
¼ cup maple syrup
2 teaspoons rosemary
1 teaspoon salt
½ teaspoon pepper

In a large bowl, toss the sprouted buckwheat groats with the chopped kale, dried cranberries, and chopped pecans.

Pour olive oil and maple syrup over the salad and mix together.

Stir in the rosemary, salt, and pepper. Let the salad sit for 30 minutes before serving.

PER SERVING | Calories: 337 | Fat: 16 g | Protein: 3 g | Sodium: 393 mg | Fiber: 4 g | Carbohydrates: 51 g | Sugar: 32 g

Kale, Uncooked

Kale, like the majority of leafy greens, is usually cooked before serving. But kale is much more tender than other greens and doesn't have a bitter flavor. As long as you remove the thicker stems, the leaves themselves are a fun addition to any salad recipe.

Buckwheat, Raspberry, and Oat Snack Cakes

This snack cake takes minutes to mix together and bakes in just over 30 minutes. Make a pan on the weekend and enjoy all week long as an afternoon snack or a quick breakfast.

INGREDIENTS | SERVES 4

1 cup oat bran
½ cup oat flour
½ cup sprouted buckwheat groats
1 tablespoon ground flaxseed
1 teaspoon baking powder
1 teaspoon cinnamon
1 teaspoon vanilla extract
½ teaspoon salt
1 cup milk
½ cup unsweetened applesauce
1 cup raspberries

Preheat the oven to 350°F.

In a medium bowl, mix together the oat bran, oat flour, buckwheat groats, flaxseed, baking powder, cinnamon, vanilla, and salt.

Stir the milk and applesauce into the dry ingredients.

Gently fold in the raspberries.

Divide batter into four greased baking ramekins or pour into 1 greased 8" × 8" baking dish. Bake for 30–40 minutes.

PER SERVING | Calories: 221 | Fat: 5 g | Protein: 10 g | Sodium: 321 mg | Fiber: 9 g | Carbohydrates: 43 g | Sugar: 8 g

Berry Buckwheat Breakfast Cake

A breakfast cake sounds like something that would need to bake for at least 20 minutes, but this quick cake is made in the microwave! Mix the dry ingredients the night before and you'll have one less step in the morning.

INGREDIENTS | SERVES 1

¼ cup oat bran

2 tablespoons oat flour

2 tablespoons sprouted buckwheat groats

½ tablespoon ground flaxseed

½ teaspoon baking powder

¼ teaspoon salt

¼ teaspoon cinnamon

¼ teaspoon vanilla extract

2 tablespoons unsweetened applesauce

¼ cup milk

½ cup berries

Mix together the oat bran, oat flour, sprouted buckwheat groats, flaxseed, baking powder, salt, and cinnamon.

Stir in the vanilla, applesauce, and milk until all the dry ingredients are incorporated.

Fold the berries into the batter.

Spray a microwave-safe baking dish or ramekin with nonstick cooking spray, and pour batter into the dish.

Heat for 1 minute and 30 seconds, pausing if needed, until the top is set. Let the cake cool for 2–3 minutes before serving.

PER SERVING | Calories: 213 | Fat: 4 g | Protein: 8 g | Sodium: 615 mg | Fiber: 7 g | Carbohydrates: 40 g | Sugar: 13 g

Customize Your Cake

Not a fan of cinnamon? Try adding ground ginger and a pinch of nutmeg. No berries in the fridge? Add some diced apple or banana. The cake base can be changed to whatever flavors you love.

Buckwheat Ginger Chip Cookies

This twist on molasses cookies will be a hit at your next cookie swap. Soft and spicy cookies filled with crunchy buckwheat, melted chocolate chips, and chewy crystallized ginger—they're full of surprises.

INGREDIENTS | YIELDS 3½ DOZEN

2 sticks butter, softened
¾ cup brown sugar
¾ cup sugar
2 eggs
1 teaspoon vanilla extract
¼ cup molasses
2¼ cups flour
1 teaspoon baking powder
1 teaspoon ground ginger
½ teaspoon cinnamon
½ teaspoon ground cloves
½ teaspoon salt
1 cup semisweet chocolate chips
½ cup sprouted buckwheat groats
½ cup chopped crystallized ginger

Preheat the oven to 350°F.

Cream the butter and sugars together with a stand or hand mixer until the mixture is light and creamy, 2–3 minutes.

Beat the eggs into the butter one at a time.

Add the vanilla and molasses to the butter mixture and mix for another minute.

Mix the flour, baking powder, ground ginger, cinnamon, ground cloves, and salt into the dough until all of the dry ingredients are incorporated.

Gently mix the chocolate chips, buckwheat groats, and crystallized ginger into the dough.

Scoop 1 tablespoon of dough for each cookie and place on a baking sheet 1"–2" apart.

Bake cookies for 10–12 minutes until the edges are golden and the center is just set. Let the cookies cool for 1 minute on the baking sheet before moving to a cooling rack.

PER SERVING (1 cookie) | Calories: 126 | Fat: 5 g | Protein: 1 g | Sodium: 33 mg | Fiber: <1 g | Carbohydrates: 18 g | Sugar: 12 g

Savory Baked Apples

Baked apples are a delicious dessert when stuffed with oats, butter, cinnamon, and nuts. But when you stuff them with a mixture of bacon, vegetables, and spices, they turn into a sweet and salty stuffed treat.

INGREDIENTS | SERVES 4

4 large Braeburn apples

2 slices bacon, diced

½ cup diced onion

½ cup sliced scallions

½ cup sprouted buckwheat groats

¼ cup dried cherries

¼ cup chopped pecans

2 tablespoons fresh parsley, chopped

1 tablespoon maple syrup

1 teaspoon apple cider vinegar

½ teaspoon salt

4 teaspoons butter

Apples to Apples

Braeburn apples are one variety that is great for baking, meaning they don't lose their shape and the apples don't break down in high heat. If you can't find Braeburns, either Rome or Honeycrisp apples are also good options.

Preheat the oven to 350°F.

Using a small spoon or melon baller, scoop out the centers of the apples beginning at the stem, leaving a ½"–1" thick shell and making sure not to cut all the way through the bottom of the apples. Remove the seeds and hard core from the apple centers. Chop the remaining apple, minus the cores, that you scooped out and set aside.

Heat a skillet over medium heat and add the diced bacon. Cook, stirring occasionally, for 5 minutes until the bacon is starting to crisp. Remove the bacon from the pan.

Add the onions and scallions to the bacon fat in the pan and cook for 5 minutes until the vegetables begin to soften. Stir in the chopped apple you set aside. Cook, stirring occasionally, for 3–5 minutes until the apple is softened.

Remove the pan from heat and stir in the buckwheat groats, dried cherries, pecans, parsley, maple syrup, apple cider vinegar, and salt.

Place the apples in a baking dish. Fill each apple with the stuffing mixture. Place 1 teaspoon of butter on top of the stuffing in each apple.

Bake the apples for 40–45 minutes until they are tender.

PER SERVING | Calories: 259 | Fat: 10 g | Protein: 4 g | Sodium: 351 mg | Fiber: 7 g | Carbohydrates: 43 g | Sugar: 30 g

Energy-Boosting Buckwheat Cereal Mix

Store-bought cereals are often full of added sugars, preservatives, and strange ingredients. Making your own cereal mix is quick and easy to do at home, and you can control the options.

INGREDIENTS | SERVES 4

3 cups spelt or corn flake cereal, low-sugar variety

¾ cup sprouted buckwheat groats

½ cup raisins

½ cup chopped walnuts or almonds

2 tablespoons ground flaxseed

1 teaspoon cinnamon

Pour all ingredients into a large bowl. Gently toss together.

Put cereal mixture into an airtight container to store.

Pour just over 1 cup of the cereal mixture into a bowl and serve with your favorite milk and fresh fruit.

PER SERVING | Calories: 280 | Fat: 14 g | Protein: 9 g | Sodium: 14 mg | Fiber: 6 g | Carbohydrates: 37 g | Sugar: 6 g

Sprouted-Grain Cereal

*This is a hearty breakfast made with sprouted grains that can be served
with almond milk and a little honey or agave nectar as a sweetener.
You can add a touch of vanilla extract or cocoa powder to change up the flavor.*

INGREDIENTS | SERVES 4

2 cups total of sprouted grains made up of buckwheat, rye, oats, barley, millet, quinoa, wheat, or sunflower seeds (around ¼ cup each)

1 cup apple, cut into small chunks

½ teaspoon salt

1–2 teaspoons cinnamon (to taste)

½ teaspoon vanilla extract or cocoa powder (optional)

In a large bowl, stir all ingredients together. Serve in cereal bowls with almond milk and garnish with slices of fresh fruit.

PER SERVING | Calories: 124 | Fat: 1 g | Protein: 4 g | Sodium: 300 mg | Fiber: 15 g | Carbohydrates: 27 g | Sugar: 3 g

The Staff of Life

Whole grains are often called the Staff of Life because they are a nutritious food source that can be safely stored for long periods of time. Unfortunately, modern food manufacturing often processes these nutritious grains into devitalized white flour, removing the beneficial vitamins and minerals. Whole grains are naturally high-nutrient, low-glycemic foods that are digested more slowly and sustain energy levels for longer periods of time.

Pumpkin Seed Crunch Cereal

This recipe uses soaked or sprouted seeds and buckwheat groats and is slow-baked in the dehydrator. It's good as a meal, a quick snack, or food to bring with you when you go traveling. If you don't have a dehydrator, you can make this on the lowest setting in your oven until the mixture is crunchy.

INGREDIENTS | SERVES 4

½ tablespoon pumpkin pie spice

¼ teaspoon salt

½ cup pumpkin seeds

1 cup sprouted buckwheat groats

¼ cup slivered almonds

½ cup sunflower seeds, soaked

1–2 tablespoons maple syrup

1 tablespoon lemon juice

2 cups almond milk

In a bowl, mix together the spices with the pumpkin seeds, buckwheat sprouts, almonds, sunflower seeds, maple syrup, and lemon juice.

Spread mixture onto dehydrator trays and dehydrate at 115°F for 24 hours until crunchy. Serve in cereal bowls with almond milk and slices of fresh fruit.

PER SERVING | Calories: 548 | Fat: 46 g | Protein: 13 g | Sodium: 174 mg | Fiber: 6 g | Carbohydrates: 31 g | Sugar: 9 g

Buckwheat Fruit Porridge

This is a delicious breakfast that will sustain your energy through the morning. The prunes can be replaced with other dried fruits including dates, apricots, or figs. The cinnamon may be replaced with maca, nutmeg, vanilla, cardamom, mesquite powder, or freshly grated ginger.

INGREDIENTS | SERVES 2

½ cup sprouted buckwheat groats

¼ cup chia seeds, soaked

2 cups sliced banana

¼ cup dried prunes

¼ cup dried cherries

1 teaspoon cinnamon

¼ teaspoon salt

¼ teaspoon vanilla extract

Prunes

Prunes are plums that have been dehydrated into a wrinkled, chewy, dried fruit. They are great additions to smoothies, jams, compotes, and other sauces. They can be used as a sweetener to replace dates or raisins. Prunes are a nutritious option for a quick afternoon snack; they are high in antioxidants, phytonutrients, vitamin A, potassium, iron, and copper.

Soak the buckwheat in water at room temperature for 6–8 hours. Soak the chia seeds in a separate bowl in ¾ cup water in the refrigerator for 6–8 hours. Stir the chia seeds a few times for the first 10 minutes.

Rinse and drain the buckwheat a few times, until the water is clear.

In a food processor or blender, blend the buckwheat until smooth. Add just enough water, a tablespoon at a time, to help it blend.

Add the banana, prunes, dried cherries, cinnamon, salt, and vanilla extract to the buckwheat and continue blending until smooth.

Stir in the chia seeds. Pour the porridge into serving bowls and serve.

PER SERVING | Calories: 671 | Fat: 20 g | Protein: 19 g | Sodium: 297 mg | Fiber: 36 g | Carbohydrates: 125 g | Sugar: 43 g

Kasha Porridge

This mix is both a hearty breakfast or a filling afternoon snack. If you want a little more liquid, try using something with a touch of sweetness like apple juice, coconut water, or almond milk.

INGREDIENTS | SERVES 2

2 cups soaked or sprouted buckwheat groats (soaked for 6–8 hours)

1 cup apple, chopped

1 tablespoon cinnamon

½ teaspoon salt

2 teaspoons orange zest

Place all ingredients in a food processor and process with the S blade until smooth and creamy.

PER SERVING | Calories: 627 | Fat: 6 g | Protein: 23 g | Sodium: 584 mg | Fiber: 21 g | Carbohydrates: 95 g | Sugar: 9 g

Kasha

Kasha is a traditional recipe from Europe using toasted buckwheat. The recipe is over 1,000 years old and is a staple dish in Russia and Eastern Europe. There is a Russian proverb that says "Cabbage soup and porridge are all we need to live on."

Buckwheat Snack Bites

Spirulina is one of the most protein rich foods on Earth.
These bites are a crunchy snack that will help give you energy and keep you satisfied.
They're also easy to travel with and will stay fresh for a few weeks when refrigerated.

INGREDIENTS | SERVES 4

2 cups sprouted buckwheat
1 cup dried coconut
1 cup pistachios
¼ cup dates, pitted and chopped
2 tablespoons honey
1 tablespoon spirulina
1 tablespoon carob

Soak the buckwheat for 6–8 hours. Drain and rinse until the water is clear.

Dehydrate the buckwheat until crunchy, about 6 hours at 110°F.

In a coffee grinder, grind the dried coconut to a flour.

In a food processor, process all ingredients together until well blended and chunky. Form into little square nuggets.

Dehydrate at 145°F for 2 hours. Turn down the temperature to 110°F and flip the nuggets. Continue dehydrating for 12 hours or until dry.

PER SERVING | Calories: 528 | Fat: 25 g | Protein: 16 g | Sodium: 26 mg | Fiber: 12 g | Carbohydrates: 47 g | Sugar: 21 g

Traditional Sprouted Essene Bread

This nutritious bread is full of flavor and can be eaten plain, with a nut butter spread, or used to make sandwiches. You can substitute other sprouted grains such as rye, barley, and Kamut. Looking for a twist on this recipe? Mix in some fresh herbs or chopped vegetables such as celery, carrots, or peppers.

INGREDIENTS | SERVES 4

2 cups wheatberries, sprouted 2 days

1½ cups water

2 tablespoons raw honey or agave nectar

1 tablespoon olive oil

1 teaspoon salt

Essene Bread

The Essenes were a Jewish religious group who lived from 200 B.C.E. to A.D. 100. They were the first to create this sprouted-grain bread, which was dried in the hot desert sun. The sprouting process activates the enzymes in the grain and makes the grains easier to digest.

In a food processor with an S blade, grind the sprouted wheat and water together until a dough forms.

Mix in the honey, olive oil, and salt. Briefly process until all the ingredients are mixed together.

Spread the mixture with a spatula onto dehydrator trays with nonstick sheets. Spread the mixture evenly, about ½" thick, and score into squares.

Dehydrate at 145°F for 3 hours. Flip the bread over and continue dehydrating at 110°F for 8 hours.

PER SERVING | Calories: 169 | Fat: 4 g | Protein: 4 g | Sodium: 592 mg | Fiber: 1 g | Carbohydrates: 32 g | Sugar: 9 g

Cinnamon Autumn Fruit in Sprouted Wheat Cups

Using a dehydrator means the machine does the majority of the work. This is a crispier crust, dehydrated for 8–12 hours, and is a great balance with the sweet cinnamon fruit.

INGREDIENTS | SERVES 4

1½ cups wheatberries, sprouted for 2 days

¼ cup raisins or dried cherries

1 teaspoon salt

1 teaspoon vanilla

Water to achieve the desired consistency

¼ cup pitted dried dates

2 tablespoons agave nectar

1 teaspoon cinnamon

½ teaspoon nutmeg

1 cup peeled and grated apple

1 cup peeled and grated pear

Sprouted Wheat

Sprouting wheat activates enzymes in the grain and brings the wheat to life. Sprouted wheat can help those who are underweight gain weight and build muscle. It is rich in vitamins B, C, and E and the minerals magnesium and phosphorus.

Prepare the sprouted wheat 2 days in advance.

Soak the raisins or dried cherries for 20 minutes.

To make a crust, mix together the sprouted wheat, salt, vanilla, and raisins. If you are making this dish in a juicer, use the blank plate for homogenizing. You probably won't need to add water. If you're making it in a food processor, gradually add water to create the consistency of dough, using the S blade until blended.

Spread a thin layer of the sprouted-wheat dough onto a dehydrator tray with a nonstick sheet. Dehydrate at 145°F for 2 hours. Flip the dough over, score the batter into round shapes, and dehydrate for another 2 hours at 115°F.

Soak the dates for 20 minutes in water. Remove the dates and set their soak water aside. Blend the dates with the agave nectar, cinnamon, nutmeg, and ½ cup of the soak water until smooth.

Grate the apple and pear and mix with the blended date mixture. Place the round wheat crust into dessert cups. Fill with the fruit and date mixture and serve.

PER SERVING | Calories: 212 | Fat: 1 g | Protein: 4 g | Sodium: 590 mg | Fiber: 4 g | Carbohydrates: 52 g | Sugar: 27 g

Sprouted Veggie Spread

This spread is full of healthy sprouted grains, fresh vegetables, and flavorful seasonings. Whip this up to serve on toasted bread, crudités, or sandwiched in your favorite bread.

INGREDIENTS | SERVES 4

1 cup sunflower seeds, soaked
1 cup buckwheat groats, sprouted
½ cup cashews, soaked
½ cup cauliflower, chopped
½ cup pickles, chopped
½ cup carrots, chopped
¼ cup scallions, chopped
3 tablespoons lemon juice
1 tablespoon ume plum vinegar or balsamic vinegar
½ teaspoon salt
2 teaspoons garlic, minced
1 tablespoon dill, minced
½ teaspoon cayenne pepper powder
2 tablespoons agave nectar
1 tablespoon Italian seasoning

Process the sunflower seeds, buckwheat groats, and cashews in a food processor until well broken down.

Process all remaining ingredients together in the food processor until they are well broken down but still chunky.

Place spread in a bowl and serve with your favorite sliced veggies, toasted bread, or crackers.

PER SERVING | Calories: 329 | Fat: 16 g | Protein: 10 g | Sodium: 549 mg | Fiber: 6 g | Carbohydrates: 43 g | Sugar: 12 g

Raw Sprouted-Grain Crust

Treat this crust as you would with any other homemade pizza crust.
You can use your favorite toppings on this dish, whatever they may be.

INGREDIENTS | SERVES 4

2 cups buckwheat groats, sprouted

1 cup sunflower seeds, soaked

½ cup sun-dried tomatoes, soaked

1 tablespoon olive oil

2 tablespoons honey

¼ teaspoon cayenne pepper powder

1 tablespoon Italian seasoning

½ teaspoon salt

Pizza

The first recipe for pizza originated in Italy. The basic pizza is a round, flat bread topped with tomato sauce and mozzarella cheese. It is one of the most popular foods in North America, and different regions of the United States specialize in unique recipes. New York style is a thin, flexible crust with minimal toppings. Chicago style specializes in a deep-dish and doughy crust. California style features nontraditional ingredients such as a peanut sauce, bean sprouts, and carrots.

Make the pizza dough using a food processor with an S blade or a heavy-duty juicer with a masticating screen. Process the buckwheat, sunflower seeds, sun-dried tomatoes, olive oil, honey, cayenne pepper, Italian seasoning, and salt until ingredients are well mixed with small chunks. They should be mixed long enough to form a batter-like consistency.

Form the dough into rectangular shapes, about ¼" thick. Make the edges a little thicker to form a crust. Dehydrate at 145°F for 2 hours. Flip over the dough and continue dehydrating at 110°F for 4 hours.

Garnish the pizza with toppings of your choice. Dehydrate at 110°F for 2 hours or until warm.

PER SERVING | Calories: 344 | Fat: 12 g | Protein: 10 g | Sodium: 301 mg | Fiber: 7 g | Carbohydrates: 55 g | Sugar: 11 g

Spicy Sprout Salad

Radish sprouts taste just like the actual vegetable, and they give a spicy kick to this dressing. If you would rather have a vegetable-based salad, leave out the buckwheat groats. You can also use it as a dip for vegetables or spread on crackers or sandwiches.

INGREDIENTS | SERVES 4

¼ cup radish sprouts

¼ cup alfalfa sprouts

1 tablespoon lemon juice

½ cup avocado

½ cup red bell pepper

½ cup tomato

½ teaspoon garlic powder

½ teaspoon salt

¼ teaspoon pepper

2–4 tablespoons water, as needed

2 cups buckwheat groats, sprouted

Place all the ingredients into a blender and blend together until smooth.

Toss the dressing with the buckwheat groat sprouts and serve.

PER SERVING | Calories: 241 | Fat: 5 g | Protein: 8 g | Sodium: 303 mg | Fiber: 8 g | Carbohydrates: 46 g | Sugar: 3 g

Preparing Sprouts

To prepare these sprouts, soak 3 tablespoons alfalfa seeds and radish seeds for 8–12 hours. Drain and rinse. Then transfer the seeds to a sprouter. Sprout for 5 days, and rinse the seeds two or three times a day. Rinse the sprouts to remove the hard hulls and they are ready to use.

CHAPTER 12

Sprouted Kamut and Rye Recipes

Kamut Salad with Cherries and Goat Cheese

Tangy goat cheese pairs perfectly with the sweet cherries, but feel free to substitute dried cherries if it's not the season for fresh cherries. Other dried fruits like dried cranberries or dried apricots would be delicious, as well.

INGREDIENTS | SERVES 6

1½ cups sprouted Kamut

3 cups water

1 cup fresh cherries, pitted and halved

½ cup goat cheese, crumbled

¼ cup fresh parsley

2 tablespoons olive oil

1 tablespoon maple syrup

2 teaspoons salt

½ teaspoon pepper

Place Kamut and water in a medium saucepan and bring to a boil. Simmer, covered, for 15–20 minutes until the Kamut is chewy and tender.

Pour Kamut into a bowl and toss together with the remaining ingredients.

Serve warm or chilled.

PER SERVING | Calories: 197 | Fat: 10 g | Protein: 7 g | Sodium: 872 mg | Fiber: 1 g | Carbohydrates: 20 g | Sugar: 5 g

Goat Cheese—Plain or Flavored?

Goat cheese is a soft, tangy cheese made from goat's milk and typically comes in a log shape. For most recipes, it's simply crumbled on top, just like in this salad. Plain goat cheese is delicious in this salad, but there are also herbed versions and varieties flavored with cranberries and other fruits that would be a great addition if you can find them in your grocery store.

Warm Kamut Salad with Spinach and Apple

Diced apples and maple syrup give a hint of sweetness that makes the Dijon mustard stand out even more in this warm salad.

INGREDIENTS | SERVES 4

1½ cups sprouted Kamut

3 cups water

2 teaspoons salt, divided use

1 medium apple, diced

2 cups baby spinach, torn into bite-sized pieces

2 tablespoons olive oil

1 tablespoon maple syrup

2 teaspoons Dijon mustard

½ teaspoon pepper

Pairing Suggestion

This warm salad would be perfect with roasted chicken or pork. You could also pair the salad with a mild fish or with roasted vegetables.

In a medium saucepan, bring Kamut, water, and 1 teaspoon of the salt to a boil. Simmer for 10–15 minutes.

Drain the Kamut and pour into a large bowl.

Add the diced apple and baby spinach; toss together.

In a separate small bowl, whisk together the olive oil, maple syrup, Dijon mustard, remaining 1 teaspoon salt, and pepper. Pour over the salad and stir so all of the salad is coated with the dressing.

Serve warm.

PER SERVING | Calories: 196 | Fat: 7 g | Protein: 5 g | Sodium: 776 mg | Fiber: 2 g | Carbohydrates: 30 g | Sugar: 8 g

Roasted Vegetable and Kamut Pilaf

The mix of red onion, carrots, and butternut squash makes this pilaf a great fall and winter option. When the seasons change, use different vegetables and herbs to transition this recipe into a year-round dish.

INGREDIENTS | SERVES 6

1 medium red onion
2 medium carrots
½ medium butternut squash
3 garlic cloves, peeled and left whole
2 tablespoons olive oil
3 teaspoons salt, divided
1½ teaspoons pepper, divided
3 cups vegetable broth
1 cup sprouted Kamut
1 cup quick-cooking brown rice
¼ cup fresh parsley, chopped

Traveling Salads

Non-mayo-based grain salads are great options for picnics and holiday get-togethers. Since you don't have to worry about refrigeration, you can leave the salads at room temperature, which helps bring out the flavors of the vegetables and herbs.

Preheat the oven to 425°F.

Chop onion, carrots, and butternut squash into 1" pieces. Toss the vegetables and whole garlic cloves with the olive oil, 2 teaspoons of the salt, and 1 teaspoon of the pepper. Spread out in a single layer on a greased baking sheet and roast for 35–40 minutes, stirring occasionally, until the vegetables and garlic are browning and tender.

While the vegetables are roasting, bring broth to a boil in a medium saucepan.

Add the Kamut and brown rice to the broth and return them to a boil. Lower the heat and let the Kamut and rice simmer for 10 minutes until the majority of the liquid has been absorbed. Remove the pan from the heat and let it sit, covered, for 5 minutes.

When the vegetables are done roasting, stir the vegetables into the Kamut and brown rice. Add the parsley, remaining 1 teaspoon of salt, and ½ teaspoon of pepper. Serve.

PER SERVING | Calories: 268 | Fat: 6 g | Protein: 8 g | Sodium: 932 mg | Fiber: 3 g | Carbohydrates: 47 g | Sugar: 5 g

Summer Berry Kamut Salad

Fruit salads don't have to be boring anymore! Tossing the fresh fruit with chewy Kamut and herbs is a fun way to spice up a fruity side dish.

INGREDIENTS | SERVES 6

1½ cups sprouted Kamut

3 cups water

1 teaspoon salt

1 cup fresh raspberries

1 cup fresh blueberries

1 cup strawberries, chopped

½ cup walnuts, chopped

¼ cup fresh basil, chopped

¼ cup fresh parsley, chopped

1 tablespoon agave nectar

1 tablespoon neutral oil such as safflower

Agave Nectar

Agave nectar is a sweetener that is made from the nectar of the agave plant, which is native to Mexico. It has a texture similar to that of honey, but agave is a bit sweeter than honey so you can use a little less to achieve the same sweetness in your dishes.

In a medium saucepan, bring Kamut, water, and salt to a boil. Simmer for 10–15 minutes.

Once the Kamut is tender, drain the grains and pour into a bowl.

Gently stir the raspberries, blueberries, strawberries, walnuts, basil, and parsley into the Kamut.

Drizzle the salad with the agave nectar and the oil. Toss together.

Serve at room temperature or cool.

PER SERVING | Calories: 190 | Fat: 9 g | Protein: 5 g | Sodium: 392 mg | Fiber: 3 g | Carbohydrates: 25 g | Sugar: 7 g

Kamut and Lentil Bean Soup

Lentil and bean soups are typically hearty dishes on their own; adding the Kamut bumps up the volume of this soup and gives another texture to contrast with the smooth and creamy beans.

INGREDIENTS | SERVES 8

2 tablespoons olive oil

1 medium onion, diced

2 carrots, sliced

2 cloves garlic, minced

1 cup sprouted Kamut

1 cup sprouted lentils

4 cups vegetable broth

2 cups water

1 bay leaf

2 teaspoons cumin

2 teaspoons smoked paprika

2 teaspoons oregano

2 teaspoons salt

1 teaspoon pepper

Heat oil in a large pot and add the onion and carrots. Cook, stirring occasionally, for 5–6 minutes until they are starting to soften.

Stir in the minced garlic and cook for another minute until the garlic is fragrant.

Add remaining ingredients and bring soup to a boil.

Lower the heat and let the soup simmer for 20–30 minutes.

Serve with a drizzle of olive oil.

PER SERVING | Calories: 108 | Fat: 4 g | Protein: 4 g | Sodium: 871 mg | Fiber: 1 g | Carbohydrates: 17 g | Sugar: 2 g

Add Pistou to Your Soup

Pistou is a cold sauce, traditionally made from garlic, herbs, and olive oil, and is used as a garnish on vegetable soups. To add some additional color and flavor to this soup, mince 2 garlic cloves and mash those together in a bowl with 2 tablespoons fresh basil, 2 tablespoons fresh parsley, 1 table-spoon fresh cilantro, 1 teaspoon sea salt, and ½ teaspoon pepper. Drizzle in 4 table-spoons of olive oil and serve 1 spoonful on each bowl of soup.

(Serves 8. Per Serving: Calories: 62; Fat: 6 g; Protein: <1 g; Sodium: 311 mg; Fiber: <1 g; Carbohydrates: <1 g; Sugar: <1 g)

Roasted Kamut and Apple Sundaes

Oatmeal isn't the only whole grain you can use to introduce a new texture to a dessert. A bit different than a normal apple crisp, this mix of Kamut, apples, nuts, and spices is delicious when paired with vanilla ice cream.

INGREDIENTS | SERVES 4

1 cup sprouted Kamut
1 large apple, diced
2 tablespoons maple syrup
1 teaspoon cinnamon
½ teaspoon salt
2 cups vanilla ice cream
½ cup chopped pecans

A Touch of Salt

Want to add another layer of flavor to these sundaes? Try drizzling a spoonful of caramel over the top and adding a pinch of sea salt for the ultimate topping. The salt will be the perfect balance with the sweet apples and cool vanilla ice cream.

Preheat the oven to 325°F.

Toss together Kamut, apple, maple syrup, cinnamon, and salt; spread out on a baking sheet lined with parchment paper.

Bake, stirring occasionally, for 15–20 minutes.

Remove the Kamut and apple mixture from the oven and let cool for 5–10 minutes.

Split the ice cream into four bowls. Top with the Kamut and apple mixture and some of the chopped pecans.

PER SERVING | Calories: 323 | Fat: 17 g | Protein: 6 g | Sodium: 340 mg | Fiber: 3 g | Carbohydrates: 40 g | Sugar: 21 g

Kamut and Turkey Sausage Casserole

*Using precooked turkey sausage links makes this recipe a great weeknight option,
but you could use your favorite chicken or pork sausage in this recipe, too.*

INGREDIENTS | SERVES 6

2 cups sprouted Kamut

4 cups water

1 tablespoon butter

2 tablespoons olive oil

1 medium onion, diced

2 carrots, thinly sliced

2 cloves garlic, minced

1 pound precooked turkey sausage links, diced

1 cup vegetable broth

¼ cup fresh parsley, chopped

1 teaspoon crushed red pepper

2 teaspoons salt

1 teaspoon pepper

½ cup Parmesan cheese, grated

Preheat the oven to 375°F.

In a medium saucepan, bring the sprouted Kamut and water to a boil. Let the Kamut cook, simmering, for 20 minutes. Drain the grains and place them in a greased 2-quart baking dish.

While the Kamut is simmering, place a deep skillet over medium heat and add the butter and olive oil. Once the butter is melted, toss the diced onion and sliced carrots into the skillet. Cook, stirring, until the vegetables are softened, about 4–5 minutes.

Add the minced garlic to the onion and carrots and cook, stirring, for another minute until the garlic is fragrant.

Stir the diced turkey sausage into the vegetables and let them cook together over medium heat for 5–6 minutes. Turn off the heat.

Add the broth, parsley, crushed red pepper, salt, and pepper to the sausage mixture and stir together. Pour the sausage and vegetable mixture into the Kamut and mix together. Stir the grated Parmesan into the dish.

Cover the dish with foil and bake at 375°F for 30 minutes. Remove the foil and bake for another 10 minutes until the liquid is absorbed.

PER SERVING | Calories: 357 | Fat: 18 g | Protein: 26 g | Sodium: 1,601 mg | Fiber: <1 g | Carbohydrates: 22 g | Sugar: 1 g

Kamut with Tuna and Roasted Red Peppers

Taking a flavorful tuna salad and placing it on Kamut rather than mixed greens or bread adds a new texture to the dish. Using sprouted wheatberries or bulgur would also work well.

INGREDIENTS | SERVES 4

1½ cups sprouted Kamut

3 cups water

2 teaspoons salt, divided

¾ cup albacore tuna, drained and flaked

2 roasted red peppers, diced

½ cup cannellini beans, drained and rinsed

¼ cup scallions, sliced

¼ cup fresh parsley, chopped

¼ cup olive oil

1 tablespoon red wine vinegar

1 teaspoon oregano

½ teaspoon pepper

Bring Kamut, water, and 1 teaspoon of the salt to a boil over medium heat. Simmer for 15 minutes.

While the Kamut is cooking, place the flaked tuna into a medium bowl.

Stir the roasted peppers, beans, scallions, parsley, olive oil, vinegar, remaining 1 teaspoon salt, oregano, and pepper into the tuna mixture and set aside.

Drain the Kamut and divide between four plates.

Top with the tuna mixture and serve.

PER SERVING | Calories: 312 | Fat: 15 g | Protein: 17 g | Sodium: 756 mg | Fiber: 3 g | Carbohydrates: 28 g | Sugar: 1 g

Why Albacore?

When buying tuna (both canned and fresh), search for albacore or white tuna that was taken from the U.S. Pacific, Canadian Pacific, Hawaii, or South Atlantic. These are the locations where catches are considered the most sustainable by the Monterey Bay Aquarium Seafood Watch.

Curried Potatoes and Peas with Kamut and Yogurt

When making curry recipes, don't skimp on the spices. Curries don't have to be spicy-hot, but you definitely want the mix of flavors to give the dish that authentic flavor.

INGREDIENTS | SERVES 6

1½ cups sprouted Kamut

3 cups water

2 tablespoons oil

1 tablespoon ground coriander

2 teaspoons ground cumin

2 teaspoons turmeric

½ teaspoon crushed red pepper

¼ teaspoon cinnamon

1½ pounds Yukon Gold potatoes, cut into ½" pieces

1 cup canned crushed tomatoes or tomato purée

½ cup coconut milk

½ cup water

½ cup fresh cilantro, chopped, divided

2 teaspoons salt

1 cup frozen peas

½ cup plain yogurt

Toasting and Grinding Your Own Spices

Although it creates one more step, you can definitely toast and grind your own spices for dishes like this or for any spice rubs or mixtures. To toast your whole spices, toss the seeds or spices into a dry pan over low-medium heat and cook, stirring often, for 3–5 minutes until the spices are fragrant. Pour the whole spices into a coffee grinder and grind them up, then use as usual. You'll have a much deeper flavor from using freshly ground spices—it's worth the extra time, especially in recipes like this curry.

In a medium saucepan, bring the Kamut and water to a boil. Cover and simmer for 15–20 minutes until the Kamut is tender. Drain and set aside.

In a large skillet, heat the oil over medium heat. Add the coriander, cumin, turmeric, crushed red pepper, and cinnamon; stir. Let the spices cook, stirring, for 1–2 minutes until fragrant.

Add the potatoes to the pan and cook, stirring frequently, until the potatoes start to soften, 5–10 minutes.

Stir in the tomatoes, coconut milk, water, ¼ cup of the cilantro, and salt. Bring the mixture to a simmer and cook on low, covered, until the potatoes are tender, about 15 minutes.

Add the frozen peas to the potato mixture and place the cover back on the skillet. Let the mixture cook for another 2–3 minutes until the peas are tender and bright green.

Remove the pan from heat. Pour potato mixture over Kamut. Sprinkle with remaining cilantro and add a dollop of yogurt before serving.

PER SERVING | Calories: 285 | Fat: 9 g | Protein: 7 g | Sodium: 1,029 mg | Fiber: 4 g | Carbohydrates: 45 g | Sugar: 5 g

Coconut Cauliflower Curry Stew

Cauliflower is a fantastic quick-cooking vegetable that works well in soups and stews. If you don't have any on hand, sweet potatoes would also be delicious in this stew. Just make sure to add another 10 minutes of cooking time.

INGREDIENTS | SERVES 8

2 tablespoons coconut oil

1 medium onion, diced

2 carrots, diced

2 garlic cloves, minced

2 teaspoons fresh ginger, minced

2 teaspoons turmeric

2 teaspoons ground coriander

2 teaspoons ground cumin

1 teaspoon crushed red pepper

½ teaspoon cinnamon

2 tablespoons tomato paste

1½ cups sprouted Kamut

3 cups water

2 cups vegetable broth

1 head cauliflower, chopped into bite-sized pieces

1 (14-ounce) can coconut milk

½ cup fresh cilantro, chopped

2 teaspoons salt

½ teaspoon pepper

Make It a Meal

This soup is hearty enough to stand alone with a nice salad, but if you want a little more protein, feel free to add your favorite meat, beans, or some tofu to the stew before serving.

Heat coconut oil in a large pot over medium heat. Once the oil is melted, add the diced onion and carrots and cook, stirring, for 5–6 minutes until the vegetables have started to soften.

Add the garlic and ginger to the vegetables, stirring for 1 minute, until they are fragrant.

Stir in the turmeric, coriander, cumin, red pepper, and cinnamon. Cook, stirring constantly, for 1–2 minutes until the spices are fragrant and the vegetables are coated with the spices.

Add the tomato paste and stir together with the vegetables for 1 minute, letting the tomato paste coat the vegetables.

Pour the sprouted Kamut, water, and broth into the pot with the vegetables and bring mixture to a boil. Let the Kamut and vegetables cook for 5–10 minutes, then add the chopped cauliflower and coconut milk.

Return the stew to a simmer and let it cook for another 5–10 minutes until the Kamut and cauliflower are tender.

Stir in the cilantro, salt, and pepper before serving.

PER SERVING | Calories: 212 | Fat: 15 g | Protein: 5 g | Sodium: 889 mg | Fiber: 3 g | Carbohydrates: 19 g | Sugar: 4 g

Italian Chicken and Kamut Bake

Using Kamut as the base of a casserole brings a new texture that's just a bit different than rice or pasta.

INGREDIENTS | SERVES 6

2 cups sprouted Kamut

4 cups water

1 tablespoon olive oil

1 pound chicken breast, diced into 1" pieces

1 tablespoon dried parsley

2 teaspoons dried oregano

2 teaspoons dried basil

3 teaspoons salt, divided

1½ teaspoons pepper, divided

1 medium onion, diced

2 garlic cloves, minced

1 cup canned crushed tomatoes

1 (15-ounce) can cannellini beans, drained and rinsed

¼ cup fresh parsley

¼ cup fresh oregano

½ cup Parmesan cheese, grated

Preheat the oven to 375°F.

In a medium saucepan, bring the Kamut and water to a boil. Simmer, covered, for 20 minutes. Drain and pour into a greased 2-quart baking dish.

While the Kamut is cooking, heat the oil in a large skillet.

Sprinkle the diced chicken with the dried parsley, dried oregano, dried basil, 1 teaspoon salt, and ½ teaspoon pepper. Add the chicken to the pan and cook for 2–3 minutes on each side until the chicken is browned.

Add the diced onions and minced garlic to the chicken and cook, 3–4 minutes, stirring frequently, until the onions begin to soften.

Remove the pan from heat and pour the chicken and vegetable mixture into the Kamut. Stir the tomatoes, beans, fresh parsley, fresh oregano, 2 teaspoons salt, 1 teaspoon pepper, and Parmesan into the Kamut mixture.

Cover the baking dish with foil and bake for 30 minutes. Remove the foil and bake for another 10 minutes until the liquid has been absorbed and the chicken is cooked through.

PER SERVING | Calories: 338 | Fat: 7 g | Protein: 31 g | Sodium: 1,399 mg | Fiber: 8 g | Carbohydrates: 40 g | Sugar: 0 g

Summer Pesto, Tomato, and Kamut Salad

Instead of making the typical tomato, basil, and mozzarella salad this summer, try this twist on a pesto salad. The Kamut gives a nice chew to the salad and makes it a bit more filling as a side dish or a light lunch.

INGREDIENTS | SERVES 4

1½ cups sprouted Kamut

3 cups water

2 teaspoons salt, divided

2 cups fresh basil

½ cup fresh parsley

½ cup walnuts, toasted

¼ cup olive oil

¼ cup Parmesan cheese, grated

1 clove garlic, chopped

½ teaspoon pepper

1½ cups cherry or Roma tomatoes, diced

Toasting Walnuts

To get the most flavor out of your walnuts, toast them before you add them to the dish. You can bake them on a sheet pan in the oven for 10–15 minutes until they are warmed and fragrant, or you can toast them in a skillet on the stovetop, stirring often, for 7–10 minutes. Either way, make sure you keep an eye on them as they can burn very quickly.

Bring Kamut, water, and 1 teaspoon of the salt to a boil in a medium saucepan. Simmer for 15 minutes.

While the Kamut is cooking, place the basil, parsley, walnuts, olive oil, Parmesan, garlic, 1 teaspoon salt, and pepper in the bowl of a food processor. Pulse until the mixture comes together and the nuts and herbs are chopped.

Drain the Kamut and pour into a bowl.

Pour the pesto over the Kamut and toss together.

Gently stir the tomatoes into the Kamut. Serve at room temperature.

PER SERVING | Calories: 290 | Fat: 21 g | Protein: 8 g | Sodium: 680 mg | Fiber: 2 g | Carbohydrates: 21 g | Sugar: 2 g

Cinnamon Raisin and Kamut Granola

This granola has a great crunchy texture and is delicious on top of yogurt, in milk, or eaten alone as a quick afternoon snack. If you're not a fan of almonds, switch them out for sunflower seeds, pecans, or walnuts.

INGREDIENTS | SERVES 10

1 cup rolled oats

1 cup sprouted Kamut

1 cup buckwheat groats

2 tablespoons ground flaxseed

2 tablespoons chia seeds

½ cup chopped almonds

¾ cup raisins

2 teaspoons cinnamon

1 teaspoon salt

½ cup maple syrup

½ cup coconut oil, melted

Preheat the oven to 225°F.

In a large bowl, mix together the oats, Kamut, buckwheat groats, flaxseed, chia seeds, chopped almonds, and raisins.

Stir in the cinnamon and salt. Pour the maple syrup and melted coconut oil over the granola and toss to combine.

Spread the granola on a baking sheet lined with parchment paper.

Bake granola for 50–60 minutes. Let it cool for 5–10 minutes before breaking into bite-sized pieces or crumbling.

PER SERVING | Calories: 320 | Fat: 16 g | Protein: 6 g | Sodium: 236 mg | Fiber: 5 g | Carbohydrates: 41 g | Sugar: 16 g

Ch-, Ch-, Ch-, Chia!

Chia seeds are the tiny seeds of the chia plant, and they are incredibly high in omega-3 fatty acids. They can be used in baking or can be eaten raw. They also form a gel-like consistency when placed into liquids, which can act as a binder in baking or as a thickener in smoothies.

Vegetable and Egg Fried Kamut

This twist on Chinese fried rice is much healthier than anything you can get off the takeout menu. Full of vegetables, whole grains, and protein from the eggs, this dish is a filling and fun way to make takeout at home.

INGREDIENTS | SERVES 4

1 tablespoon olive oil

1 medium onion, diced

½ cup sliced scallions

2 carrots, thinly sliced

1 clove garlic, minced

1 cup frozen peas, thawed

1½ cups sprouted Kamut

4 eggs, beaten

2 teaspoons sesame oil

3 tablespoons soy sauce

Make It a Meal

While the eggs do provide protein in this dish, you could also add in leftover meat from another meal or diced and sautéed tofu. Serve this with a salad or steamed edamame on the side.

In a large skillet or wok, heat the oil over medium heat and add the onion, scallions, and carrots. Cook the vegetables, 5–6 minutes, until they are beginning to brown and soften.

Stir in the garlic and frozen peas, and cook for 1–2 minutes until the garlic is fragrant.

Add the Kamut and toss together with the vegetables in the pan.

Push the Kamut and vegetables to the sides of the pan, making a well in the center. Pour in the eggs and cook, scrambling until the eggs are cooked through.

Stir in the sesame oil and soy sauce. Serve hot.

PER SERVING | Calories: 261 | Fat: 10 g | Protein: 13 g | Sodium: 866 mg | Fiber: 3 g | Carbohydrates: 30 g | Sugar: 4 g

Kamut with Leeks and Parmesan

This is a simple, warm grain side dish, full of the timid flavor of leeks and a bit of salt from the Parmesan.

INGREDIENTS | SERVES 4

1 tablespoon olive oil
3 leeks, trimmed, sliced, and rinsed
1½ cups sprouted Kamut
½ cup vegetable broth
1 teaspoon salt
½ teaspoon pepper
½ cup Parmesan cheese, grated

Heat oil in a large skillet over medium heat.

Cook the sliced leeks in the olive oil for 5–7 minutes, stirring occasionally, until they are softened.

Stir in the Kamut, broth, salt, and pepper. Bring the mixture to a simmer and let it cook for 5–10 minutes until the broth has been absorbed.

Remove the pan from heat and stir in the Parmesan.

Serve warm.

PER SERVING | Calories: 221 | Fat: 7 g | Protein: 10 g |
Sodium: 855 mg | Fiber: 1 g | Carbohydrates: 30 g | Sugar: 3 g

Zucchini, Tomato, and Kamut Frittata

Frittatas are one of the easiest meals to make. They are delicious for breakfast and even better for lunch or dinner. The Kamut gives this frittata a bit more texture, but you could use any whole grain you have on hand.

INGREDIENTS | SERVES 4

1 tablespoon olive oil

½ medium onion, diced

1 medium tomato, diced

1 clove garlic, minced

½ cup sprouted Kamut

6 eggs

½ cup milk

1 teaspoon salt

½ teaspoon pepper

½ teaspoon dried oregano

½ teaspoon dried rosemary

¼ cup Parmesan cheese, grated

Breakfast for Dinner

The frittata itself is packed with protein from the eggs. Pair slices of the frittata with a green salad and roasted potatoes or fresh fruit for an easy weeknight meal.

Preheat the oven to 375°F.

In a medium, oven-safe skillet, heat the oil over medium heat.

Add the onion and tomato, and cook for 5 minutes until they are beginning to soften. Stir in the garlic and Kamut.

In a separate bowl, whisk the eggs with the milk, salt, pepper, oregano, rosemary, and Parmesan.

Pour egg mixture into the vegetables and cook on the stovetop for 2 minutes.

Move the pan to the oven and bake for 15–18 minutes or until the eggs are set and the top is golden.

PER SERVING | Calories: 207 | Fat: 12 g | Protein: 14 g | Sodium: 783 mg | Fiber: 1 g | Carbohydrates: 11 g | Sugar: 3 g

Kamut and Sausage Stuffed Squash

One of the best things about cooking during the fall is being able to use all the beautiful types of squash that are in season. In this recipe, sweet squash is stuffed with a savory filling and topped with a layer of cheese for the ultimate comfort meal.

INGREDIENTS | SERVES 4

4 buttercup or golden nugget squash, 1 pound each

½ pound spicy Italian sausage, casings removed

½ medium onion, chopped

2 medium carrots, chopped

1 clove garlic, minced

1 tablespoon tomato paste

1½ cups sprouted Kamut

¼ cup fresh parsley, chopped

1 teaspoon dried thyme

1 teaspoon salt

½ teaspoon pepper

1 cup mozzarella cheese, shredded

Removing Sausage Casings

To remove the casings from your sausage, cut a small slit down the length of the sausage with a small paring knife. Pull the casing away from the sausage and crumble the meat into the pan to cook.

Preheat the oven to 350°F.

Cut the top quarter off each squash and discard the seeds. Slice a section from the bottom of each squash so it will sit up evenly in the baking dish.

Bake the squash cut side up for 20 minutes. Remove from the oven and set aside.

While the squash is baking, heat a skillet over medium heat and add the sausage. Brown the meat, stirring to break it up as it cooks.

When the sausage is browned, remove the meat from the pan and leave the drippings behind. Stir the onions and carrots into the drippings and cook for 5–7 minutes until the vegetables are tender.

Add the garlic and tomato paste and stir into the vegetables, letting the mixture cook for another 2 minutes.

Stir the Kamut, parsley, thyme, salt, and pepper into the vegetable mixture. Add the sausage back into the stuffing mixture and stir together.

Remove the pan from heat. Divide the stuffing between the four squash and fill each to the top.

Sprinkle the tops of each squash with mozzarella and bake for 25–35 minutes until the squash is tender and the cheese is melted.

PER SERVING | Calories: 475 | Fat: 17 g | Protein: 23 g | Sodium: 1,118 mg | Fiber: 14 g | Carbohydrates: 63 g | Sugar: 2 g

Homemade Rejuvelac

Rejuvelac has a tart flavor and contains beneficial bacteria; it can be made with any sprouted hard grain, including wheat, rye, quinoa, or buckwheat. Rejuvelac can also be used as a starter culture to make seed cheese or as a liquid base for smoothies.

INGREDIENTS | SERVES 4

2 cups rye
6 cups water

Rejuvelac

Rejuvelac should taste like sour lemonade. Sometimes it will not culture properly because of factors in the environment. Avoid any batch that has mold on the seeds or bad bacteria in the air. If the batch goes bad and spoils, it will have a nasty smell and taste. Don't give up! Simply discard the batch and start over.

Soak the rye seeds and sprout them for 1–2 days.

Drain and rinse the rye sprouts. Place them into a ½ gallon glass jar and fill the jar with water.

Fasten a cheesecloth over the opening of the jar with a rubber band.

Let the jar sit at room temperature for 2 days.

Pour the rejuvelac into a new jar, straining out the rye seeds. The rejuvelac will keep in the refrigerator for 2–3 days, but ideally it should be consumed within 24 hours.

The same rye seeds can be used to make a second batch. Fill the jar with fresh water and let it sit for 24 hours. Pour into a new container and discard the seeds.

PER SERVING | Calories: 93 | Fat: 0 g | Protein: 3 g | Sodium: 8 mg | Fiber: 3 g | Carbohydrates: 15 g | Sugar: >1 g

Rye Bread

This bread can be used to make sandwiches, served with a salad, or used as croutons. The flavor you expect from regular rye bread is here—you just get more nutritional value in this loaf. Once dehydrated, the rye bread will stay fresh in an airtight container for 3–4 weeks.

INGREDIENTS | SERVES 4

2 cups rye, sprouted 2 days

Water for blending

1 teaspoon caraway seeds

½ teaspoon coriander

In a food processor with an S blade, grind the sprouted rye to a dough. Add just enough water to help it blend. Alternatively, homogenize the rye with a heavy-duty juicer.

Stir in the caraway seeds and coriander.

Form the dough into small, flat, round loafs. Dehydrate at 145°F for 2 hours.

Turn down the temperature to 110°F. Flip the bread over and continue dehydrating for 12 hours or until crisp.

PER SERVING | Calories: 285 | Fat: 2 g | Protein: 13 g | Sodium: 5 mg | Fiber: 13 g | Carbohydrates: 59 g | Sugar: >1 g

CHAPTER 13

Sprouted Chickpeas Recipes

Baked Sweet Potato and Chickpea Falafel

Traditional falafel are chickpea-based patties that are deep-fried before serving.
This baked version still has the great flavor without the high calories and fat.

INGREDIENTS | SERVES 4

2 medium sweet potatoes (about 1 pound), cooked and peeled

1½ cups sprouted chickpeas

2 tablespoons ground flaxseed

2 teaspoons garlic powder

2 teaspoons parsley

1 teaspoon cumin

1 teaspoon ground coriander

1 teaspoon salt

½ teaspoon turmeric

½ teaspoon pepper

¼ teaspoon cinnamon

Preheat the oven to 400°F.

In a large bowl (or in a food processor), mash the cooked and peeled sweet potatoes with the chickpeas until the mixture is combined and mostly smooth.

Stir the flaxseed, garlic powder, parsley, cumin, coriander, salt, turmeric, pepper, and cinnamon into the sweet potato mixture.

Form dough into 1"–2" rounds and place on a greased or parchment paper–lined baking sheet.

Bake for 20–30 minutes until golden.

PER SERVING | Calories: 228 | Fat: 8 g | Protein: 7 g | Sodium: 609 mg | Fiber: 7 g | Carbohydrates: 32 g | Sugar: 7 g

Quick Greek Salad

These falafel are delicious stuffed into pitas with hummus, but they're also fantastic on top of this quick Greek salad for a light lunch or dinner. Chop 2 heads of romaine lettuce, 3 medium tomatoes, ½ medium red onion, ½ cup pitted olives, and ½ cup feta cheese. Toss everything together in a large bowl and stir in 2 tablespoons olive oil, 1 tablespoon red wine vinegar, 1 teaspoon dried oregano, 1 teaspoon salt, and ½ teaspoon pepper.

(Serves 4. Per Serving: Calories: 204; Fat: 13 g; Protein: 7 g; Sodium: 963 mg; Fiber: 8 g; Carbohydrates: 17 g; Sugar: 7 g)

Ancho Chile Hummus

Hummus is a staple of the Mediterranean diet and is a dish based on chickpeas and Tahini. This version would be a delicious spread to serve with chopped vegetables and pita chips.

INGREDIENTS | SERVES 8

2 cups sprouted chickpeas

2 tablespoons olive oil

2 tablespoons Tahini

½ tablespoon ancho chile powder

½ tablespoon smoked paprika

1½ teaspoons salt

1 clove garlic

What Is Tahini?

Tahini is a smooth and creamy ingredient that is always used in traditional hummus recipes. It is a paste made up of ground sesame seeds. Tahini is sold prepared, but you can also make your own in a food processor.

Place all the ingredients in the bowl of a food processor.

Process the mixture until all the chickpeas are broken down and the hummus is smooth. You can add more oil, if needed.

Pour into a bowl and serve with tortilla chips, pita chips, celery, jicama, or carrots.

PER SERVING | Calories: 116 | Fat: 6 g | Protein: 4 g | Sodium: 430 mg | Fiber: 3 g | Carbohydrates: 12 g | Sugar: 2 g

Vanilla Maple Chickpea Dip

Because chickpeas don't have a strong flavor of their own, they are a great base for sweet dips as well as savory ones. The flavors of the maple syrup and vanilla turn this "vegetable dip" into a sweet spread that's perfect on sliced apples or toast.

INGREDIENTS | SERVES 8

2 cups sprouted chickpeas

2 tablespoons coconut oil or neutral oil like safflower

2 tablespoons maple syrup

1 teaspoon vanilla extract

1 teaspoon salt

Place the chickpeas, oil, maple syrup, vanilla, and salt in the bowl of a food processor.

Process the mixture until the chickpeas are broken down and the mixture is smooth. You can add more oil or maple syrup, if needed.

Pour into a bowl. Serve chilled or at room temperature.

PER SERVING | Calories: 106 | Fat: 4 g | Protein: 3 g | Sodium: 280 mg | Fiber: 3 g | Carbohydrates: 14 g | Sugar: 5 g

Cinnamon Pita Chips

The sweet chickpea dip makes for a great afternoon snack or lunchtime dessert with sliced apples, graham crackers, carrots, or Cinnamon Pita Chips. To make the chips, take four whole-wheat pitas and cut each one of them into six pieces. Brush them with a little oil and sprinkle with cinnamon and sugar. Bake the pita pieces in the oven at 350°F for 6–8 minutes until they are toasted.

(Serves 8. Per Serving: Calories: 87; Fat: 1 g; Protein: 3 g; Sodium: 160 mg; Fiber: 2 g; Carbohydrates: 17 g; Sugar: <1 g)

Radish, Spinach, and Chickpea Salad

*Radishes and spinach are some of the earliest spring crops.
The tender flavor of the spinach balances the crisp and peppery radish slices in this salad.*

INGREDIENTS | SERVES 4

3 cups sprouted chickpeas

½ red onion, diced

½ cup radishes, sliced

1 teaspoon lemon zest

1 teaspoon lemon juice

1 tablespoon olive oil

1 teaspoon salt

½ teaspoon pepper

2 cups spinach, chopped

In a large bowl, toss the chickpeas with the red onion, radishes, and lemon zest.

Stir in the lemon juice, olive oil, salt, and pepper.

Add chopped spinach just before you serve the salad. This salad can be served cold or at room temperature.

PER SERVING | Calories: 251 | Fat: 6 g | Protein: 11 g |
Sodium: 610 mg | Fiber: 10 g | Carbohydrates: 38 g | Sugar: 8 g

Olive and Chickpea Salad

Kalamata and green olives pair nicely together, even though they differ in flavor and texture. This salad can be mixed up with any of your favorite olives—the brininess is delicious with the salty feta and mild chickpeas.

INGREDIENTS | SERVES 4

10 ounces pitted green and kalamata olives

1½ cups sprouted chickpeas

4 ounces feta cheese, cubed or crumbled

1 tablespoon olive brine (from olive jar) or vinegar

1 tablespoon olive oil

¼ cup fresh parsley, chopped

½ teaspoon pepper

In a medium bowl, toss olives with chickpeas and feta cheese.

Gently stir in the olive brine (or vinegar), olive oil, fresh parsley, and pepper.

Refrigerate until ready to serve.

PER SERVING | Calories: 289 | Fat: 18 g | Protein: 10 g | Sodium: 939 mg | Fiber: 7 g | Carbohydrates: 23 g | Sugar: 4 g

Serving Suggestion

The olive salad can be mixed up ahead of time and baked on top of chicken breast or a mild fish. If you're already serving a green salad with your meal, top the greens with a scoop of the olive salad and you can leave your salad dressing in the refrigerator.

Chopped Chicken and Chickpea Greek Salad

Typical Greek salads don't include chickpeas, but they are a staple of the typical Greek diet in hummus and other dishes. Adding the chickpeas to this salad gives it additional texture and protein.

INGREDIENTS | SERVES 4

1 pound chicken breast, cut into 1" pieces

1 tablespoon oregano

1 tablespoon garlic powder

1½ teaspoons salt, divided

¾ teaspoon pepper, divided

1 tablespoon plus ¼ cup olive oil, divided

4 cups romaine lettuce, chopped

1 cup sprouted chickpeas

1 cup tomatoes, diced

½ cup olives, chopped

½ red onion, diced

½ cup feta, crumbled

2 tablespoons red wine vinegar

1 teaspoon Dijon mustard

Toss diced chicken with oregano, garlic powder, 1 teaspoon salt, and ½ teaspoon pepper.

Heat 1 tablespoon olive oil in a large skillet over medium heat and add chicken. Brown chicken on all sides and cook on medium, 7–10 minutes, until it is fully cooked.

Remove chicken from pan and place in a large bowl.

Toss chicken with chopped lettuce, chickpeas, tomatoes, olives, red onion, and feta.

In a small bowl, whisk the ¼ cup olive oil, vinegar, mustard, ½ teaspoon salt, and ¼ teaspoon pepper together.

Pour dressing over the salad and toss to coat right before serving.

PER SERVING | Calories: 348 | Fat: 14 g | Protein: 34 g | Sodium: 890 mg | Fiber: 7 g | Carbohydrates: 23 g | Sugar: 7 g

Quick Chana Masala

Chana masala is a popular vegetarian dish in India and Pakistan. Chana masala's main ingredients are chickpeas and aromatics, including a spicy mix of flavors that add some oomph to the chickpeas.

INGREDIENTS | SERVES 4

1 tablespoon olive oil

1 medium onion, diced

2 cloves garlic, minced

1" piece of fresh ginger, peeled and chopped

1 tablespoon tomato paste

2 cups sprouted chickpeas

½ cup water

1 tablespoon cumin

2 teaspoons curry powder

1 teaspoon turmeric

1 teaspoon salt

½ teaspoon cayenne pepper

1 tablespoon fresh lemon juice

Peeling Fresh Ginger

The easiest way to peel fresh ginger is either with a spoon or by setting it on a cutting board and cutting off thin slices of the peel with a paring knife.

Heat olive oil over medium heat in a large skillet.

Add diced onion and cook, stirring frequently, for 5–6 minutes until the onions are softened and beginning to caramelize.

Stir in the garlic and ginger, and cook for another minute until fragrant.

Add the tomato paste and stir into the onions until all of the onion pieces are coated with the paste. Cook for 1–2 minutes.

Stir the chickpeas, water, cumin, curry powder, turmeric, salt, and cayenne pepper into the skillet.

Let the chickpeas simmer for 5–10 minutes until the water has reduced and the sauce is thickened around the chickpeas. Remove from heat, stir in the lemon juice, and serve.

PER SERVING | Calories: 185 | Fat: 6 g | Protein: 8 g | Sodium: 595 mg | Fiber: 7 g | Carbohydrates: 26 g | Sugar: 4 g

Roasted Tomato Pesto, Chickpea, and Pasta Salad

This is a perfect summer salad; the fresh pesto bursts with flavor from the basil and pine nuts. Roasting the tomatoes brings out their sweetness and concentrates the flavor.

INGREDIENTS | SERVES 4

1 pound Roma or cherry tomatoes

2 tablespoons olive oil, divided

1 teaspoon plus 1 tablespoon salt, divided

½ teaspoon pepper

¼ cup pine nuts

1 clove garlic

¼ cup Parmesan cheese, grated

6 cups water

½ pound short whole-wheat pasta

1 cup sprouted chickpeas

2 cups fresh spinach, chopped

½ cup fresh basil, chopped

Extras for Roasted Tomatoes

Roasted tomatoes have so much more flavor than the raw version. They're a fantastic addition to salads, pizza, pasta, soups, and sandwiches. Try adding some roasted tomatoes to a grilled cheese sandwich or chopped and whipped into butter for a new spread.

Preheat the oven to 400°F.

Slice tomatoes in half, place on a baking sheet, and drizzle with 1 tablespoon olive oil, 1 teaspoon salt, and pepper. Roast for 25–30 minutes until the tomatoes have softened.

Remove the tomatoes from the oven and let them cool for 5 minutes.

Place tomatoes, pine nuts, garlic, 1 tablespoon olive oil, and Parmesan in a food processor or blender, and process until the mixture is combined.

Bring water to a boil in a large pot. Add 1 tablespoon salt and pasta, and cook, stirring occasionally, for 7–10 minutes until the pasta is al dente. Drain pasta and pour into a large dish or bowl.

Stir chickpeas and roasted tomato pesto into the warm pasta.

Gently stir the spinach and basil into the pasta. Serve warm or at room temperature.

PER SERVING | Calories: 423 | Fat: 13 g | Protein: 16 g | Sodium: 872 mg | Fiber: 8 g | Carbohydrates: 63 g | Sugar: 5 g

Lemony Couscous with Chickpeas

*Israeli couscous is made of semolina, just like regular couscous,
but the pieces of pasta are much larger. Also known as ptitim, Israeli couscous is a round,
toasted pasta and is typically served by itself or in salads like this dish.*

INGREDIENTS | SERVES 6

1 cup Israeli couscous

2 cups water

2 tablespoons lemon juice

3 teaspoons salt, divided

2 cups sprouted chickpeas

½ cup scallions, sliced

½ cup sun-dried tomatoes, diced

2 tablespoons olive oil

1 tablespoon lemon zest

In a medium saucepan, bring Israeli couscous, water, lemon juice, and 1 teaspoon salt to a boil. Cover the pot and simmer for 5 minutes. Remove the pan from heat and let the couscous steam for 10 minutes.

In a medium bowl, toss the chickpeas with the scallions, sun-dried tomatoes, olive oil, lemon zest, and 2 teaspoons salt.

Fluff the couscous with a fork and divide between four plates.

Top with the chickpea salad.

PER SERVING | Calories: 232 | Fat: 4 g | Protein: 9 g |
Sodium: 1,260 mg | Fiber: 6 g | Carbohydrates: 40 g | Sugar: 4 g

Sweet and Smoky Roasted Chickpeas

These crunchy roasted chickpeas are an easy snack to take to work or school and are quick and easy to make on the weekends or after work.

INGREDIENTS | YIELDS 2 CUPS

2 cups sprouted chickpeas
1 tablespoon olive oil
1 tablespoon maple syrup
2 teaspoons chili powder
1 teaspoon smoked paprika
1 teaspoon salt

Storing Roasted Chickpeas

Once the roasted chickpeas have cooled completely, place them into an airtight container and store for 3–4 days.

Preheat the oven to 375°F.

Toss chickpeas with the olive oil, maple syrup, chili powder, smoked paprika, and salt.

Place in a single layer on a greased or parchment paper–lined baking sheet.

Roast for 35–45 minutes until the chickpeas are toasted and crunchy.

Cool before serving.

PER SERVING | Calories: 91 | Fat: 3 g | Protein: 4 g | Sodium: 300 mg | Fiber: 3 g | Carbohydrates: 13 g | Sugar: 4 g

Cinnamon Sugar Roasted Chickpeas

Do you find yourself reaching for sweet snacks in the afternoon or after dinner?
Try these roasted chickpeas for a healthy and sweet new treat.

INGREDIENTS | YIELDS 2 CUPS

2 cups sprouted chickpeas
1 tablespoon safflower oil
2 tablespoons sugar
1 teaspoon cinnamon
½ teaspoon salt

Mix It Up

Want a little more flavor in your afternoon snack? Make a healthier trail mix by tossing these sweet roasted chickpeas with dried cherries, sliced almonds, and a sprinkle of chocolate chips.

Preheat the oven to 375°F.

Toss chickpeas with safflower oil, sugar, cinnamon, and salt.

Place in a single layer on a greased or parchment paper–lined baking sheet.

Roast chickpeas for 35–45 minutes until they are toasted and crunchy.

Cool before serving.

PER SERVING | Calories: 93 | Fat: 3 g | Protein: 4 g | Sodium: 144 mg | Fiber: 3 g | Carbohydrates: 14 g | Sugar: 5 g

Chickpea, Tomato, and Olive Spread

A touch of brightness from the lemon zest gives this spread a light flavor when paired with the tomatoes and olives.

INGREDIENTS | SERVES 6

1 cup sprouted chickpeas
¼ cup sun-dried tomatoes
¼ cup pitted olives
1 teaspoon lemon zest
½ teaspoon salt
½ teaspoon pepper
1 tablespoon olive oil
Garlic Toast (see sidebar recipe)

Garlic Toast

Since this spread can be served chilled or at room temperature, it makes for a great appetizer for dinners or parties. Take 1 large baguette and slice into 1" slices. Pre-heat the oven to 350°F, place the sliced bread on a baking sheet, and bake for 7–10 minutes until the edges are crispy and the bread is warmed through. Remove from the oven and rub each piece with a halved clove of garlic. Drizzle the bread with olive oil.

Place chickpeas, sun-dried tomatoes, olives, lemon zest, salt, and pepper in the bowl of a food processor.

Pulse until the vegetables are chopped and mixed together.

While the food processor is running, stream in the olive oil.

Once everything is combined, scrape into a bowl and chill until ready to serve.

Top each toast with olive spread.

PER SERVING | Calories: 225 | Fat: 6 g | Protein: 8 g | Sodium: 599 mg | Fiber: 3 g | Carbohydrates: 35 g | Sugar: 3 g

Maple Roasted Vegetables with Chickpeas

Most roasted vegetable dishes typically stick with the same options: onions, peppers, potatoes. This blend of hearty fall vegetables is a delicious mix of colors, flavors, and textures.

INGREDIENTS | SERVES 6

1 medium sweet yellow onion

1 medium red onion

½ pound carrots

½ medium butternut squash

2 medium sweet potatoes

2 cups sprouted chickpeas

2 tablespoons olive oil

2 tablespoons maple syrup

2 teaspoons dried rosemary

2 teaspoons salt

1 teaspoon pepper

Veggies for Dinner

Since this mix of roasted vegetables is full of hearty options with fiber and protein, these would make a delicious fall dinner alongside a green salad and some rice or couscous. You could also toss the roasted vegetables with some whole-wheat pasta and fresh cheese.

Preheat the oven to 425°F.

Peel the onions, carrots, butternut squash, and sweet potatoes. Cut the onions, sweet potatoes, carrots, and butternut squash into 1"–2" pieces, making sure that all the vegetables are about the same size.

Toss the vegetables and chickpeas with the olive oil and maple syrup. Stir the rosemary, salt, and pepper into the vegetable mixture.

Roast the vegetables, uncovered, for 40–50 minutes, stirring twice during the cooking time, until the vegetables are browned and tender.

PER SERVING | Calories: 230 | Fat: 6 g | Protein: 6 g | Sodium: 820 mg | Fiber: 6 g | Carbohydrates: 40 g | Sugar: 12 g

Herbed Chickpea, Onion, and Tomato Salad

When people hear "onion and tomato salad," they almost always think of cucumbers. This twist on a fresh vegetable salad adds in creamy chickpeas and a sweet and salty dressing that is perfect on a warm summer day.

INGREDIENTS | SERVES 4

1 cup sprouted chickpeas
½ medium red onion, thinly sliced
2 medium tomatoes, halved and diced
2 tablespoons olive oil
2 teaspoons balsamic vinegar
1 teaspoon brown sugar
1 teaspoon salt
½ teaspoon pepper
¼ cup fresh parsley, chopped
¼ cup fresh basil, chopped

Toss the chickpeas with the sliced red onion and diced tomatoes in a medium bowl.

In a small dish, whisk the olive oil, balsamic vinegar, brown sugar, salt, and pepper together.

Pour the dressing over the chickpea salad and toss to combine.

Stir the chopped parsley and basil into the salad.

Let the salad sit at room temperature for 30 minutes before serving.

PER SERVING | Calories: 163 | Fat: 8 g | Protein: 4 g | Sodium: 586 mg | Fiber: 4 g | Carbohydrates: 19 g | Sugar: 7 g

The Older, the Better

Balsamic vinegar is one of those items that gets better with age. True aged balsamic vinegar has a texture closer to that of a syrup and has a sweet quality to it that most vinegars lack. You can simmer regular balsamic vinegar and let it reduce to a syrupy texture to use in your recipes, although the result won't be quite the same as the aged varieties.

Spiced Bulgur and Chickpeas

The crunch from the almonds paired with the fluffy bulgur and creamy chickpeas gives this salad a texture that will keep you coming back for more.

INGREDIENTS | SERVES 6

1½ cups water

1 cup bulgur wheat

1 teaspoon salt

1 cup sprouted chickpeas

½ cup slivered almonds

1 teaspoon garam masala

1 teaspoon ground coriander

½ teaspoon turmeric

½ teaspoon mint

¼ teaspoon cayenne pepper

¼ teaspoon ginger

2 tablespoons coconut oil

Bring water to a boil in a medium saucepan. Place bulgur and salt in a heatproof bowl and pour the water over the bulgur. Cover the bowl and let it sit for 15–20 minutes until the liquid is absorbed.

Stir the chickpeas, slivered almonds, garam masala, coriander, turmeric, mint, cayenne pepper, ginger, and coconut oil into the bulgur.

Serve warm or at room temperature.

PER SERVING | Calories: 160 | Fat: 9 g | Protein: 5 g | Sodium: 387 mg | Fiber: 4 g | Carbohydrates: 15 g | Sugar: 2 g

Garam Masala

Similar to curry powders, the actual mix of spices in garam masala can differ between areas and producers. Even among the small variations, a typical garam masala mix will contain pepper, cloves, cumin, cardamom, nutmeg, coriander, and star anise.

Chickpea and Rice Soup

Next time you're feeling under the weather, put this soup on the stovetop to make you feel better. A twist on chicken and rice soup, this version is perfect for vegetarians (and vegans, depending on the broth you use) and adds in nutrient-rich brown rice for an extra punch of fiber.

INGREDIENTS | SERVES 6

2 tablespoons olive oil

1 medium onion, diced

3 celery stalks, diced

3 carrots, sliced

2 cloves garlic, minced

5 cups chicken or vegetable broth

1 cup water

1 bay leaf

1 teaspoon salt

½ teaspoon pepper

½ cup quick-cooking brown rice

1½ cups sprouted chickpeas

½ cup fresh parsley, chopped

Heat oil in a large pot over medium heat.

Add onion, celery, and carrots; cook for 5–7 minutes until the vegetables are softened. Stir in the garlic and cook another minute until fragrant.

Add the broth, water, bay leaf, salt, and pepper to the pot and bring to a boil.

Stir the rice and chickpeas into the pot and return to a boil. Lower the heat to a simmer and cook for 7–10 minutes, until rice is tender.

Add the fresh parsley and serve warm.

PER SERVING | Calories: 197 | Fat: 6 g | Protein: 8 g | Sodium: 901 mg | Fiber: 5 g | Carbohydrates: 28 g | Sugar: 4 g

Cinnamon Chickpea Peanut Butter Spread

What might seem like an unusual mix of ingredients turns into a creamy and delicious dip after a quick whir in the food processor. Using a mix of peanut butter and chickpeas gives you the great flavor you want but with fewer calories and more health benefits.

INGREDIENTS | SERVES 8

½ cup sprouted chickpeas

½ cup peanut butter

1 tablespoon neutral oil (like safflower or canola)

½ teaspoon cinnamon

½ teaspoon vanilla extract

¼ teaspoon salt

Healthy Dippers

Even though this peanut butter spread has a sneaky healthy addition, it will still give you the great peanut butter flavor with your favorite dippers. Carrots, sliced apples, and celery are delicious options, but the spread is also a fun way to sneak in veggies on toast at breakfast.

Place all ingredients into the bowl of a food processor.

Pulse the mixture until the chickpeas are broken down and the mixture is smooth and creamy.

Pour into a bowl and refrigerate until ready to eat. Store in the refrigerator.

PER SERVING | Calories: 126 | Fat: 10 g | Protein: 5 g | Sodium: 145 mg | Fiber: 2 g | Carbohydrates: 6 g | Sugar: 2 g

Sprout Medley Salad with Green Goddess Dressing

This is a delicious fresh salad to start your meal. The dressing is delicious with finely chopped fresh herbs blended in, such as dill, chives, cilantro, or basil—use whatever herbs you like or have on hand.

INGREDIENTS | SERVES 2

2 tablespoons Tahini

2 tablespoons lemon juice

1 tablespoon nama shoyu

¼ cup olive oil

½ clove garlic, minced

½ teaspoon salt

¾ cup water

1 cup green sunflower sprouts

2 cups microgreen sprouts (alfalfa, clover, broccoli, arugula, cabbage, cress, and radish sprouts)

1 cup sprouted chickpeas

½ cup celery hearts, diced

½ cup red cabbage, shredded fine

Microgreen Sprouts

Microgreens start as tiny seeds and grow into little plants in a few days. They are high in protein, antioxidants, enzymes, vitamins, and phytonutrients. For this recipe you can use a mixture of microsprout varieties. Soak them for 8–12 hours and sprout for 2–3 days.

To make the salad dressing, blend together the Tahini and lemon juice. Gradually add the nama shoyu, olive oil, garlic, salt, and water.

Rinse the sunflower sprouts and arrange them in salad bowls. Top with the microgreen sprouts, sprouted chickpeas, diced celery hearts, and shredded red cabbage.

Drizzle the dressing over the salad and serve.

PER SERVING | Calories: 434 | Fat: 13 g | Protein: 23 g | Sodium: 1,086 mg | Fiber: 21 g | Carbohydrates: 62 g | Sugar: 12 g

CHAPTER 14

Sprouted Lentils Recipes

Lentil Pizza Salad

Lentils and pizza aren't two words normally associated with each other. But this salad takes all the great flavors of pizza and mixes them together with heart-healthy and filling lentils.

INGREDIENTS | SERVES 4

2 tablespoons olive oil, divided
1 red bell pepper, diced
½ medium red onion, diced
2 cloves garlic, minced
1 cup sprouted lentils
¼ cup vegetable broth
1 cup cherry tomatoes, halved
4 ounces fresh mozzarella, diced
1 tablespoon oregano
1 tablespoon parsley
1 tablespoon basil
1 teaspoon salt
½ teaspoon pepper

Pizza on Pizza

Want to try this salad on an actual pizza? Lentils are a fantastic source of protein and make a great pizza topping. Just spread a layer of olive oil on your favorite pizza dough, layer on the lentil salad, and bake until the cheese is melted.

Heat pan over medium heat and add 1 tablespoon of the olive oil.

Sauté the red pepper, red onion, and garlic for 3–4 minutes, stirring occasionally until the vegetables are softened and the garlic is fragrant.

Stir the lentils and broth into the vegetables and cover the pan. Simmer for 5 minutes, covered.

Take the pan off the heat and pour the lentils and vegetables into a large bowl. Let the lentil mixture cool for 5 minutes.

Toss the lentils with the cherry tomatoes, diced mozzarella, oregano, parsley, basil, 1 tablespoon olive oil, salt, and pepper. Serve warm or at room temperature.

PER SERVING | Calories: 148 | Fat: 7 g | Protein: 5 g | Sodium: 737 mg | Fiber: 2 g | Carbohydrates: 18 g | Sugar: 4 g

Sprouted Lentil Pasta Salad

While most pasta salads are served as side dishes, the protein from the lentils makes this dish filling enough to serve as a main dish and is a great option for dinner or a weekday lunch.

INGREDIENTS | SERVES 6

6 cups water

1 pound sprouted whole-wheat pasta

2 tablespoons salt

2 tablespoons olive oil

1 onion, diced

1 clove garlic, minced

1 (15-ounce) can crushed tomatoes

1 cup sprouted lentils

2 tablespoons butter

¼ cup fresh parsley, chopped

2 tablespoons fresh oregano, chopped

½ cup pitted olives, chopped

½ cup fresh Parmesan cheese, grated

Sprouted-Grain Pasta

Most sprouted-grain pastas on the market are a mix of different grains, which gives the pasta a balanced flavor and texture. Sprouted-grain pasta normally needs less cooking time than regular wheat pasta, so make sure to watch it carefully and not overcook.

Bring 6 cups of water to a boil, and add the pasta and salt. Stirring occasionally, simmer for 6–8 minutes or until the pasta is al dente. Drain and set aside.

While the pasta is cooking, heat a pan over medium heat and add the olive oil. Sauté the onion and garlic for 2–3 minutes until they are softened and fragrant.

Stir the tomatoes, lentils, and butter into the onion and garlic, and cook on low for 10 minutes.

Remove the sauce from the heat and stir in the parsley, oregano, and olives.

Toss pasta with the sauce and top with Parmesan before serving.

PER SERVING | Calories: 443 | Fat: 13 g | Protein: 18 g | Sodium: 1,017 mg | Fiber: 2 g | Carbohydrates: 70 g | Sugar: <1 g

Curried Lentils with Cilantro Rice

Curries are usually made or served with coconut milk or yogurt to help temper the heat of the spices and peppers used in most recipes. While this curry isn't very hot, a dollop of yogurt helps balance the flavors and gives a nice cooling effect to the warm spices in the lentils.

INGREDIENTS | SERVES 4

2 cups water

1½ cups brown rice

1 tablespoon plus 1 teaspoon salt, divided

½ cup fresh cilantro

2 tablespoons olive oil

1 medium onion, diced

1 clove garlic, minced

1" piece of ginger, minced (about 2 teaspoons)

2 tablespoons tomato paste

1 teaspoon curry powder

1 teaspoon turmeric

1 teaspoon cumin

1 teaspoon salt

½ teaspoon paprika

¼ teaspoon cayenne

¼ teaspoon cinnamon

1½ cups sprouted lentils

1 cup chickpeas

½ cup vegetable broth

1 tablespoon lemon juice

A Note on Curry

Curry powder isn't just one spice; it's actually a ground mixture of spices that is traditionally used in curry dishes. Although curry mixes differ depending on the region and producer, most include turmeric, coriander, cumin, fenugreek, and red pepper and can also have ginger, garlic, fennel seed, caraway, cinnamon, cardamom, and black pepper.

In a medium saucepan, bring water to a boil. Stir in rice and 1 tablespoon salt and cover. Simmer the rice for 25–30 minutes until the water has been absorbed and the rice is fluffy. Remove from the heat, stir in the cilantro, and keep warm.

Place a large skillet over medium heat and add the olive oil. Cook the onion, stirring frequently, for 5–10 minutes until it is beginning to caramelize.

Stir the garlic and ginger into the onion, cooking for 2–3 minutes until fragrant.

Add the tomato paste, curry powder, turmeric, cumin, 1 teaspoon salt, paprika, cayenne, and cinnamon. Cook, stirring, for 2–3 minutes until the tomato paste is coating the onions.

Stir the lentils, chickpeas, and broth into the pan and bring to a low simmer. Let the mixture cook, simmering on low, for 5–10 minutes until the broth has cooked down and the mixture has thickened.

Remove the pan from the heat and stir the lemon juice into the lentils.

Serve lentils over cilantro rice with extra cilantro on top.

PER SERVING | Calories: 480 | Fat: 10 g | Protein: 15 g | Sodium: 2,633 mg | Fiber: 7 g | Carbohydrates: 85 g | Sugar: 5 g

Sprouted Lentil Tacos

Tacos are an easy dinner meal for most people. Swapping out the usual ground meat or chicken for iron-rich lentils still gives you the protein you're looking for while adding extra fiber and nutrients.

INGREDIENTS | SERVES 4

1 tablespoon olive oil
1 medium onion, thinly sliced
1 clove garlic, minced
2 tablespoons tomato paste
1½ cups sprouted lentils
1 tablespoon chili powder
1 tablespoon cumin
2 teaspoons smoked paprika
2 teaspoons salt
½ teaspoon pepper
½ cup water
8 tortillas (corn or flour)
2 cups shredded lettuce
½ cup chopped tomatoes
½ cup shredded cheese
½ cup sour cream
Quick Guacamole (see sidebar recipe)

Place a pan over medium heat and add the olive oil.

Sauté the onion in the olive oil for 4–5 minutes until the slices are softened and beginning to brown.

Add the garlic to the onion and cook for another minute.

Stir the tomato paste into the onion and garlic, and cook for 1–2 minutes until the onions are coated with the tomato paste.

Pour the lentils, chili powder, cumin, smoked paprika, salt, pepper, and water into the pan and bring to a simmer. Cook the lentils for 5–10 minutes until the water has reduced into a thick sauce with the lentils.

To serve, place a layer of lentils in a tortilla and top with lettuce, tomatoes, cheese, sour cream, and Quick Guacamole.

PER SERVING | Calories: 527 | Fat: 30 g | Protein: 28 g | Sodium: 2,034 mg | Fiber: 10 g | Carbohydrates: 55 g | Sugar: 7 g

Quick Guacamole

For a fast and fresh guacamole, mash 2 ripe avocados in a medium bowl. Stir 1 minced garlic clove, 2 tablespoons sliced scallions, ¼ cup chopped fresh cilantro, 1 teaspoon salt, 1 teaspoon cumin, and 1 teaspoon lime juice into the avocados. Dollop on tacos or serve with tortilla chips and sliced veggies on the side.

Greek Lentil Salad

The Mediterranean diet is one that is based on heart-healthy grains, vegetables, proteins, and fats. Olive oil lends a rich flavor to the salad, and the naturally salty olives and feta mean you don't have to add as much salt to the dish as you would otherwise.

INGREDIENTS | SERVES 6

2 cups sprouted lentils

4 ounces feta cheese, crumbled

½ cup pitted olives, chopped

1 cup cherry tomatoes, halved

½ cup roasted red peppers, diced

¼ cup fresh parsley, chopped

¼ cup fresh oregano, chopped

¼ cup fresh lemon juice

¼ cup olive oil

1 tablespoon fresh lemon zest

1 teaspoon salt

½ teaspoon pepper

In a large bowl, toss the sprouted lentils with the feta cheese, chopped olives, chopped tomatoes, roasted red peppers, parsley, and oregano.

Add the lemon juice, olive oil, lemon zest, salt, and pepper; gently stir to combine.

Let the salad chill, covered, in the refrigerator for 30 minutes.

Serve chilled.

PER SERVING | Calories: 218 | Fat: 15 g | Protein: 8 g | Sodium: 705 mg | Fiber: 1 g | Carbohydrates: 17 g | Sugar: 2 g

Roasting Peppers at Home

The roasted peppers you can buy in the store are much more expensive than buying your own fresh peppers at the market, and it's easy to roast them in your own kitchen. Preheat the oven to 400°F and place the peppers on a large baking sheet. Roast for 45 minutes to 1 hour, turning them on the pan every 15 minutes until the skins are dark and roasted. When the skins are cooked, remove them from the oven and cover the pan and peppers with a sheet of foil and let them cool. Peel the skins and use as directed in the recipe.

Sausage, Swiss Chard, and Lentil Bake

Lentils themselves have an earthy flavor that makes a delicious base for soups and casseroles. This hearty dish is full of spicy sausage and winter greens, and is a warming dinner for a cool winter night.

INGREDIENTS | SERVES 4

2 teaspoons olive oil

½ pound Italian pork or turkey sausage, casing removed

1 medium onion, diced

1 clove garlic, minced

2 cups Swiss chard, finely chopped

1½ cups sprouted lentils

¾ cup vegetable broth

1 cup diced tomatoes

1 tablespoon oregano

1 tablespoon parsley

1 teaspoon salt

½ teaspoon pepper

¾ cup mozzarella cheese, shredded

Preheat the oven to 350°F.

Place a large sauté pan over medium heat and add the olive oil. Add the sausage and onion; cook, stirring to break up the sausage, for 5 minutes until the onion is softened.

Add the garlic and Swiss chard and cook, stirring occasionally, for 5–10 minutes until the chard is beginning to wilt.

Stir the lentils, broth, tomatoes, oregano, parsley, salt, and pepper into the sausage. Pour the mixture into a greased 9" × 13" baking dish and top with the shredded mozzarella.

Bake for 25–35 minutes until the casserole is heated through and the cheese is melted and browned.

PER SERVING | Calories: 230 | Fat: 11 g | Protein: 21 g | Sodium: 1,314 mg | Fiber: 1 g | Carbohydrates: 12 g | Sugar: 2 g

Preshredded or Block Cheese?

While preshredded cheese is definitely more convenient, shredding your own will give you better melting and browning results when you cook with it. Bagged and shredded cheese are often treated with other ingredients and sometimes tossed with cornstarch or flour, which makes it harder for the cheese to melt and brown on dishes like casseroles or pizza. If you're looking for a nice cheesy crust, it's worth the work to grate your own cheese.

Coconut Red Curry and Lentil Soup

Green, brown, and red lentils can typically be traded out in any recipe, depending on the type you have on hand. For soups and stews, red lentils break down more than the other varieties, which lends a creamier and smoother texture for soups.

INGREDIENTS | SERVES 6

2 tablespoons coconut oil

1" piece of fresh ginger, minced (about 2 teaspoons)

½ cup scallions, sliced

2 carrots, sliced

1 tablespoon red curry paste

2 tablespoons tomato paste

2 teaspoons turmeric

2 teaspoons salt

1 cup sprouted green lentils

1 cup red lentils

1 (14-ounce) can coconut milk

4 cups water

¼ cup fresh cilantro, chopped

Red Curry Paste

Red curry paste is something you can make at home, but it does require a good deal of ingredients and spices. If you can't find things like fresh lemongrass, Thai chiles, shrimp paste, or fish sauce in stores near you, buying the premade curry paste is the best option. It keeps well in the fridge and will last through a few recipes.

Heat a large pot over medium heat and add the coconut oil.

Once the coconut oil is melted, toss the fresh ginger, scallions, and carrots into the pot and cook, stirring, for 5–10 minutes until the carrots begin to soften and the ginger is fragrant.

Stir the red curry paste, tomato paste, turmeric, and salt into the vegetables until the carrots, ginger, and scallions are coated.

Pour in the green lentils, red lentils, coconut milk, and water. Bring mixture to a boil and simmer for 30–45 minutes until the soup has thickened and the lentils and carrots are tender.

Serve with fresh cilantro.

PER SERVING | Calories: 285 | Fat: 19 g | Protein: 9 g | Sodium: 1,080 mg | Fiber: 7 g | Carbohydrates: 24 g | Sugar: 4 g

Lentil Enchilada Casserole

Since lentils have a subtle flavor of their own, using them in Mexican-spiced recipes transforms them into a dish where lentils wouldn't normally be used.

INGREDIENTS | SERVES 8

1 tablespoon olive oil

½ cup scallions, sliced (about 4–5)

1½ cups sprouted red lentils

2 cups vegetable broth

2 cups kale, finely chopped

3½ cups green enchilada sauce, divided

2 cloves garlic, minced

1 tablespoon cumin

1 tablespoon chili powder

2 teaspoons smoked paprika

2 teaspoons salt

1 (8-ounce) jar picante sauce or salsa

16 corn tortillas, cut into quarters (or see homemade recipe in sidebar)

1 cup queso fresco, shredded

Homemade Corn Tortillas

To make your own corn tortillas, you only need three ingredients: 2 cups masa harina, 1 teaspoon salt, and 2 cups hot water. Mix the masa and salt, and stir in the water until everything comes together. Let the dough sit for 30 minutes, then roll it into 2"–3" rounds. Flatten each round between parchment paper with a tortilla press or a rolling pin. Cook each tortilla for 2–3 minutes on each side in a skillet over medium heat, flipping once.

Preheat the oven to 375°F.

Heat oil in a large skillet over medium heat and add the scallions. Cook for 2–3 minutes until they are softened.

Add the lentils and broth to the pan, and bring to a simmer. Cook for 10 minutes.

Stir in the chopped kale, 1 cup of the enchilada sauce, garlic, cumin, chili powder, smoked paprika, salt, and picante sauce.

Let the lentil and kale mixture simmer for another 5–10 minutes until the kale starts to wilt and most of the liquid has been absorbed.

In the bottom of a greased 9" × 13" pan, pour ½ cup of the remaining enchilada sauce and top with ⅓ of the tortilla pieces.

Pour ½ of the lentil mixture on top of the tortillas. Add another layer of enchilada sauce, tortillas, and the rest of the lentil mixture. Top with the remaining tortilla pieces, and pour the rest of the enchilada sauce over the top.

Sprinkle the queso fresco on top of the casserole and bake for 30–35 minutes until the cheese is melted.

PER SERVING (filling with 2 Homemade Corn Tortillas) | Calories: 273 | Fat: 8 g | Protein: 10 g | Sodium: 2,271 mg | Fiber: 3 g | Carbohydrates: 42 g | Sugar: 10 g

Spiced Salmon with Lentils

Leeks have a mild and timid flavor that provides depth to any dish you use them in. Before adding leeks to your pan, make sure to clean them thoroughly, however. Leeks are grown in sandier soil and need to be swished around in cold water after slicing to remove the dirt and sand.

INGREDIENTS | SERVES 4

¼ pound bacon, diced

2 leeks, sliced and rinsed

2 carrots, sliced

2 cloves garlic, minced

1½ cups sprouted lentils

2 cups vegetable broth

1 cup crushed tomatoes

1 bay leaf

1 tablespoon parsley

3 teaspoons salt, divided

1½ teaspoons pepper, divided

1 teaspoon dried thyme

1 pound salmon, cut into 4 portions

1 teaspoon cumin

1 teaspoon ground coriander

1 teaspoon smoked paprika

2 tablespoons olive oil

Sustainable Salmon

When looking for salmon, choose wild-caught Alaskan salmon whenever possible. It is considered the best choice and is certified as sustainable.

In a medium saucepan over medium-high heat, cook the diced bacon until brown and crisp, stirring occasionally. Remove the bacon from the pan.

Add the leeks and carrots to the bacon fat and cook for 3–4 minutes until softened. Stir in the garlic and cook for another minute until fragrant.

Stir the lentils, broth, tomatoes, bay leaf, parsley, 2 teaspoons salt, 1 teaspoon pepper, and thyme into the vegetables and bring to a boil. Lower the heat and simmer for 15 minutes.

While the lentils are cooking, set a cast-iron pan (or other frying pan) over medium heat. Season the salmon with the cumin, coriander, smoked paprika, 1 teaspoon salt, and ½ teaspoon pepper.

Add the olive oil to the cast-iron pan and place the salmon in, skin side down. Sear for 3–4 minutes before flipping. Cook for another 1–2 minutes, depending on how done you like your salmon.

Serve salmon over lentils.

PER SERVING | Calories: 326 | Fat: 15 g | Protein: 30 g | Sodium: 1,209 mg | Fiber: 3 g | Carbohydrates: 20 g | Sugar: 3 g

Smoky Lentil Dip

Lentils will break down easily on their own, but adding the cannellini beans and olive oil help this dip purée into a super smooth and creamy dip.

INGREDIENTS | SERVES 8

1½ cups sprouted lentils

1 cup cannellini beans, drained and rinsed

2 tablespoons olive oil

1 clove garlic, minced

2 teaspoons salt

1½ teaspoons smoked paprika

1½ teaspoons cumin

Garlic Herb Toasted Pita Chips (see sidebar recipe)

Garlic Herb Toasted Pita Chips

To make Garlic Herb Toasted Pita Chips, preheat the oven to 350°F. Take four to six whole-wheat or sprouted-grain pitas and cut into quarters. Brush each piece with olive oil and sprinkle with garlic powder, dried oregano, salt, and pepper. Bake on a cookie sheet for 8–12 minutes until the chips are toasted.

Place lentils, cannellini beans, olive oil, garlic, and spices in the bowl of a food processor.

Pulse the mixture until the lentils and beans are broken down and the mixture is creamy, streaming in more olive oil if needed.

Serve chilled or at room temperature with crackers, Garlic Herb Toasted Pita Chips, celery, and carrots.

PER SERVING | Calories: 166 | Fat: 5 g | Protein: 6 g | Sodium: 810 mg | Fiber: 3 g | Carbohydrates: 25 g | Sugar: 1 g

Triple Lentil Soup

Most lentil soups are only made with one type of lentil. Using brown, green, and red lentils gives this soup a true lentil flavor and shows off the textures of each type.

INGREDIENTS | SERVES 6

2 tablespoons olive oil

2 leeks, sliced and rinsed

1 medium onion, diced

2 carrots, diced

3 celery stalks, diced

2 cloves garlic, minced

1 cup sprouted brown lentils

1 cup sprouted green lentils

1 cup sprouted red lentils

5 cups vegetable broth

1 (15-ounce) can diced tomatoes

1 cup red wine

1 bay leaf

1 tablespoon fresh thyme

2 teaspoons cumin

2 teaspoons salt

1 teaspoon pepper

Heat the olive oil in a large pot over medium heat and add the leeks, onion, carrots, and celery. Cook the vegetables for 5–6 minutes until they have softened. Add the garlic and cook for another minute until fragrant.

Stir the lentils, broth, tomatoes, red wine, bay leaf, thyme, cumin, salt, and pepper into the vegetables, and bring the soup to a boil.

Lower the heat and simmer for 20–30 minutes until the red lentils have broken down and the brown and green lentils are tender.

Remove the bay leaf from the pot and serve.

PER SERVING | Calories: 164 | Fat: 5 g | Protein: 5 g | Sodium: 1,285 mg | Fiber: 2 g | Carbohydrates: 21 g | Sugar: 5 g

Roasted Carrot, Pear, and Lentil Salad

This salad is full of fall flavors, textures, and colors. Try starting a new holiday tradition by bringing new dishes like this one to family gatherings for everyone to sample.

INGREDIENTS | SERVES 4

2 medium pears

4 medium carrots

1 medium red onion

2 tablespoons olive oil

1 tablespoon maple syrup

2 teaspoons salt

½ teaspoon pepper

1 cup sprouted lentils

¼ cup dried cranberries

¼ cup fresh parsley

1 tablespoon fresh rosemary

The Right Pear

When choosing pears to use for this salad, pick two that are medium-ripe. Since you'll be roasting the fruit, you don't want ones that are too soft or they'll break down in the high heat of the oven.

Preheat the oven to 425°F.

Chop pears, carrots, and onion into 1" pieces and toss with olive oil, maple syrup, salt, and pepper. Spread out on a baking sheet lined with parchment paper and roast for 35–45 minutes, stirring every 15 minutes.

Once the pears and vegetables are roasted, pour them into a large bowl.

Toss lentils, cranberries, parsley, and rosemary with the pears and vegetables.

Serve warm or at room temperature.

PER SERVING | Calories: 221 | Fat: 7 g | Protein: 3 g | Sodium: 1,215 mg | Fiber: 6 g | Carbohydrates: 40 g | Sugar: 23 g

Cranberry, Bacon, and Lentil Rice Pilaf

The more flavorful the bacon, the deeper the flavor will be in this pilaf. If you can, find locally made bacon or the thickest cut you can get. Seasoned bacon like cracked pepper is also a good option.

INGREDIENTS | SERVES 4

¼ pound bacon, diced
1 medium onion, diced
2 cloves garlic, minced
1 cup quick-cooking brown rice
1 cup sprouted lentils
2½ cups vegetable broth
½ cup dried cranberries
¼ cup fresh parsley, diced
1 tablespoon apple cider vinegar
2 tablespoons olive oil
2 teaspoons salt
½ teaspoon pepper

Leave the Bacon, Keep the Smoke

If you'd rather not use the bacon, leave it out of the recipe and instead add 1 table-spoon more olive oil for richness and ½ teaspoon liquid smoke to replicate the flavor.

Heat a large saucepan over medium heat and cook the diced bacon until crisp. Remove the bacon from the pan and set aside.

Add the onion and garlic to the bacon fat and cook, stirring frequently, for 5–6 minutes until the onions are softened and the garlic is fragrant.

Stir the brown rice, lentils, and broth into the onions and garlic, and bring the mixture to a boil. Let the lentils and rice simmer, covered, for 10–15 minutes until the rice is tender.

Toss the cranberries, parsley, vinegar, olive oil, salt, and pepper into the rice and lentils. Add the diced bacon and serve warm.

PER SERVING | Calories: 354 | Fat: 2 g | Protein: 8 g | Sodium: 1,706 mg | Fiber: 3 g | Carbohydrates: 56 g | Sugar: 11 g

Pasta with Lentils, Mushrooms, and Goat Cheese

Don't get stuck in a pasta rut. Tomato sauce isn't the only topping option! This rustic mix of flavors showcases the earthy lentils, meaty mushrooms, and tangy goat cheese, and is hearty enough to serve as a main dish.

INGREDIENTS | SERVES 6

6 cups water

1 pound whole-wheat shell pasta

1 tablespoon plus 1 teaspoon salt, divided

4 tablespoons olive oil, divided

1 tablespoon butter

1 pound cremini mushrooms, sliced

1 cup sprouted lentils

½ cup goat cheese, crumbled

¼ cup fresh parsley, chopped

2 teaspoons thyme

½ teaspoon pepper

2 tablespoons olive oil

Bring water to a boil and stir in the pasta and 1 tablespoon salt. Cook the pasta for 8–10 minutes until al dente. Drain and set aside.

While the pasta is cooking, set a pan over medium heat and add 2 tablespoons olive oil and butter.

Toss the sliced mushrooms into the pan with the oil and butter, and cook for 2–3 minutes before turning. Brown the mushrooms on both sides.

Stir the mushrooms, lentils, goat cheese, parsley, thyme, 1 teaspoon salt, and pepper into the hot pasta.

Drizzle with 2 tablespoons olive oil before serving.

PER SERVING | Calories: 441 | Fat: 15 g | Protein: 18 g | Sodium: 602 mg | Fiber: 1 g | Carbohydrates: 64 g | Sugar: 2 g

How to Clean Mushrooms

Bringing mushrooms home from the market means you'll always have the step of cleaning them before cooking. The quickest and easiest way to do this is to dampen a paper towel and brush off the mushrooms over the sink or trash can, knocking off the dirt. Submerging the mushrooms in water can make them soggy if you leave them in too long—the less water to touch the mushrooms, the better their texture will be.

Red Lentil, Couscous, and Kale Soup

Red lentils, as opposed to green and brown, completely break down while cooking, giving this soup a silky base. Adding the couscous and cashews gives it some additional texture and flavor.

INGREDIENTS | SERVES 8

2 tablespoons coconut oil
1 tablespoon olive oil
1 medium onion, diced
3 carrots, sliced
4 celery stalks, sliced
2 cloves garlic, minced
1 tablespoon cumin
1 tablespoon turmeric
2 teaspoons salt
2 tablespoons tomato paste
1½ cups sprouted red lentils
4 cups vegetable broth
½ cup whole-wheat Israeli couscous
4 cups kale, chopped into bite-sized pieces
1 cup light coconut milk
¼ cup fresh cilantro, chopped
¼ cup cashews, chopped

In a large pot, heat coconut oil and olive oil over medium heat until the coconut oil is melted.

Add onion, carrots, celery, and garlic; cook until softened, stirring occasionally.

Stir in the cumin, turmeric, salt, and tomato paste; cook for 1–2 minutes until fragrant.

Add in the lentils and vegetable broth, and bring to a boil. Reduce heat to medium and cook for 15 minutes.

Stir in couscous and kale, and cook for 10–15 minutes more or until lentils and couscous are cooked.

Turn off the heat and stir in the coconut milk and fresh cilantro. Serve topped with chopped cashews.

PER SERVING | Calories: 226 | Fat: 14 g | Protein: 6 g | Sodium: 974 mg | Fiber: 3 g | Carbohydrates: 24 g | Sugar: 4 g

Did You Know?

Cashew nuts are actually a seed that grows on the bottom of the cashew fruit, which is native to Central American countries. The cashew fruit is not popular in the United States, but the fruit and fruit juice are very popular in Central America.

Curried Butternut Squash, Apple, and Red Lentil Soup

Butternut squash, apple, and curry are a classic combination. To keep this soup smooth and rich, red lentils are simmered and the entire pot of soup is blended together before serving.

INGREDIENTS | SERVES 6–8

2 tablespoons olive oil

1 medium onion, diced

2 carrots, sliced

1 medium apple, shredded

2 cups butternut squash, peeled and diced into 1" pieces

2 cups sprouted red lentils

5 cups vegetable broth

1 cup apple cider

2 tablespoons brown sugar

1 tablespoon curry powder

2 teaspoons turmeric

2 teaspoons salt

1 teaspoon pepper

Cherry Nut Relish (see sidebar recipe)

Cherry Nut Relish

Mix together ¼ cup chopped dried cherries, ¼ cup chopped pecans, 2 tablespoons diced red onion, 1 teaspoon honey, and ¼ teaspoon ground ginger.

Heat olive oil over medium heat in a large pot.

Sauté the onion and carrots for 5–6 minutes until they are softened.

Add the apple, butternut squash, lentils, broth, apple cider, brown sugar, curry powder, turmeric, salt, and pepper to the pot and bring to a boil.

Let the soup simmer for 30–40 minutes until the lentils have broken down and the butternut squash is tender.

In batches, carefully purée the soup in a blender, or directly in the pot with an immersion blender, until the soup is smooth.

Serve warm with a spoon of relish on top.

PER SERVING | Calories: 192 | Fat: 7 g | Protein: 3 g | Sodium: 991 mg | Fiber: 2 g | Carbohydrates: 32 g | Sugar: 14 g

Lentil and Rice Cakes

These cakes can serve as the base for your protein, as a twist on a grain side dish, or as the main dish for your meal. They're delicious on top of a salad or topped with salsa or pesto.

INGREDIENTS | SERVES 6

3 tablespoons olive oil, divided
½ medium onion, diced
1 clove garlic, minced
½ cup quick-cooking brown rice
1 cup sprouted red lentils
2 cups water
1 tablespoon oregano
1 tablespoon basil
2 teaspoons salt
1 teaspoon pepper
2 eggs, beaten
¼ cup sprouted-grain bread crumbs
½ cup mozzarella cheese

A New Way to Start the Day

This recipe will make ten to twelve cakes, depending on how much of the mixture you use for each cake. If you have leftovers, reheat two cakes in the oven or toaster oven, top them with some salsa, sautéed greens, and over-easy eggs for a delicious breakfast.

In a medium saucepan, heat 1 tablespoon oil and add the onions. Cook for 3–4 minutes until they are beginning to soften.

Stir in the garlic and cook for another minute until fragrant.

Add the brown rice, lentils, and water to the pot. Bring the mixture to a boil, cover, and lower the heat to a simmer. Let the mixture cook on low for 15–20 minutes until the rice is tender and the lentils begin to break down.

Remove the pan from the heat and stir in the oregano, basil, salt, and pepper. Pour the mixture into a bowl and add the beaten eggs, bread crumbs, and mozzarella. Let this sit for 10 minutes to allow the rice and lentils to cool.

Heat a skillet over medium heat and add 1–2 teaspoons of oil. Scoop the mixture by ⅓ cup and place into the pan, spreading out to form a round. Cook for 4–5 minutes or until lightly browned. Carefully flip the cakes over and cook for another 3–5 minutes. Remove the cakes from the pan and repeat with the remaining oil and cakes.

Serve warm.

PER SERVING | Calories: 221 | Fat: 12 g | Protein: 9 g |
Sodium: 936 mg | Fiber: 1 g | Carbohydrates: 20 g | Sugar: 1 g

Quick Spicy Lentil Chili

*You can select your favorite onion for this recipe—
red onions, scallions, or sweet onions are all delicious options.*

INGREDIENTS | SERVES 4

½ cup soaked sun-dried tomatoes

1 cup red bell pepper, chopped

2 cups tomatoes, diced

1 clove garlic

1 teaspoon cumin

2 teaspoons chili powder

1 teaspoon oregano

½ teaspoon cayenne pepper

½ teaspoon crushed red pepper

¼ cup onion, diced

1 cup lentils, sprouted 2 days

Soak the sun-dried tomatoes in 2 cups water for 3 hours. Remove tomatoes and save the soak water.

In a blender, blend the sun-dried tomatoes, red bell pepper, 1 cup tomato, garlic, cumin, chili powder, oregano, cayenne, crushed red pepper, and 1 cup of the soak water from the sun-dried tomatoes.

In a large mixing bowl, mix together the prepared sauce, onion, remaining 1 cup tomato, and lentils. The dish will keep for 2 days in the refrigerator.

PER SERVING | Calories: 103 | Fat: 1 g | Protein: 7 g | Sodium: 166 mg | Fiber: 3 g

Lentils

Lentils are a small legume popular in Middle Eastern and Indian cuisine, valued by vegetarians as a good, inexpensive source of protein, fiber, B vitamins, iron, magnesium, and phosphorus. They are one of the first cultivated foods and have been found at archeological sites dating back 8,000 years. Lentils are also described in stories and parables found in the Old Testament of the Bible.

Moroccan Lentil Soup

To speed up prep time, you can use fresh raw almonds and cashews (without soaking them), and sun-dried tomatoes, available marinated in olive oil, which are ready to use when you're ready to cook. This spicy soup is delicious served with couscous.

INGREDIENTS | SERVES 2

½ cup sun-dried tomatoes, soaked

½ cup almonds, soaked

½ cup cashews, soaked

3 cups water

1 cup lentil sprouts

2 tablespoons lemon juice

1 teaspoon cinnamon

1 teaspoon cumin

½ teaspoon salt

½ teaspoon turmeric

1 tablespoon miso (optional)

1 cup portobello or crimini mushrooms, diced

Blend the sun-dried tomatoes, almonds, and cashews with water until smooth. Add in the lentil sprouts, lemon juice, cinnamon, cumin, salt, and turmeric and blend until smooth. As an option, you could add 1 tablespoon miso at this point.

If you want the soup to have a chunky texture, save out ½ cup of the sprouted lentils.

Pour soup into serving bowls and stir in the diced portobello (or reserved ½ cup whole lentil sprouts).

Garnish with fresh cilantro or parsley.

PER SERVING | Calories: 720 | Fat: 30 g | Protein: 38 g | Sodium: 930 mg | Fiber: 36 g | Carbohydrates: 83 g | Sugar: 7 g

Cumin

Cumin is a culinary spice native to Syria, the Middle East, and India. It is a seed with a strong, spicy flavor popular in gourmet cuisine. It is commonly used in spice blends such as curry, chili powder, and garam masala.

Lentil Burgers

These burgers are delicious served on a bun or on top of a fresh summer salad. If you're not a fan of garam masala, you can add in some fresh parsley or another fresh herb that you enjoy.

INGREDIENTS | SERVES 4

1 tablespoon coconut oil

2 cups lentil sprouts

¼ cup flaxseed, ground

¼ cup carrot, shredded

2 tablespoons olive oil

1 clove garlic

1 teaspoon garam masala powder

3 tablespoons lemon juice

¼ cup scallions

Melt the coconut oil by warming it in a bowl or warm water or placing it in the microwave for 15–20 seconds.

Add all ingredients to a food processor with an S blade and process until the ingredients become a chunky paste.

Form the mixture into burger patty shapes. Place them on dehydrator trays and dehydrate at 145°F for 2 hours. Flip over patties and continue dehydrating for 8–12 hours at 110°F. If you don't have a dehydrator, you can also bake these at 325°F on a parchment paper–lined baking sheet for 30–40 minutes, flipping once in the middle of the cook time.

PER SERVING | Calories: 488 | Fat: 15 g | Protein: 27 g | Sodium: 16 mg | Fiber: 32 g | Carbohydrates: 32 g | Sugar: 3 g

Tomato and Almond Stew

This hearty stew requires some advance preparation with the lentils, but it's worth the time. Serve this soup with a sprinkling of chopped parsley and cilantro and some fresh flatbread on the side for dipping.

INGREDIENTS | SERVES 4

1 cup sun-dried tomatoes, soaked

½ cup almonds, soaked

½ cup pine nuts

2 tablespoons olive oil

1 teaspoon salt

½ tablespoon Berber spice

3 cups water

½ cup zucchini, chopped

¼ cup celery, minced

1 cup lentils, sprouted

1 cup tomato, chopped

2 tablespoons lemon juice

Prepare the stew base by blending together the sun-dried tomatoes, almonds, pine nuts, olive oil, salt, Berber spice, and water.

Mix the stew base, vegetables, lentils, and lemon juice together in a large bowl and serve.

PER SERVING | Calories: 434 | Fat: 25 g | Protein: 18 g | Sodium: 688 mg | Fiber: 18 g | Carbohydrates: 38 g | Sugar: 5 g

Ethiopian Cuisine

Ethiopian food is popular in the vegetarian community because it has many meat-free, plant-based meals. Berber is a spice blend commonly used in Ethiopian dishes and is available at most spice stores. Wat is the name for the hearty Ethiopian stew traditionally eaten with sourdough flatbread called injera.

New Orleans "Beans and Rice"

This dish packs your favorite flavors in the classic New Orleans dish,
but it also offers some different texture and more nutritional benefits than the traditional recipe.
If you're not a fan of parsnips, try subbing in cauliflower.

INGREDIENTS | SERVES 2

¼ cup sun-dried tomatoes, soaked

2 tablespoons onion

1 clove garlic

2 tablespoons lemon juice, divided

1½ teaspoons fresh jalapeño pepper

¼ cup red bell peppers

¼ cup celery

½ teaspoon salt

¼ teaspoon black pepper

1 teaspoon thyme

1 cup parsnips, peeled and chopped

½ teaspoon salt

1 cup sprouted lentils

2 slices bacon, cooked and crumbled (optional)

To prepare the sauce, blend together the sun-dried tomatoes, onion, garlic, 1 tablespoon lemon juice, jalapeño, red bell pepper, celery, salt, black pepper, and thyme. Add just enough of the sun-dried tomato soak water to create a thick sauce.

Process the parsnips with ½ teaspoon salt and 1 tablespoon lemon juice in a food processor with the S blade. Using the pulse function, process them just enough to make the mixture look like rice.

Make a bed of parsnip rice on a plate. Pour the sauce on top of the parsnip rice, and sprinkle the sprouted lentils (and bacon, if using) on top.

PER SERVING (WITHOUT BACON) | Calories: 113 | Fat: 1 g | Protein: 5 g | Sodium: 1,188 mg | Fiber: 5 g | Carbohydrates: 26 g | Sugar: 5 g

Parsnips

Parsnips are nutritious root vegetables that are delicious raw. They are good substitutions for starchy foods like rice, pasta noodles, and mashed potatoes. They are in the same family as carrots and are a good source of complex carbohydrates, fiber, potassium, and beta-carotene.

Pecan and Lentil Sprout Loaf

To prepare this recipe in less than 30 minutes, use mung sprouts in place of the homegrown cabbage sprouts. You can use the pecans without soaking them and add ½–1 teaspoon mustard powder.

INGREDIENTS | SERVES 4

½ cup cabbage sprouts, mung sprouts, or other sprouts

1 cup pecans

½ cup sprouted red lentils

1 tablespoon tamari

¼ cup red or white onions, chopped

¼ cup sweet bell pepper, chopped

¼ cup celery hearts, chopped

2 tablespoons fresh parsley

Water for blending

To use cabbage sprouts in this recipe, soak the cabbage seeds for 8–12 hours and sprout them for 3 days.

Soak the pecans for 2–4 hours. Drain and rinse.

Grind the pecans and sprouts together in a food processor with the tamari.

Add the onion, bell pepper, celery, and parsley to the food processor. Briefly process with enough water to help the ingredients stick together in a loaf.

Form the ingredients into a loaf or into croquettes, and dehydrate at 145°F for 2 hours. Then turn down the heat to 110°F and continue dehydrating for 12 hours.

PER SERVING | Calories: 287 | Fat: 20 g | Protein: 10 g | Sodium: 262 mg | Fiber: 10 g | Carbohydrates: 21 g | Sugar: 2 g

Pecan and Herb Dip

Serving this dip rather than the usual ranch dressing will give you a new flavor and texture to enjoy with your vegetables and crackers.

INGREDIENTS | SERVES 2

1½ cups raw pecans

2 tablespoons liquid coconut oil

1 tablespoon Italian seasoning

1 tablespoon miso

½ clove garlic, minced

½ teaspoon salt

1 cup diced fresh vegetable mix (zucchini, red bell pepper, carrots, onion, asparagus tips)

1 cup small sprouts (fenugreek, alfalfa, clover, lentil)

½ cup Tahini

Using the S blade, process the pecans until they break down and begin to stick to the walls of the food processor.

Into the food processor, add the coconut oil, Italian seasoning, miso, minced garlic, and salt with the pecans and process until they are well mixed.

Mix the vegetables and sprouts with ½ cup Tahini. Fold in the pecan mixture until everything is combined.

Garnish with fresh herbs and serve.

PER SERVING | Calories: 543 | Fat: 54 g | Protein: 10 g | Sodium: 490 mg | Fiber: 8 g | Carbohydrates: 15 g | Sugar: 3 g

Fenugreek

Fenugreek has culinary uses as both an herb (the leaves and sprouts) and as a spice (made from the seeds). A nutritious sprout, fenugreek contains about 30 percent protein, iron, niacin, calcium, and vitamin A. This herb has some medicinal uses and is popular as a digestive aid. The seed is a popular spice in Indian cuisine.

Sprout Burgers

If you don't have nama shoyu, you can substitute 1 teaspoon salt,
1 tablespoon miso, Bragg's Liquid Aminos, or regular soy sauce.

INGREDIENTS | SERVES 6

1½ cups sunflower seeds, soaked

2 tablespoons flaxseed, ground

1 cup mixed sprouts (alfalfa, fenugreek, mung, lentil, green pea)

¼ cup red pepper, chopped

¼ cup red or white onion, chopped

4 tablespoons agave nectar

1 clove garlic, minced

1 tablespoon nama shoyu

1 tablespoon Italian seasoning

Nama Shoyu

This is a raw and unpasteurized soy sauce. It has a rich, salty flavor and is delicious with Asian meals. It does contain a little wheat, so it is not appropriate for those with gluten intolerance.

Using a food processor with an S blade, mix all ingredients together. Leave some texture and chunks in the mixture.

Form the mixture into 4–6 burger patties and dehydrate at 110°F for 4 hours. Flip over burgers and continue to dehydrate for 2–4 more hours.

PER SERVING | Calories: 133 | Fat: 8 g | Protein: 3 g | Sodium: 154 mg | Fiber: 2 g | Carbohydrates: 15 g | Sugar: 12 g

Oriental Spring Rolls

This is a great recipe that can be made in less than 30 minutes. These wraps capture the flavor of spring rolls found in Asian restaurants. The wraps can be dipped in nama shoyu, soy sauce, or your favorite salad dressing.

INGREDIENTS | SERVES 4

4 large romaine lettuce leaves
¼ cup mint leaves
¼ cup cilantro leaves
½ cup mung bean sprouts
½ cup red lentils, sprouted
¼ cup slivered almonds
½ cup carrot, julienned
½ cup sliced avocado or julienned radishes

Lay the romaine lettuce leaves flat. Place a layer of mint and cilantro onto one side. Top with the mung beans, sprouted lentils, almonds, carrot, and avocado.

Roll up the wraps tightly. Place a toothpick through the middle to hold it together. Serve with sauce.

PER SERVING | Calories: 165 | Fat: 6 g | Protein: 9 g | Sodium: 17 mg | Fiber: 10 g | Carbohydrates: 21 g | Sugar: 2 g

CHAPTER 15

Store-Bought Sprouted-Grain Flour Recipes

Multigrain Buttermilk Pancakes

Buttermilk pancakes are always a hit on the breakfast table, no matter what mix of flours you use. Letting the whole oats soak helps give these pancakes a nutty and fluffy texture.

INGREDIENTS | SERVES 6

1 cup sprouted oats

1 cup buttermilk

¼ cup sprouted oat flour

½ cup sprouted whole-wheat flour

1 tablespoon sugar

1½ teaspoons baking powder

1 teaspoon baking soda

½ teaspoon salt

1 egg, beaten

2 tablespoons oil or melted butter

Maple syrup and Quick Berry Topping
(see sidebar recipe), for serving

Quick Berry Topping

For a fast pancake topping, take 2 cups of your favorite berries (fresh or frozen) and place in a medium saucepan with 1 table-spoon water and 1 tablespoon honey. Bring the berry mixture to a boil, then lower to simmer and cook, stirring frequently, for 10 minutes, until the berries have broken down and the sauce has thickened.

Mix the oats and buttermilk in a medium bowl. Cover with plastic wrap and refrigerate for 45 minutes or overnight.

In a separate bowl, whisk the flours, sugar, baking powder, baking soda, and salt together.

Once the oats and buttermilk have thickened and the oats have soaked up most of the liquid, stir the beaten egg and oil (or butter) into the oats.

Add the dry ingredients to the wet, and stir just until the batter comes together and all of the flour is incorporated.

Heat a large griddle (or skillet) over medium heat and add a thin layer of oil if the surface is not nonstick. Scoop the batter, ¼–⅓ cup at a time, onto the hot griddle.

When the bottoms of the pancakes are golden and the top is set around the edges, flip them over. Cook for another 1–2 minutes until the second side is golden brown. Serve warm.

PER SERVING | Calories: 233 | Fat: 8 g | Protein: 9 g |
Sodium: 262 mg | Fiber: 4 g | Carbohydrates: 30 g | Sugar: 4 g

Double Oat Chocolate Chip Cookies

There aren't many things that can beat a homemade, fresh-out-of-the-oven chocolate chip cookie. This batch has everything that a good cookie needs, but it's also full of healthy whole grains.

INGREDIENTS | YIELDS 3 DOZEN COOKIES

2 sticks butter, softened to room temperature

¾ cup brown sugar

¾ cup sugar

2 eggs

1 teaspoon vanilla extract

1 cup sprouted oat flour

1¼ cups sprouted whole-wheat flour

1 cup sprouted oats

1 teaspoon baking soda

¼ teaspoon baking powder

1 teaspoon cinnamon

½ teaspoon salt

2 cups chocolate chips

Chocolate Choices

Dark chocolate has the most health benefits, but feel free to alternate the types of chocolate you use in these cookies. A blend of dark and milk chocolate is delicious together, and semisweet chocolate goes really well with white chocolate.

Preheat the oven to 375°F.

Cream the butter and sugars together, and then blend together with a mixer on medium until the mixture is light and fluffy, about 3 minutes.

Add the eggs, one at a time, to the sugar mixture. Once the eggs are blended into the sugar and butter, mix in the vanilla.

In a separate bowl, stir together the oat flour, whole-wheat flour, oats, baking soda, baking powder, cinnamon, and salt. Slowly add the flour mixture to the butter and sugar mixture, mixing on medium speed, until the flour is just combined in the butter and sugar.

On low speed, mix the chocolate chips into the dough.

Scoop the dough by rounded tablespoons onto a greased baking sheet, 2" apart, and bake for 11–13 minutes.

Cool the cookies on the pan for 2 minutes, and then move them to a cooling rack.

PER SERVING (1 cookie) | Calories: 174 | Fat: 8 g | Protein: 3 g | Sodium: 72 mg | Fiber: 2 g | Carbohydrates: 23 g | Sugar: 14 g

Strawberry Rhubarb Coffee Cake

Strawberry and rhubarb aren't only meant for pies.
Tart and sweet, the fruit bakes into a soft filling for this sprouted whole-grain coffee cake.

INGREDIENTS | SERVES 9

1 cup buttermilk
¼ cup melted butter or oil
⅓ cup sugar
1 teaspoon vanilla extract
1½ cups sprouted whole-wheat flour
1½ teaspoons baking powder
½ teaspoon salt
1 cup chopped rhubarb
1 cup chopped strawberries
⅓ cup brown sugar
1 teaspoon cinnamon
⅔ cup sprouted oat flour
¼ cup melted butter
¼ cup chopped pecans

Preheat the oven to 375°F.

In a large bowl, mix together the buttermilk, butter or oil, sugar, and vanilla.

Stir the wheat flour, baking powder, and salt into the buttermilk mixture. Gently fold the rhubarb and strawberries into the coffee cake batter.

Pour the batter into a greased 8" × 8" baking dish.

In a medium bowl, mix the brown sugar, cinnamon, oat flour, melted butter, and pecans until all of the flour is incorporated and the mixture is crumbly.

Sprinkle the crumb topping over the batter and bake for 30–40 minutes until a toothpick comes out clean.

PER SERVING | Calories: 307 | Fat: 14 g | Protein: 6 g | Sodium: 159 mg | Fiber: 4 g | Carbohydrates: 40 g | Sugar: 16 g

DIY Buttermilk

Buttermilk is one of the best ingredients for baking. It's thick and rich, and has a fantastic tangy flavor. If you don't have any buttermilk on hand, you can make a quick version at home. For every cup of buttermilk you need for a recipe, add 1 tablespoon of lemon juice to 1 cup of milk and let it sit for 5 minutes before adding to your batter.

Dense Chocolate and Quinoa Cake

Think you can't have whole grains and chocolate together? Think again. This chocolate loaf cake is full of deep chocolate flavor and is intensely rich. It is a quick and easy dessert option—just serve with a dollop of whipped cream or a small scoop of ice cream.

INGREDIENTS | SERVES 12

4 ounces semisweet chocolate

6 tablespoons butter

3 eggs

½ cup sugar

1 teaspoon vanilla extract

¼ cup sprouted whole-wheat flour

3 tablespoons sprouted quinoa flour

½ cup dark chocolate chips

½ cup walnuts, chopped

½ teaspoon salt

Spiced Whipped Cream

For an easy topping with this chocolate cake, you can whip this spiced cream together in less than 5 minutes. Pour 1½ cups cold heavy cream into a bowl. Using a hand mixer or egg beater, whip the cream for 3–4 minutes until it begins to thicken. Pour in ½ tablespoon bourbon, ¼ teaspoon cinnamon, and ¼ teaspoon vanilla. Continue beating until the cream is thick and forms stiff peaks when you pick the egg beater up out of the cream.

(Serves 12. Per Serving: Calories: 104; Fat: 11 g; Protein: <1 g; Sodium: 11 mg; Fiber: <1 g; Carbohydrates:<1 g; Sugar: <1 g)

Preheat the oven to 350°F.

Melt the chocolate and butter together in a double-boiler or in the microwave.

In two medium bowls, separate the yolks from the egg whites.

Beat the egg yolks with the sugar and vanilla until the mixture is light and pale in color. Add the chocolate and butter to the egg mixture, and mix until the chocolate is incorporated.

Stir the wheat flour, quinoa flour, chocolate chips, and walnuts into the flour mixture until all of the flour is incorporated.

Add the salt to the egg whites and beat them until they're light and fluffy. Gently fold the egg whites into the rest of the batter.

Pour batter into a greased loaf pan and bake for 45–55 minutes or until a toothpick comes out clean when inserted into the center.

PER SERVING | Calories: 232 | Fat: 16 g | Protein: 3 g | Sodium: 68 mg | Fiber: 2 g | Carbohydrates: 21 g | Sugar: 15 g

Multigrain Waffles

The trick to light and crispy waffles is the melted butter and the whipped egg whites. Without the lightness from the egg whites, the waffle batter would be too thick and the waffles would be very dense and heavy.

INGREDIENTS | SERVES 6

¾ cup sprouted whole-wheat flour

¾ cup all-purpose flour

½ cup sprouted buckwheat flour

2 tablespoons sugar

1½ teaspoons baking powder

¼ teaspoon salt

2 eggs, separated

1¾ cups buttermilk

4 tablespoons butter

1 teaspoon vanilla extract

Separating Eggs

The easiest way to separate eggs is to use your hands. Put two bowls next to each other on the counter in front of you. Crack the egg and hold it over the bowl where you want your egg whites. Once the egg shell is broken in two, pour the yolk from one half of the shell to the other, letting the whites drip down into the bowl. When all the whites are in the bowl, pour the yolk into the other bowl. Toss the shells and repeat.

Turn on your waffle maker and set aside.

In a large bowl, whisk together the sprouted whole-wheat flour, all-purpose flour, buckwheat flour, sugar, baking powder, and salt.

After you've separated the eggs, whisk the buttermilk into the egg yolks.

In a microwave-safe bowl, heat the butter for 45 seconds–1 minute until the butter has melted. Let it cool for 5 minutes.

Once the butter has cooled, stir it into the buttermilk and egg yolk mixture. Add the vanilla and stir together.

Take your separated egg whites and beat (in a stand mixer or with a hand mixer) until the egg whites are glossy and form stiff peaks when you remove the beater.

Pour the buttermilk mixture into the flour and stir together until all the flour is incorporated.

Fold the beaten egg whites into the batter, being careful to keep as much air in the batter as possible.

Pour 4 tablespoons of batter into each waffle space and cook in the waffle iron for 3–5 minutes until golden brown.

PER SERVING | Calories: 276 | Fat: 10 g | Protein: 9 g | Sodium: 197 mg | Fiber: 3 g | Carbohydrates: 38 g | Sugar: 8 g

Baked Greek Pasta

This isn't a typical baked pasta dish. Full of herbs, olives, and artichokes,
this baked Greek pasta is a fun twist on an easy weeknight meal.

INGREDIENTS | SERVES 8

6 cups water

1 pound sprouted-grain penne pasta

1 tablespoon plus 1 teaspoon salt, divided

1 (28-ounce) can crushed tomatoes

¼ cup fresh oregano, chopped

¼ cup fresh basil, chopped

2 tablespoons olive oil

1 teaspoon fresh lemon zest

½ teaspoon pepper

½ cup kalamata olives, chopped

½ cup artichoke hearts, chopped

½ cup feta cheese, crumbled

½ cup mozzarella cheese, shredded

Preheat the oven to 375°F.

Bring water to a boil in a large pot, and add the pasta and 1 tablespoon salt. Cook, stirring occasionally, for 7–10 minutes until the pasta is al dente. Drain the pasta and return it to the pot.

Gently stir the tomatoes, oregano, basil, olive oil, lemon zest, 1 teaspoon salt, pepper, olives, and artichoke hearts into the pasta.

Pour pasta into a greased 9" × 13" pan and top with the crumbled feta and shredded mozzarella.

Bake for 30–40 minutes until the cheese is melted and beginning to brown.

PER SERVING | Calories: 320 | Fat: 8 g | Protein: 13 g |
Sodium: 814 mg | Fiber: 3 g | Carbohydrates: 53 g | Sugar: <1 g

Sprouted Pasta with Rosemary Walnuts and Ricotta

Sweet and savory candied walnuts aren't something you normally find on pasta, but they pair well with the nutty flavor of the sprouted-grain pasta and the creamy texture of the ricotta.

INGREDIENTS | SERVES 6

6 cups water

1 pound sprouted-grain pasta

1 tablespoon plus 1 teaspoon salt, divided

1 tablespoon olive oil

1 tablespoon fresh rosemary, chopped

1 cup walnuts, chopped

1 teaspoon garlic, minced

1 tablespoon brown sugar

1 cup ricotta cheese, store-bought or homemade (see sidebar recipe)

Quick 10-Minute Ricotta Cheese

Making your own ricotta cheese is easy! To make enough for this recipe, pour 4½ cups of milk into a large microwave-safe bowl, and add 1 cup of yogurt and 1 tablespoon of apple cider vinegar. Heat the milk mixture on high in the microwave for 6–7 minutes. Remove and stir, slowly, for 2–3 minutes until the curds begin to separate from the whey (liquid). Pour the mixture into a colander lined with cheesecloth or paper towels, and let it drain for 3–4 minutes. Scrape the cheese out of the colander, season with 1 teaspoon salt, and dollop onto your pasta.

Bring water to a boil in a large pot and add the pasta and 1 tablespoon salt. Cook, stirring occasionally, for 7–10 minutes until the pasta is al dente. Drain and set aside.

While the pasta is cooking, heat the olive oil in a skillet over medium heat. Add the chopped rosemary and cook for 1 minute until fragrant.

Stir the chopped walnuts into the oil and rosemary, and cook, stirring frequently, for 4–5 minutes, until the walnuts are coated with the oil and rosemary and begin to toast.

Stir the garlic, brown sugar, and 1 teaspoon salt into the walnuts. Cook for another 2–3 minutes until the sugar is melted and coating the walnuts. Remove the pan from the heat.

Divide pasta into six bowls. Top each bowl with a scoop of the walnuts and a dollop of ricotta. Gently toss together before serving.

PER SERVING | Calories: 469 | Fat: 18 g | Protein: 18 g | Sodium: 646 mg | Fiber: 1 g | Carbohydrates: 64 g | Sugar: 3 g

Sprouted Bread and Sausage Stuffing

One of the easiest ways to add more sprouted and whole grains to your diet is to simply take recipes you already know and love, and add in those sprouted grains. Keeping the rest of this holiday stuffing recipe the same will leave all the familiar flavors while bumping up the nutritional value.

INGREDIENTS | SERVES 10

1 loaf sprouted-grain bread, diced into cubes

4 tablespoons butter

1 medium onion, diced

1 cup celery, diced (about 3 stalks)

1 medium apple, cored and diced

2 tablespoons fresh parsley, chopped

2 teaspoons salt

1 teaspoon pepper

½ pound sweet Italian sausage, casings removed

1 cup vegetable broth

1 cup dried cherries

Tart Versus Sweet

Using the dried cherries in this stuffing gives a punch of sweet flavor to the dish. If you like having a tart bite in your stuffing, switch them out for dried cranberries.

Preheat the oven to 325°F.

Spread the cubed bread in a single layer on a baking sheet and bake for 5–7 minutes. Remove the bread from the oven and pour into a large bowl.

In a large skillet, melt the butter. Add the onion, celery, and apple to the butter and cook, stirring over medium heat, for 10 minutes until the vegetables and apple are softened. Stir the parsley, salt, and pepper into the apple mixture and pour it into the bowl with the cubed bread.

In the same pan, cook the sausage over medium heat for 10–15 minutes, crumbling it as it cooks, until it's browned and cooked through. Add the sausage to the bread cubes.

Pour the broth and dried cherries into the stuffing mixture and toss together.

Put the stuffing in a greased 9" × 13" baking dish. Bake for 35–40 minutes until the stuffing is browned on top and is heated through. Serve warm.

PER SERVING | Calories: 292 | Fat: 9 g | Protein: 13 g | Sodium: 985 mg | Fiber: 6 g | Carbohydrates: 41 g | Sugar: 14 g

Pumpkin and Molasses Quinoa Cookies

Molasses cookies are a holiday staple. Try this version of the spicy cookies on your dessert plate this year—it's a healthier spin on an autumn treat.

INGREDIENTS | YIELDS 3 DOZEN

1 tablespoon ground flaxseed

2 tablespoons water

½ cup neutral oil (like safflower or canola)

½ cup pumpkin purée

1 cup brown sugar

¼ cup blackstrap molasses

1½ cups sprouted whole-wheat flour

½ cup sprouted quinoa flour

2 teaspoons baking soda

1 teaspoon cinnamon

1 teaspoon ground ginger

½ teaspoon cloves

¼ teaspoon salt

1 tablespoon sugar

Blackstrap Molasses

This type of molasses is the best choice in terms of health benefits. The calories in blackstrap molasses are still mostly from the sugar content, but blackstrap molasses also contains small amounts of vitamins and significant amounts of calcium, magnesium, potassium, and iron.

In a large bowl, mix the ground flaxseed and water, and let the mixture sit for 5 minutes to thicken.

Add the oil, pumpkin purée, brown sugar, and molasses to the flaxseed mixture, and stir until combined.

Stir in the wheat flour, quinoa flour, baking soda, cinnamon, ground ginger, cloves, and salt until the flours and spices are incorporated.

Cover the bowl and let the dough chill in the refrigerator for 30 minutes.

While the dough is chilling, preheat the oven to 375°F.

Place the sugar into a shallow dish.

Once the dough is chilled, roll 1 tablespoon of dough at a time into rounds and dip the tops of the cookies in the sugar.

Place on a baking sheet, 1"–2" apart. Bake for 8–10 minutes and cool for 1–2 minutes before eating.

PER SERVING (1 cookie) | Calories: 72 | Fat: 3 g | Protein: 1 g | Sodium: 73 mg | Fiber: 1 g | Carbohydrates: 11 g | Sugar: 6 g

Baked Minestrone Pasta

Minestrone soup is typically a mix of vegetables, broth, and pasta or rice. This baked pasta has all the flavors of a minestrone soup packed into a cheesy-topped casserole.

INGREDIENTS | SERVES 10

2 tablespoons olive oil

¼ pound bacon, diced

1 medium onion, diced

2 carrots, peeled and diced

2 celery stalks, chopped

2 cloves garlic, minced

1 pound kale, washed and finely chopped

1 (14-ounce) can diced tomatoes

1 (15-ounce) can cannellini beans, drained and rinsed

2 cups beef broth

1 cup sprouted-grain short pasta (macaroni or rigatoni)

¼ cup fresh parsley, chopped

1 teaspoon salt

½ teaspoon pepper

½ cup mozzarella cheese, grated

½ cup Parmesan cheese, grated

How to Prep Kale

When you buy a bunch of kale at the market, the greens will still be on the thick stems. Pull the kale leaves off the stems and rinse the leaves in a colander. Once the kale leaves are cleaned, either tear into bite-sized pieces or chop with a knife before adding to the dish.

Preheat the oven to 375°F.

Heat oil in a large pot over medium heat. Add the bacon, onion, carrots, and celery. Cook, stirring, for 7–10 minutes until the bacon is cooked and the vegetables are softened. Add the garlic and cook for another minute until fragrant.

Stir the kale, diced tomatoes, and cannellini beans into the vegetable mixture and cook, stirring occasionally, for 10 minutes until the kale has wilted.

Add the broth and pasta and bring the mixture to a boil. Cook for 5 minutes or until the pasta is just al dente.

Remove the pot from the heat and stir in the parsley, salt, and pepper. Pour the mixture into a 9" × 13" pan and cover the top with the mozzarella and Parmesan.

Bake for 35–40 minutes until the cheese is melted and beginning to brown. Serve hot.

PER SERVING | Calories: 307 | Fat: 11 g | Protein: 18 g | Sodium: 816 mg | Fiber: 4 g | Carbohydrates: 35 g | Sugar: 3 g

Vanilla Maple French Toast Casserole

The nutty flavor and texture of the sprouted-grain bread provides a nice balance to the creamy and rich base of this baked breakfast casserole.

INGREDIENTS | SERVES 9

½ cup brown sugar

2 tablespoons butter

2 tablespoons maple syrup

6 slices sprouted-grain bread, diced into 1" pieces

4 eggs

1 cup heavy cream

½ cup milk

1 teaspoon vanilla extract

¼ teaspoon salt

Heavy on the Cream?

Using heavy cream in this casserole gives it a flavor similar to vanilla ice cream, but if this is too heavy a breakfast dish for you, swap out the cream for your choice of milk.

Place the brown sugar, butter, and maple syrup in the bottom of an 8" × 8" microwave-safe baking dish. Heat in the microwave for 30 seconds–1 minute or until the butter is melted. Stir the mixture together to let the sugar dissolve.

Place the diced bread on top of the sugar mixture in the baking dish.

In a separate bowl, beat the four eggs. Stir in the cream, milk, vanilla, and salt.

Pour the cream mixture over the diced bread. Press the top of the bread mixture into the pan to let the cream mixture soak into all of the bread.

Cover the dish and let it sit in the refrigerator overnight.

In the morning, preheat the oven to 375°F. Remove the dish from the refrigerator and cover with foil.

Bake the bread pudding in the oven, covered, for 25 minutes. Remove the foil and bake for another 5–10 minutes. Serve warm with a drizzle of maple syrup.

PER SERVING | Calories: 279 | Fat: 16 g | Protein: 5 g | Sodium: 233 mg | Fiber: 1 g | Carbohydrates: 28g | Sugar: 16 g

Chocolate Cherry Sprouted Bread Pudding

A great option for dessert or breakfast, this bread pudding combines dark chocolate and tart cherries for a sweet and tangy treat.

INGREDIENTS | SERVES 9

6 slices sprouted-grain bread, diced into 1" pieces

4 eggs

1 cup milk

½ cup cream

½ cup sugar

1 teaspoon vanilla extract

¼ teaspoon salt

½ cup dried cherries

½ cup chocolate chips

Preheat the oven to 375°F.

Place the diced bread into a large bowl.

In a smaller bowl, beat the eggs. Add the milk, cream, sugar, vanilla, and salt to the eggs. Pour over the bread cubes and toss together.

Add the dried cherries and chocolate chips to the bread mixture.

Pour bread pudding mixture into a greased 8" × 8" pan.

Cover the pan with foil and bake for 30 minutes. Remove the foil and bake for another 5–10 minutes. Serve warm.

PER SERVING | Calories: 240 | Fat: 10 g | Protein: 5 g | Sodium: 208 mg | Fiber: 2 g | Carbohydrates: 33 g | Sugar: 22 g

Raspberry and Cream Cheese Stuffed French Toast

This baked French toast casserole is the perfect breakfast to make on busy weekends or when you have overnight guests. The dish can be prepped the night before, placed in the fridge, and baked in the morning.

INGREDIENTS | SERVES 6

12 slices sprouted-grain bread

8 ounces cream cheese, softened or cubed

1 cup fresh raspberries

½ cup raspberry jam

1 dozen eggs

½ cup maple syrup

1 cup milk

1 cup cream

1 teaspoon cinnamon

1 teaspoon vanilla extract

½ teaspoon salt

Fresh or Frozen?

If it's not raspberry season, you can use frozen raspberries in this dish. Thaw them in the fridge or at room temperature until the berries are softened. Drain off most of the liquid before using the berries in the recipe.

Preheat the oven to 375°F.

Place six slices of the bread on the bottom of a 9" × 13" baking dish.

Add the cream cheese to the bottom layer of bread, either by spreading some on each slice or by adding cubes of cream cheese to each piece.

Sprinkle the fresh raspberries on top of the cream cheese.

On the remaining slices of bread, spread a layer of raspberry jam on each piece and place, jam side down, on top of the other slices of bread in the pan.

In a medium bowl, beat the eggs with the maple syrup, milk, cream, cinnamon, vanilla, and salt. Pour the egg mixture over the bread.

Cover the pan with foil and bake for 35–40 minutes. Remove the foil and bake for another 5–10 minutes or until the egg mixture is cooked and set. Serve warm.

PER SERVING | Calories: 694 | Fat: 38 g | Protein: 20 g | Sodium: 765 mg | Fiber: 5 g | Carbohydrates: 70 g | Sugar: 33 g

Spring Panzanella Salad with Sprouted Bread

Panzanella salad is typically made with day-old bread and fresh tomatoes, but any fresh vegetable will work. This mix of spring vegetables and flavors highlights the best of the season.

INGREDIENTS | SERVES 4

5 cups sprouted-grain bread, diced

3 tablespoons plus ¼ cup olive oil, divided

2 teaspoons salt, divided

1 leek, cleaned and sliced

½ cup scallions, sliced

1 cup asparagus, trimmed into 1" pieces

½ cup fresh parsley, chopped

½ cup fresh basil, chopped

1 tablespoon red wine vinegar

1 tablespoon lemon juice

1 teaspoon lemon zest

1 teaspoon Dijon mustard

1 teaspoon garlic, minced

¼ teaspoon pepper

Trimming Asparagus

To find the perfect spot to trim the ends of the asparagus, take one spear and hold one end in each hand. Slowly start bending the spear in half until it breaks off. Lay that spear next to the remaining spears and trim the rest at the same spot.

Preheat the oven to 350°F. Toss the cubed bread with 2 tablespoons olive oil and 1 teaspoon salt and place in a single layer on a baking sheet. Toast for 8–10 minutes until the bread is crisp.

While the bread is toasting, heat 1 tablespoon olive oil in a skillet over medium heat. Add the sliced leeks, scallions, and asparagus. Cook, stirring occasionally, for 7–10 minutes until the leeks are softened and the asparagus is crisp-tender.

Remove the vegetables from the pan and pour into a large bowl.

Once the bread is toasted, add it to the vegetables. Toss in the parsley and basil.

In a small bowl, whisk together ¼ cup olive oil, red wine vinegar, lemon juice, lemon zest, Dijon mustard, garlic, 1 teaspoon salt, and pepper. Pour the dressing over the bread and vegetables, and gently toss together.

Serve warm or at room temperature.

PER SERVING | Calories: 462 | Fat: 22 g | Protein: 11 g | Sodium: 1,748 mg | Fiber: 7 g | Carbohydrates: 58 g | Sugar: 2 g

Sprouted-Grain Sandwich Bread

The smell of freshly baked bread is one that can't be replicated.
A mix of bread flour and sprouted grains gives this bread a nutty flavor and a great texture.

**INGREDIENTS | YIELDS 2 LOAVES,
12 SLICES EACH**

3 cups bread flour

⅓ cup honey

¼ cup neutral oil

1 tablespoon salt

4½ teaspoons active dry yeast

2¼ cups warm water

3 cups sprouted-wheat flour

1 tablespoon olive oil

Make Your Own Grain Mix

If you can find other whole grains and sprouted-grain flours, try out your own mix of flavors in this bread recipe. Just make sure to always use the 3 cups of bread flour—it keeps the loaves light and helps give them their fluffy texture.

In the bowl of a stand mixer (or other large bowl), mix the bread flour with the honey, neutral oil, salt, and yeast.

Add the water to the bread flour mixture and blend together for 2–3 minutes.

Add the sprouted-wheat flour, 1 cup at a time, to the dough. Once the flour is incorporated, knead the dough for 5 minutes until it is smooth and easy to handle.

Pour the olive oil into a large bowl and turn the dough around in the oil in the bottom of the bowl. Cover the bowl and let the dough rise in a warm place until doubled, about 1–2 hours.

Once the dough has doubled, punch it down and divide it into two pieces. Pat each piece out lengthwise and roll it up. Place each loaf, seam side down, in a greased 9" × 5" loaf pan. Cover the pans and let the dough rise again until doubled, about 40 minutes–1 hour.

Preheat the oven to 375°F. Uncover loaves and bake on the bottom rack for 40–45 minutes or until the tops are golden and the loaves sound hollow when you tap the tops.

PER SERVING (per 1 slice) | Calories: 153 | Fat: 3 g | Protein: 4 g | Sodium: 290 mg | Fiber: 2 g | Carbohydrates: 27 g | Sugar: 4 g

Sprouted-Grain Pizza Crust

Adding small amounts of sprouted grains to your regular go-to recipes is the easiest way to start getting sprouted grains into your daily diet. This sprouted-grain pizza crust is a healthier option, but still makes a delicious base for your favorite pizza combination.

INGREDIENTS | YIELDS 2 PIZZA CRUSTS, 8 SLICES EACH

2¼ teaspoons (1 package) active dry yeast

2 cups warm water

3 cups sprouted-wheat flour

2 teaspoons salt

2 cups all-purpose flour

1 tablespoon olive oil

Freezing for Later

If you're making this crust recipe and only need to use one crust, wrap the other dough round (before the second rise) in plastic wrap and place in a Zip-top bag in the freezer. Then when you're ready to use it, thaw the dough in the refrigerator and let it rest at room temperature for 30 minutes before stretching out to bake.

In a large bowl, dissolve the yeast in the warm water and let it stand for 5 minutes or until it's creamy.

Stir the sprouted-wheat flour and salt into the water and yeast.

Add in the all-purpose flour, 1 cup at a time, until the dough is smooth and no longer sticky, adding additional flour if needed.

Pour 1 tablespoon olive oil into a large bowl and add the dough, tossing to coat in the oil. Cover the bowl and let the dough rise in a warm place until doubled, about 1–2 hours.

Once the dough has doubled, punch it down and divide it into two rounds.

Place the rounds on a baking sheet or cutting board and cover. Let the rounds sit in a warm spot for 30 minutes before stretching out.

Preheat the oven to 475°F. Stretch or roll out the dough, place on a pizza stone or baking sheet, and top with your favorite pizza toppings. Bake for 12–15 minutes until your toppings are cooked and the crust is golden.

PER SERVING (crust only) | Calories: 138 | Fat: 1 g | Protein: 4 g | Sodium: 286 mg | Fiber: 3 g | Carbohydrates: 28 g | Sugar: <1 g

Chili Beans and Corn Bread Casserole

This recipe features three comfort dishes baked into one casserole. The chili bean mixture combines the best flavors of baked beans and chili, and the top is a cheesy corn bread studded with spicy jalapeños.

INGREDIENTS | SERVES 12

4 slices bacon, diced

1 medium onion, diced

2 cloves garlic, minced

1 pound ground buffalo or beef

2 tablespoons tomato paste

1 tablespoon chili powder

2 teaspoons cumin

2 teaspoons smoked paprika

2½ teaspoons salt, divided

1 teaspoon pepper

1 tablespoon apple cider vinegar

2 tablespoons molasses

1 tablespoon Dijon mustard

1 (28-ounce) can crushed tomatoes

1 (15-ounce) can kidney beans, drained and rinsed

1 (15-ounce) can pinto beans, drained and rinsed

1 (15-ounce) can cannellini beans, drained and rinsed

¾ cup cornmeal

½ cup sprouted-corn flour

¾ cup sprouted-wheat flour

2 tablespoons honey

1 teaspoon baking powder

½ teaspoon baking soda

1 egg

1½ cups buttermilk

2 tablespoons neutral oil (like safflower or canola)

1 jalapeño pepper, seeds removed and diced

1 cup Cheddar cheese, shredded

In a large pot, cook the bacon on medium heat, stirring occasionally for 5–7 minutes until the bacon begins to crisp.

Add the onion to the pan and cook for 5 minutes until it begins to soften. Stir in the garlic and cook for 1 minute.

Crumble the ground buffalo into the pot and cook, stirring to break up the meat while it browns. Cook for 5–7 minutes until the juices are running clear.

Stir the tomato paste into the meat and cook for 3–4 minutes on medium heat. Add the chili powder, cumin, smoked paprika, 2 teaspoons salt, and pepper to the pot and stir everything together. Cook for 3–4 minutes.

Pour the apple cider vinegar, molasses, Dijon mustard, crushed tomatoes, and all the beans into the pot. Let the chili bean mixture simmer on low while you mix the corn bread topping.

Preheat the oven to 400°F.

In a medium bowl, mix together the cornmeal, sprouted corn flour, and sprouted-wheat flour. Stir in the honey, baking powder, baking soda, and ½ teaspoon salt.

In a small bowl, whisk the egg with the buttermilk and oil, and pour into the cornmeal mixture. Fold the diced jalapeño and Cheddar into the corn bread mixture.

Pour the chili bean mixture into a greased 9" × 13" pan. Scoop the corn bread batter over the chili bean mixture and spread it out to cover as much of the chili beans as possible.

Bake for 20–25 minutes until the chili is bubbling around the edges and the corn bread is golden brown.

PER SERVING | Calories: 422 | Fat: 9 g | Protein: 30 g | Sodium: 819 mg | Fiber: 13 g | Carbohydrates: 57 g | Sugar: 7 g

Buttercup Squash Spoon Bread

Spoon bread is a dish often saved for holiday tables, but this version would be perfect any time during fall or winter. The sweetness from the squash and maple syrup is a delicious match with the sage and rosemary.

INGREDIENTS | SERVES 8

1 tablespoon butter, softened

1 buttercup squash

2 cups milk

½ cup half and half

1 tablespoon fresh sage, chopped

1 tablespoon fresh rosemary, chopped

2 tablespoons maple syrup

2 teaspoons salt

1 teaspoon pepper

1 cup sprouted-corn flour or sprouted cornmeal

4 eggs, separated

2 tablespoons butter, melted and cooled

1½ teaspoons baking powder

Preheat the oven to 425°F. Spread 1 tablespoon of softened butter in a 2-quart soufflé or casserole dish.

Cut the squash in half, remove the seeds, and roast in the oven for 40–45 minutes until the flesh is tender. When the squash is cool enough to handle, scrape the flesh away from the peel and mash the squash flesh in a large bowl.

Turn the oven down to 350°F.

In a medium saucepan, heat the milk, half and half, sage, rosemary, maple syrup, salt, and pepper to a low simmer. Slowly whisk the sprouted-corn flour into the milk mixture, stirring constantly until the mixture thickens and starts to pull away from the sides of the pan.

Remove the pan from heat and stir in the mashed squash, 4 egg yolks, 2 tablespoons of melted butter, and baking powder into the corn flour mixture.

In a large bowl, beat the egg whites until soft peaks form. Gently fold the whipped egg whites into the squash mixture.

Pour spoon bread batter into the greased baking dish. Bake for 35–45 minutes, until the internal temperature of the bread reaches 165°F. The bread edges will be firm, but the center will be slightly soft. Remove from the oven and let cool before serving.

PER SERVING | Calories: 193 | Fat: 9 g | Protein: 6 g | Sodium: 649 mg | Fiber: 1 g | Carbohydrates: 22 g | Sugar: 7 g

Sprouted Pasta with Romesco Sauce and Goat Cheese

Romesco sauce is a condiment that originated in Spain and is eaten with fish, poultry, vegetables, and grains. It has a gorgeous color, thanks to the tomatoes and peppers, and is a fun sauce to make for pasta.

INGREDIENTS | SERVES 6

6 cups water

1 tablespoon salt

1 pound sprouted-grain pasta

¼ cup olive oil

1 slice sprouted-grain bread, cubed

½ cup blanched almonds, slivered or chopped

5 cloves garlic, minced

1½ teaspoons salt

1 (15-ounce) can crushed tomatoes

1 (8-ounce) jar roasted red peppers, drained

1 tablespoon smoked paprika

2 tablespoons sherry vinegar

¼ cup goat cheese

Only Almonds?

While almonds are traditionally used in Romesco sauce, feel free to try using hazelnuts or walnuts in the sauce. Substitutions will give the sauce a different flavor, but the texture will be the same.

Bring the water to a boil. Stir in salt and pasta, and cook, stirring occasionally, for 6–8 minutes until the pasta is al dente. Drain and set aside while the sauce cooks.

In a large pot, heat the olive oil over medium heat. Stir the diced bread and almonds into the oil and cook, stirring often, until they begin to brown.

Stir in the garlic and cook for another minute until fragrant.

Pour the bread and almond mixture into a food processor or blender, and add the salt, tomatoes, roasted red peppers, smoked paprika, and vinegar. Purée the mixture until smooth.

Pour the sauce back into the pot and cook on medium heat, stirring frequently, for 15 minutes. Serve tossed with the sprouted-grain pasta and a sprinkle of goat cheese.

PER SERVING | Calories: 584 | Fat: 26 g | Protein: 21 g | Sodium: 1,094 mg | Fiber: 5 g | Carbohydrates: 76 g | Sugar: 1 g

Apple Pecan Salad with Grilled Gruyère Croutons

Salad topped with grilled cheese? Who wouldn't want that for lunch or dinner?
Kids (and adults) will love this play on croutons.

INGREDIENTS | SERVES 4

4 cups mixed greens
1 large apple, diced
½ cup pecan halves
½ cup dried cherries
¼ cup olive oil
1 tablespoon apple cider vinegar
1 tablespoon maple syrup
1 teaspoon salt
½ teaspoon pepper
4 slices sprouted-grain bread
2 teaspoons Dijon mustard
⅔ cup Gruyère cheese, shredded
2 tablespoons butter

Gruyère Cheese

A Swiss cheese, Gruyère is sweet, salty, and has a slightly nutty flavor that pairs well with the apples, dried fruit, and pecans in this salad. If you can't find Gruyère, try a good-quality Swiss cheese or Havarti, which is super creamy.

In a large bowl, toss the mixed greens with the diced apple, pecans, and dried cherries.

In a smaller bowl, whisk together the oil, vinegar, maple syrup, salt, and pepper, and pour over the salad. Toss gently and set aside.

Place a skillet over medium heat and, on the counter, lay out the 4 slices of bread.

Spread each slice with a little of the Dijon mustard. Top 2 slices with cheese and place another piece of bread on top, making 2 sandwiches.

Spread 1 slice of bread with some butter and place butter side down in the pan. Cook on medium 3–4 minutes until the bread is toasted and the cheese is beginning to melt. Flip the sandwich and cook another 2–3 minutes on the other side. Repeat with the second sandwich.

Once the grilled cheese sandwiches are golden and the cheese is melted, set them aside to cool for 2–3 minutes.

Divide the salad between four plates. Dice the grilled cheese sandwiches into 2" pieces and top each salad with some of the grilled cheese "croutons" before serving.

PER SERVING | Calories: 502 | Fat: 36 g | Protein: 10 g | Sodium: 820 mg | Fiber: 5 g | Carbohydrates: 40 g | Sugar: 19 g

Cauliflower Gratin with Sprouted Bread Crumb Topping

People who think they don't like cauliflower haven't tried it in this gratin. The tender florets are cooked in milk and baked with herbs under a cheesy crust, making this vegetable irresistible.

INGREDIENTS | SERVES 6

1 tablespoon olive oil

½ medium onion, diced

1 (3–4 pounds) head of cauliflower, cut into medium florets

4 tablespoons butter

3 tablespoons all-purpose flour

1¼ cups milk

2 teaspoons salt

1 teaspoon pepper

1 teaspoon dried rosemary

½ cup sprouted-grain bread crumbs

¼ cup Parmesan cheese, grated

½ tablespoon dried parsley

How to Make Your Own Bread Crumbs

There are a couple of ways to make bread crumbs from fresh bread. You can either toast the bread and crush the slices in a bag, or place the bread in a food processor and pulse a few times until the bread is crumbled into the size pieces that you want.

Preheat the oven to 375°F.

In a large pot, heat the oil over medium heat and add the onion. Cook, stirring occasionally, for 5–10 minutes until the onion has softened and just begins to brown.

Stir in the cauliflower and cook for another 10–12 minutes.

Add the butter to the pan and cook for another 2 minutes or until it is melted.

Sprinkle the flour into the pan and stir the vegetable mixture until the flour is distributed evenly.

Slowly add the milk, continuing to stir, until everything is combined. Stir in the salt, pepper, and rosemary, and bring mixture to a simmer.

Let the cauliflower and milk simmer and thicken for 5–10 minutes.

Pour the mixture into a greased baking dish. Sprinkle the top of the gratin with the bread crumbs, Parmesan, and dried parsley.

Bake for 18–20 minutes or until the edges are bubbling and the top is golden. Serve warm.

PER SERVING | Calories: 251 | Fat: 14 g | Protein: 11 g | Sodium: 970 mg | Fiber: 8 g | Carbohydrates: 26 g | Sugar: 10 g

Pad Thai with Almond Sauce

Pad thai is a traditional dish from Thailand. This recipe uses a sesame seed Tahini sauce in place of the peanut sauce. If you want the traditional flavor, use your favorite peanut butter.

INGREDIENTS | SERVES 2

2 tablespoons lime juice

1 tablespoon Tahini or freshly ground sesame seeds

1 tablespoon agave nectar or honey

2 tablespoons nama shoyu

1 clove minced garlic

½ tablespoon ginger

¼ cup sun-dried tomatoes, soaked

½ cup sun-dried tomato soak water

3 medium zucchinis

2 large carrots

½ cup mung bean sprouts

½ cup snow peas

½ cup peanuts, chopped

½ cup sugar snap peas

¼ cup finely sliced scallions

¼ pound sprouted-grain spaghetti or fettuccine noodles

2–4 tablespoons minced cilantro, for garnish

To make the pad thai sauce, place the lime juice, Tahini, agave nectar, nama shoyu, garlic, ginger, and sun-dried tomatoes in a blender and blend until smooth. Gradually pour in the sun-dried tomato soak water until it blends into a thick sauce.

Using a spiral slicer, make noodles with the zucchini and carrot. Alternatively, julienne or shred them.

Place the zucchini, carrots, mung bean sprouts, snow peas, peanuts, sugar snap peas, and scallions in a large bowl and toss together.

Cook sprouted-grain pasta according to the directions on the box. Once the noodles are cooked, divide between 2 plates. Top with the vegetable mixture and toss together with the sauce. Sprinkle with cilantro before serving.

PER SERVING | Calories: 494 | Fat: 24 g | Protein: 23 g | Sodium: 1,010 mg | Fiber: 14 g | Carbohydrates: 60 g | Sugar: 23 g

APPENDIX A

Additional Resources

Books

Braunstein, Mark Mathew. *Sprout Garden, Revised Edition*. Summertown, TN: Book Publishing Co., 1999.

Meyerowitz, Steve. *Sproutman's Kitchen Garden Cookbook: Sprout Breads, Cookies, Soups, Salads and 250 Other Low Fat, Dairy-Free, Vegetarian Recipes, Fifth Edition*. Great Barrington, MA: Sproutman Publishing, 1999.

Meyerowitz, Steve; Parman, Michael; and Robbins, Beth. *Sproutman's Kitchen Garden Cookbook: 250 Flourless, Dairyless, Low Temperature, Low Fat, Low Salt, Living Food Vegetarian Recipes*. Great Barrington, MA: Sproutman Publishing, 1983.

Meyerowitz, Steve; Parman, Michael; and Robbins, Beth. *Sprouts the Miracle Food: The Complete Guide to Sprouting, Sixth Edition*. Great Barrington, MA: Sproutman Publishing, 1999.

Wigmore, Ann. *The Sprouting Book: How to Grow and Use Sprouts to Maximize Your Health and Vitality*. New York, NY: Avery Publishing for Penguin Group, 1986.

Websites

Sproutpeople

This site is a great resource for all things sprouted. Sproutpeople offers background information, tips for sprouting at home, and also sells sprouting kits, books, and the grains themselves.

www.sproutpeople.org

Handy Pantry

Handy Pantry is a fantastic resource for anything you want related to sprouting. Seeds, grains, kits, books, juicers, and supplements are all available for purchase.

www.handypantry.com

Mumm's Sprouting Seeds

Mumm's Sprouting Seeds offers Certified Organic seeds, grains, and legumes that are ready for you to sprout at home. The firm ships to both Canada and the United States.

www.sprouting.com

USA Emergency Supply

A resource for all things food, first aid, equipment, and information, USA Emergency Supply offers useful detailed information when it comes to grain storage, seed storage, and sprout storage. They also sell sprouting kits and seeds.

www.usaemergencysupply.com

Whole Grains Council

Offering anything there is to know about whole grains, the Whole Grains Council website covers the history, health benefits, recipes, and everything in between.

www.wholegrainscouncil.org

National Institutes of Health, Office of Dietary Supplements

This agency offers extensive background information about dietary supplements and about vitamins, minerals, and nutrients in our food.

http://ods.od.nih.gov

The World's Healthiest Foods

Supported by the George Mateljan Foundation, this website delivers information about a variety of whole grains, beans, legumes, seeds, fruits, vegetables, and other healthy foods.

www.whfoods.com

Brand Listing for Store-Bought Options

To Your Health Sprouted Flour Co.

1138 Highway 82
Fitzpatrick, AL 36029
1-877-401-6837
www.organicsproutedflour.net
An online store that sells both whole grains and sprouted-grain flour.

Alvarado Street Bakery

2225 S. McDowell Blvd. Ext.
Petaluma, CA 94954
(707) 283-0300
www.alvaradostreetbakery.com
Alvarado Street Bakery sells a variety of Certified Organic sprouted-grain baked goods, including breads, tortillas, bagels, rolls, buns, and granola. This brand is available in some stores; check with the local grocers in your area.

Essential Eating Sprouted Foods

P.O. Box 771
Waverly, PA 18471
(570) 586-1557
www.essentialeating.com
This company offers information and resources about sprouted foods and class opportunities, and sells its own sprouted-grain flours.

Food for Life

P.O. Box 1434
Corona, CA 92878
1-800-797-5090
www.foodforlife.com
The Food for Life Baking Company has a large variety of sprouted-grain foods for purchase, including breads, buns, English muffins, tortillas, bagels, cereals, and pastas. You can shop on the firm's website, and Food for Life products are available in some stores as well.

Shiloh Farms

191 Commerce Drive
New Holland, PA 17557
1-800-362-6832
www.shilohfarms.com
Shiloh Farms sells sprouted-grain flours, beans, seeds, cereals, whole grains, dried fruits, and sprouted breads. They also offer books and other information on the website as well.

Silver Hills Sprouted Bakery

Box 2250
Abbotsford, BC V2T 4X2
Canada
1-604-850-5600
www.silverhillsbakery.ca
A Canadian company, the Silver Hills Sprouted Bakery has the most variety in flavors when it comes to sprouted-grain breads.

Blue Mountain Organics

P.O. Box 898
Floyd, VA 24091
1-866-777-7475
www.bluemountainorganics.com/store
Blue Mountain Organics has one of the largest offerings of Certified Organic sprouted-grain flours for sale. They also sell grains that are ready for sprouting and raw, organic snack foods.

APPENDIX C

Soaking and Sprouting Guide

▼ SOAKING AND SPROUTING CHART

FOOD	SOAKING TIME	SPROUTING TIME
Alfalfa	5 hours	5 days
Almonds	8 to 12 hours	Do not sprout
Barley	6 to 8 hours	5 to 7 days
Broccoli	6 to 12 hours	3 days
Buckwheat	15 to 45 minutes	24 hours
Chickpea / Garbanzo	8 to 12 hours	1 to 2 days
Cloves	5 hours	5 days
Cabbage	8 to 12 hours	3 days
Dulse sea vegetable	5 minutes	Do not sprout
Fenugreek	6 hours	5 days
Flaxseeds	6 to 8 hours	Do not sprout
Green pumpkin seeds	4 hours	24 hours
Hemp seeds	Do not soak	Do not sprout
Lentils	8 to 12 hours	2 days
Mustard	5 hours	5 days
Macadamia	Do not soak	Do not sprout
Pecans	1 to 2 hours	Do not sprout
Pine nuts	Do not soak	Do not sprout
Pistachio	Do not soak	Do not sprout
Quinoa	3 hours	24 hours
Radish	6 hours	5 days
Raisins	1 to 3 hours	Do not sprout
Rye	6 to 8 hours	5 to 7 days
Sesame seeds	4 to 6 hours	Do not sprout
Sun-dried tomatoes	3 to 4 hours	Do not sprout
Sunflower seeds	4 to 6 hours	24 hours
Walnuts	1 to 2 hours	Do not sprout
Wakame sea vegetable	2 hours	Do not sprout
Wheat	6 to 8 hours	5 to 7 days
Wheatgrass	8 to 12 hours	7 days
Sunflower, unhulled	8 hours	7 days
Buckwheat, unhulled	6 hours	7 days

Standard U.S./Metric Measurement Conversions

VOLUME CONVERSIONS

U.S. Volume Measure	Metric Equivalent
⅛ teaspoon	0.5 milliliters
¼ teaspoon	1 milliliters
½ teaspoon	2 milliliters
1 teaspoon	5 milliliters
½ tablespoon	7 milliliters
1 tablespoon (3 teaspoons)	15 milliliters
2 tablespoons (1 fluid ounce)	30 milliliters
¼ cup (4 tablespoons)	60 milliliters
⅓ cup	90 milliliters
½ cup (4 fluid ounces)	125 milliliters
⅔ cup	160 milliliters
¾ cup (6 fluid ounces)	180 milliliters
1 cup (16 tablespoons)	250 milliliters
1 pint (2 cups)	500 milliliters
1 quart (4 cups)	1 liter (about)

WEIGHT CONVERSIONS

U.S. Weight Measure	Metric Equivalent
½ ounce	15 grams
1 ounce	30 grams
2 ounces	60 grams
3 ounces	85 grams
¼ pound (4 ounces)	115 grams
½ pound (8 ounces)	225 grams
¾ pound (12 ounces)	340 grams
1 pound (16 ounces)	454 grams

OVEN TEMPERATURE CONVERSIONS

Degrees Fahrenheit	Degrees Celsius
200 degrees F	95 degrees C
250 degrees F	120 degrees C
275 degrees F	135 degrees C
300 degrees F	150 degrees C
325 degrees F	160 degrees C
350 degrees F	180 degrees C
375 degrees F	190 degrees C
400 degrees F	205 degrees C
425 degrees F	220 degrees C
450 degrees F	230 degrees C

BAKING PAN SIZES

American	Metric
8 x 1½ inch round baking pan	20 x 4 cm cake tin
9 x 1½ inch round baking pan	23 x 3.5 cm cake tin
1 x 7 x 1½ inch baking pan	28 x 18 x 4 cm baking tin
13 x 9 x 2 inch baking pan	30 x 20 x 5 cm baking tin
2 quart rectangular baking dish	30 x 20 x 3 cm baking tin
15 x 10 x 2 inch baking pan	30 x 25 x 2 cm baking tin (Swiss roll tin)
9 inch pie plate	22 x 4 or 23 x 4 cm pie plate
7 or 8 inch springform pan	18 or 20 cm springform or loose bottom cake tin
9 x 5 x 3 inch loaf pan	23 x 13 x 7 cm or 2 lb narrow loaf or pate tin
1½ quart casserole	1.5 litre casserole
2 quart casserole	2 litre casserole

Index.

C

We Have

EVERYTHING®

on Anything!

With more than 19 million copies sold, the Everything® series has become one of America's favorite resources for solving problems, learning new skills, and organizing lives. Our brand is not only recognizable—it's also welcomed.

The series is a hand-in-hand partner for people who are ready to tackle new subjects—like you!

For more information on the Everything® series, please visit *www.adamsmedia.com*

The Everything® list spans a wide range of subjects, with more than 500 titles covering 25 different categories:

Business	History	Reference
Careers	Home Improvement	Religion
Children's Storybooks	Everything Kids	Self-Help
Computers	Languages	Sports & Fitness
Cooking	Music	Travel
Crafts and Hobbies	New Age	Wedding
Education/Schools	Parenting	Writing
Games and Puzzles	Personal Finance	
Health	Pets	